Successful Supervision and Leadership

Successful Supervision and Leadership
Ensuring High-Performance Outcomes Using the PASE™ Model

Tracey Harris

Routledge
Taylor & Francis Group

A PRODUCTIVITY PRESS BOOK

First published 2020
by Routledge
52 Vanderbilt Avenue, New York, NY 10017
and by Routledge
2 Park Square, Milton Park, Abingdon, Oxon, OX14 4RN

Routledge is an imprint of the Taylor & Francis Group, an informa business
© 2020 Amovita Enterprises Pty Ltd

Library of Congress Cataloging-in-Publication Data
Names: Harris, Tracey, author.
Title: Successful supervision and leadership: ensuring high-performance outcomes using the PASE model / Tracey Harris.
Description: 1 Edition. | New York: Routledge, 2020. |
Includes bibliographical references and index.
Identifiers: LCCN 2019052647 (print) | LCCN 2019052648 (ebook) |
ISBN 9780367178451 (paperback) | ISBN 9780367178468 (hardback) |
ISBN 9780429058028 (ebook)
Subjects: LCSH: Supervision of employees. | Leadership.
Classification: LCC HF5549.12 .H377 2020 (print) | LCC HF5549.12 (ebook) |
DDC 658.3/02—dc23
LC record available at https://lccn.loc.gov/2019052647
LC ebook record available at https://lccn.loc.gov/2019052648

ISBN: 978-0-367-17846-8 (hbk)
ISBN: 978-0-367-17845-1 (pbk)
ISBN: 978-0-429-05802-8 (ebk)

Typeset in Garamond
by codeMantra

Contents

Foreword

Fifteen years ago, in the preface of my book, *Social Work Supervision: Contexts and Concepts*, I wrote 'supervision has been identified as one of the most important factors in determining the job satisfaction levels and the quality of service to clients'. As an indirect but vital to provide quality practice, it is surprising that supervision has not received as much attention as other components of other areas of practice (Tsui, 2005). Fortunately, there have been numerous books, journal articles and conference papers to keep filling the theory and knowledge gap in the last fifteen years. Supervision has received more attention than before in various parts of the world, such as Australia, New Zealand, United Kingdom, United States, Canada, Africa, Europe, Southeast Asia and China.

Based on the existing foundation of theories and knowledge, it is time for us to think about bridging the practice gap by providing useful textbooks to supervisors and leaders in the different fields of practice and sectors. In order to fulfil this purpose, this book is crucial as one of the most recent leading books on professional supervision. It is a contemporary book that addresses key aspects of supervision and leadership that continue to draw attention. First, this book explores some of the key areas such as existing theoretical models of supervision as the guiding principles for formulating the approaches and methods in supervisory practice. Second, it considers both the cultural and organisational contexts as the environment for supervisory practice. Third, it explores the daily practice needs, from decisions to actions, of the leaders as supervisors. Fourth, it continues to provide readers with practice examples and hands-on, step-by-step skills to inform the professional practice of the supervisor. Last, and the most important, throughout this book, it preserves the values and ethics that guide the legal and professional judgements in complicated and complex situations.

There are many unique features of this book I need to highlight and recommend to potential readers. First, the art of reflection is elaborated in supervisory practice to ensure and enhance the client outcomes, which is a proactive cross-over between the art and science in getting things done effectively through supervision. Second, I am glad to see that the author integrates the use of neuroscience and supervision as the future of supervision needs to consider the literature in this area as a precursor to better support staff in the complex work they do. It is a new book to expand and extend the boundary of the knowledge and skills in supervisory practice that currently exist. Third, a chapter on feedback and conversations in supervision illustrates the micro skills in handling the face-to-face close encounter between the supervisor and the supervisee(s) using key skills that consider how to reach positive outcomes through language and the supervisor's capability. Fourth, there is a unique and valuable chapter on the subjective experience of supervision. This sharing will be very much treasured among practicing supervisors as they share their experiences in supervision and of an evidence informed supervision model. Even though supervisors, by nature, are 'managerial' and 'marginal' persons in the organisation, this book will make supervisors feel that they are not alone. At least, their voices are heard and taken as valuable advice.

Although Tracey Harris and I work in different continents, our colleagueship has drawn us together through our passion and love of supervision and leadership. I am delighted to write this foreword given the need for a book such as this. I have been deeply impressed by her commitment and momentum in her pursuit for effective supervision. She has developed an international presence through her consultancy firm for pursuing professional excellence in leadership and supervision over the last twenty-five years. She has also developed a leading supervision model that provides an integrated approach to supervision that features in this book. At present, Tracey is working on her doctoral thesis research and publishing and continuing to be a leader in her field. In my mind, she is the best and right person to write this book as it has been needed for some time now. I am sure that this book will enrich the knowledge of supervisors and leaders, enable supervisors to do an excellent job and eventually ensure the quality of the work that we all do. It advances our thinking in supervision and encourages us all to consider what is needed to provide effective supervision. Thank you for your commitment to develop the PASE™ supervision model as one of the leading models globally to support best practice in supervisory outcomes.

Ming-Sum Tsui
Editor, International Social Work Journal
Professor and Felizberta Lo Padilla Tong Dean of Social Sciences
Caritas Institute of Higher Education
Hong Kong
13 September 2019

Preface

Professional supervision is a crucial part of providing quality leadership practice. It ensures that leaders know how to get the best from their team. It provides a reflective space for staff to explore their work and it ensures that staff feel valued and supported (Tsui, 2005). Supervision is a multi-layered approach that requires leaders to have a range of specific capabilities to ensure supervision remains effective. When supervision is not valued or is absent in the workplace, there is an increased risk of staff not feeling valued, and it is more difficult to monitor or assess their performance and practices (Falender & Shafranske, 2017). Whilst there has been a lot written about supervision over many years with many books on the topic, this latest book is critical for experienced supervisors and leaders to consider how they provide supervision that is effective. It provides a clear process and system for supervisors and leaders to evaluate their supervisory practice, includes a range of supervision models to focus discussions and offers a wealth of resources to use with staff in supervision.

Including twelve chapters, this book explores the context in which supervision takes place; the importance of using a supervision model to focus discussions; the neuroscience of supervision; providing supervision to students on field practicum and how to provide brain-friendly feedback in supervision that supports open conversations. It provides supervisors with advanced practice skills in how to provide supervision at a higher level. Each chapter includes a range of activities and questions to support advanced supervisory practice and can be used with staff in supervision. This book can be read through in its entirety or specific chapters can be chosen depending on the need of the reader at the time. At the conclusion of each chapter, reflective questions assist the reader to take into their supervision meetings to explore with supervisees. They have been included to support you as the supervisor or leader to engage in further reflection, particularly if you are not receiving quality supervision or coaching yourself. I hope you enjoy reading it, as much as I have enjoyed writing this book. Remember to have your own quality supervision, continue to develop your own capabilities and be intentional in the supervision you provide.

Acknowledgements

This book has been a long time in the making. After many years of writing and facilitating supervision training; writing train the trainer programs; observing supervisors in their leadership and supervisory practice; and providing supervision to thousands of professionals both in Australia and internationally, it was time to write this book. Titled *Successful Supervision and Leadership*, this book explores many aspects of supervision to ensure it remains effective. All too often supervision is provided without a formal structure, lack of supervision model and without evaluation. This book is crucial to support supervisors and their supervisees to better understand many of the elements that ensure supervision is effective. It features the PASE™ Supervision model as one of the leading evidence-informed models internationally.

Throughout my career, there have been many amazing professionals and leaders that have encouraged me to write this book and been there with their wisdom along the journey. I would like to first say how grateful I am to have met Professor Peter Camilleri. His leadership during the years I provided lectureship at the Australian Catholic University was instrumental for writing this book. Thank you for your colleagueship and discussions over many years encouraging me to write this book. Two other amazing professionals and colleagues that I am grateful to are Professor Ming-Sum Tsui and Dr Kieran O'Donoghue. My career was just waiting for you both to come along: Two remarkable professionals and men who have been influential in my journey over the last few years. This book could not have happened without you both, thank you.

I would like to thank Ronnie Egan, Elizabeth Holloway, Alfred Kadushin, Derek Milne, Lambert Engelbrecht, Tony Morrison, Carol Falender, Edward Shafranske, Marion Bogo and many other professionals too many to name who have paved the way for this book over the decades in their research and writing. I appreciate the hard work you have done in the area of supervision and leadership. Thank you to Donna McAuliffe from Griffith University who has been a great inspiration to me in my career and a wonderful support in my current PhD journey and to Elyse Leonard, our Director Clinical Services and Programs, who reviewed the manuscript and editing process: thank you for taking the time on this important part of the project.

A special thank you to my PhD supervisor, Dr Maddy Slattery. We have been on this journey for nearly five years now and hopefully not too many to go before the PhD is completed. She is a selfless professional who believes in getting the best from her Higher Degree Research students and always finds the time to co-write, edit and read my work. I appreciate your dedication, commitment and encouragement, thank you so much.

To my late father Barry Phillips, who was one of life's gentle and authentic people taken way too early: He never compromised on quality and always held his clients at the forefront of being authentic and kind. He loved his family with a passion and loved life, which was obvious by his words and actions. I thank you for instilling in me ethics and values in a way that epitomized our relationship: thank you for being a wonderful father and mentor. Thank you to my truly wonderful children, Bruce, Mathew and Alysha. You have always supported me in my career and I thank you for your unconditional love and kindness given my busy work life. We are a great team and I am the lucky one being your mother. My life is what it is because of you all being in it. We are an awesome foursome.

Finally, I am forever grateful to the thousands of clients I have worked with over the last twenty-eight years. They put in the work through supervision and coaching. As a leader, supervisor and coach, it is so rewarding to be on their journey of discovery, celebration, achievement and challenge. To hold people's stories with care and kindness is one of the most privileged places to be. My commitment to you is to continue to provide effective and quality supervision and engage in ongoing growth so I can be my best for you.

Tracey Harris
BSW (MAASW) (Acc) Dip SocSc TAE HBDI (Acc)
Dip NSLeadership Adv Dip NSLeadership FDRP (Acc) FDRP (Acc)
PhD (Current)
CEO
Amovita International

Author

Tracey Harris is the CEO and founder of Amovita International. Amovita is a leader in providing professional consulting and business management services and programs to support high-performance outcomes in the workplace. They provide a wide range of strategy, human resource and management services and over seventy different training programs to support leaders in their roles. Testament to the work that Amovita provides, they have been awarded the 2011, 2012, 2013, 2014, 2015, 2016, 2017 and 2019 Australian Business Award for their contributions to the Australian business sector. Tracey is the developer of the PASE™, LASE™, FASE™, MASE™, VASE™, CASE™, CALD™ and MOSK™ supervision models. Tracey holds qualifications in social science, social work and neuroscience. Her career spans nearly thirty years in leadership, clinical practice and academia, and she has held senior advisory roles for Ministers and Members of Parliament. She held lectureship with the Australian Catholic University in Brisbane, Australia, where she lectured in social and public policy and a range of clinical and practice areas. Tracey works as a leadership and strategy consultant across Australia and internationally. She is currently undertaking her PhD as a Higher Degree Candidate with Griffith University in Brisbane, developing an evidence-informed framework to assess supervisor capability. She currently provides supervision to over 150 leaders and professionals and continues to develop training and resources to support leaders and supervisors to provide effective supervision.

Introduction

When we engage and communicate with others, we generally feel valued, heard, inspired and connected. Given we live busy lives and are in a time of immense pace, our brains are processing about 1,200–3,000 bits of information every second. We have somewhere between 50,000 and 60,000 thoughts a day and process each thought within 0.3–0.5 second (Neurocapability, 2019). We are spending more and more time on technology, engaging with social media each 24-hour period interrupting our sleeping patterns and connecting via other mediums rather than in person. As professionals, we do not realise that we are disconnecting from the very things that ground us, help us to feel connected and promote our health and well-being. One of the best forums to remember these things is in supervision discussions in the workplace. When we stop in the moment and reflect, it allows us to reconnect with ourselves in a way that tells our brain that we are mindful and self-caring. Whilst we are racing around our daily lives, we are busy in the moment rather than being intentional, purposeful and meaningful in the moment. Every day it is important to start the day with setting an intention, being an intentional leader and bringing intention to supervision discussions (Harris, 2018).

In my recent book published for new supervisors, I told the story of where my journey began in supervision. I was fortunate to receive quality supervision and over my career of now thirty years, I have attended a lot of supervision and leadership training, engaged in my own leadership and professional supervision, developed training to ensure that supervisors and supervisees receive quality training, developed a Train the Trainer program in supervision that sees leaders and supervisors attend three-day supervision training and four-day train the trainer training and then engage in monthly supervision. I have provided all types of supervision to thousands of professionals globally throughout my career, observed supervisors undertaking supervision, and at Amovita International we have an accreditation program where supervisors and leaders can have their supervisory practice evaluated and benchmarked from Level 1: Beginner Supervisor/Leader to Level 4: Advanced Supervisory Practice. We provide student practicums, present our work at conferences and engage in research and consulting services about leadership and supervision. So, I guess you could say that we take it fairly seriously! This is because we understand the capabilities required to provide effective supervision, know that having an evidence-informed supervision model is critical to great supervision outcomes and understand what frameworks and resources need to sit alongside supervision to ensure it remains effective.

There are many challenges that supervisors face to ensure they have the time to provide supervision. At Amovita, we know from the work we do that the first thing to be cancelled in a leader's day is supervision because other things take priority. It is often not viewed as important, valued or provide genuine outcomes. However, we know when it is provided with skill, capability, frequently and regularly, the benefits are immense, evidenced by the reduction in work cover costs, sick leave and workplace absences. Even if you are a busy leader, implementing just some of the resources outlined in this book will make a significant difference to the workplace. Having training on one of the models and using it in your own leadership and supervisory practice will definitely support staff better. Even better is attending quality training, and engaging in your own supervision will make an enormous difference. So however you view supervisory practice, provide it, receive it or understand it, there is one thing for sure: it is the one activity that can transform your workplace to maintain high-performance outcomes. I hope you enjoy reading this book and let me know how your own supervisory practice is making a difference in your workplace.

Chapter 1

Organisational Supervision Frameworks

Key focus for this chapter

- The importance of organisational frameworks for supervision
- The principles of an organisational framework
- Minimum standards
- The CAPES organisational framework
- Supervision practice guidelines
- Supervision policy frameworks

Introduction

Professional supervision is fundamental to reflecting on practice and ensuring organisational requirements are met. It supports staff to develop a framework for their professional identity and to feel appreciated and supported in their role (Milne, 2007). Supervision is a professional activity that ensures quality services are provided to clients with identified outcomes. Many organisations see the importance of supervision and provide staff with the opportunity to engage regularly with a qualified and well-trained supervisor. Despite this, many supervisors have neither attended formal supervision training, nor do they receive supervision. When supervisors attend training and engage in their own supervision on a regular basis, they are better equipped to showcase their skills and knowledge (capability framework) in a way that enables the supervisees to continue to grow and develop in their professional role (O'Donoghue & Tsui, 2017).

Supervision offers a well-structured process that allows the supervisee to critically analyse their practice in a way that cannot be undertaken in any other forum. This is particularly important where a professional is semi or fully autonomous in their role, and is required to work in complex situations. It allows them to continue to develop their skills and knowledge base in a way that contributes to their own and their colleagues practice. It also encourages supervisees to evoke organisational processes that are committed to continuous improvement (Lencioni, 2012).

Organisational Frameworks

For supervision to be valued and understood, it is important that organisations or businesses have a well-developed organisational framework that espouses key components to form a holistic way of approaching supervision. Having an organisational framework that supervisors consider in their supervisory practice provides a clear message that supervision is a crucial part of supporting professional practice. It also provides a message to all staff across the organisation that taking time out regularly to explore all aspects of their role is the most effective way to perform the role well. An organisational framework needs to be clear and concise, easy to transfer into practice and has a shared language framework that everyone understands (Egan, 2012). It also needs to relate to relevant policies and guidelines and how the organisation communicates its message. When key organisational frameworks and supervision relate to each other, everyone in the organisation can value the role that supervision plays and take it seriously. This will ensure that staff participate more readily, are better prepared for supervision discussions and provide more accurate feedback about how effective it is (Falender & Shafranske, 2017; Lencioni, 2012).

Principles

Developing and implementing an effective organisational framework for supervision needs sound principles that ensure everyone in the organisational environment knows what a framework means, what it can deliver and how to incorporate it into their practice. The following principles provide an overview on the development of an organisational framework for supervision. It needs to be simple to use yet sophisticated enough in its conceptualisation that demonstrates a sense of organisational capability.

The principles of an effective organisational framework include the following:

■ Clearly relating the framework to key aspects of the organisation's business such as position descriptions, the organisation's strategy, annual review process, vision, policy framework and governance processes;
■ Ensuring that staff are aware of the relevance of the framework and how it relates to supervision;
■ Making it interactive and relational across all roles in the organisation;
■ Ensuring it offers a collaborative language framework for all staff to value supervision and
■ Having a framework that demonstrates its generic intent, yet it is specific to relate to each supervisee's role.

The CAPES Framework

Developing an organisational framework is more effective when staff can refer to a visual representation of what the framework looks like and what it is intended to deliver. It is important to meet different learning styles in the organisational environment and therefore having a visual is helpful for the staff to follow.

The CAPES (Communication & Language, Attitudinal Positioning, Partnering & Relationships, Excellence in Practice, Skills & Capabilities) framework developed by Harris (2018) is an organisational framework that guides the way supervision is understood and provided across the organisational landscape. The CAPES framework is central to organisational policy in order for all parties to understand the key components supervision is built upon. The framework incorporates five elements:

1. (*C*) Knowing the appropriate communication and language in supervision to guide the supervisee in their practice;
2. (*A*) Knowing what attitudinal positioning is and how mindset, professional identity and qualities play an essential role in the supervisory process and relationship;
3. (*P*) Seeing supervision as a relational partnership between the supervisor and supervisee. Understanding the importance of

developing a positive and productive relationship that demonstrates a partnership approach;

4. (*E*) Understanding the fundamental role of supervision to ensure that excellence and best practice occur. The framework provides an overview of what excellence in practice is and how it is demonstrated through supervision and

5. (*S*) Provides an overview of the range of required skills and competencies the supervisor is to demonstrate to ensure their supervisory practice enhances supervision outcomes.

The CAPES framework is overviewed in Visual 1.1.

The **CAPES** framework incorporates the following:

C Communication & Language
A Attitudinal Positioning
P Partnerships & Relationships
E Excellence in Practice
S Skills & Competencies

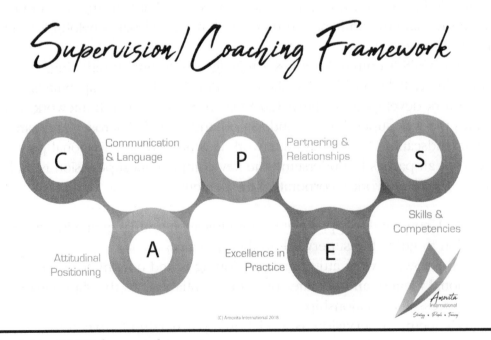

Visual 1.1 CAPES framework.

C – Communication & Language

Communication and language in supervision can influence the outcome of the supervision process, lead to better practice outcomes, provide guidance to the supervisee and change the course of a discussion. The use of language in supervision enhances the conversation, refuels the supervisee and impacts on mindset. The use of particular language and style of communication by the supervisor can also support and validate the supervisee's decision-making process. When a supervisor is well versed in different communication styles and knows how to effectively use words and language, the supervisee can feel confident in the supervisor's ability to perform the role. Supervisors need to understand how words and language impact the brain's emotional centre (i.e., flight, fight and freeze), and can evoke different responses from the supervisee in different situations (Farmer, 2009).

A – Attitudinal Positioning

Attitudinal positioning demonstrates how both parties in supervision present and engage with each other, what their mindset is like and what position they take with each other through their values. Having attitudinal positioning requires high-level insight, reflection and professional maturity. Being able to position oneself in a positive way, in respect and consideration of the other person, is a desirable quality in a professional supervisor. Understanding how cognitive and decision-making biases impact the supervisory role is another crucial skill for supervisors to utilise. We all hold different beliefs and biases, so understanding these assist the supervisory relationship to be purposeful and meaningful (Farmer, 2009).

P – Partnerships & Relationships

Supervision is a highly relational activity. Having the ability to develop, maintain and end relationships positively is an important part of an organisational framework for supervision. This requires knowledge about humanism, how relationships form and end, and the importance of any relationship cycle. The supervisor needs to demonstrate the ability to collaborate and form positive relationships with their supervisees, teams and the wider organisational system. It is important that supervisors demonstrate insight and introspection as this ensures the professional relationship is meaningful and supportive (Carroll, 2010).

E – Excellence in Practice

When supervisors remain up to date with the latest approaches in leadership and supervision, it supports supervisees to demonstrate excellence in practice. This can come from the supervisor having their own supervision, attending conferences and training, and reviewing their qualifications every few years. Being a good role model where the supervisor has congruent practice and values supports the supervisee to be a keen participant in the supervision process and can inspire the supervisee, so they are in own continual development. The supervisor's role is to value add to the supervisee's practice excellence.

S – Skills & Competencies

Professional supervisors need to be adequately trained in order to perform the supervisory role. Having key competences (skills, knowledge, attributes and tasks) provides supervisees with the confidence that the supervisor enhances their knowledge and skills in their role. It is equally important for organisations to develop minimum standards for supervisors, so that supervisors know where their supervision is benchmarked in relation to specific competencies. It is ideal for supervisors to have their supervisory practice observed at least once a year as part of the developmental process (Falender & Shafranske, 2017).

Minimum Standards

Some professions and workplaces have a set of minimum standards to support supervisors to demonstrate their capabilities in the role and guide them in their supervisory practice. Having minimum standards ensures that the supervisee can be confident about the supervision they receive and supervisors engage in their role more consciously (Falender & Shafranske, 2017). Minimum standards also need to align relevant professional association standards where available.

For example, minimum standards may include things such as

■ Supervisors are required to attend a minimum of two days supervision training prior to providing supervision in the workplace;
■ Supervisors are required to engage in their own supervision, either internal or external, to the workplace with a relevant professional who has met minimum standards;

■ Supervisors are required to sign the organisation's supervision practice guideline to demonstrate they have the required capabilities to provide supervision (i.e., skills, tasks, knowledge and attributes);

■ The supervisor has their supervision evaluated on an annual or bi-annual basis to ensure it remains effective;

■ They attend leadership/supervision refresher training every two years;

■ They can clearly articulate what aspects of their capability framework are used in supervision;

■ Supervision files are audited on an annual basis and

■ Supervisors demonstrate the use of key supervision resources such as a supervision model, schedule, document conversations, etc.

Supervision Guidelines

It is usual for organisations to have a well-defined supervision guideline or policy. I often find that supervision policies are as comprehensive as they need to be given that supervision sits within an industrial framework, i.e., records can be called upon or subpoenaed at any time. When developing a supervision policy or guideline, it is important that it links to other organisational documents such as a well-being policy, performance and conduct. If your organisation or business does not wish to have supervisees sign a supervision agreement, ensure information about engagement and participation in supervision is included in the code of conduct.

When developing professional standards for supervision, the following guideline may assist in the development process.

Supervision Guideline

1. Introduction
   Supervision is regarded as being critical to maintaining high standards of practice. It assists supervisees to reflect on their work, meet organisational requirements, feel supported and valued, and engage in ongoing development. It assists supervisees to maintain a professional identity and focus on well-being as a professional. Supervision Practice Standards aim to
   - Articulate the purpose, benefits and definitions of supervision;
   - Provide a guide for supervisors about best practice in supervision;

– Articulate the skills, knowledge, attributes and tasks that supervisors are required to hold in order to be an effective supervisor;
– Provide an overview of the process and framework for supervision;
– Outline the importance of using a supervision model to guide the discussion so that it is effective;
– Outline the requirements that supervisors must have in order to perform the supervisory role and
– Overview the supervisee's role in supervision.

2. Definition

Supervision is a professional and intentional forum that allows supervisees to critically reflect and analyse their work with an experienced supervisor. As a professional activity, it is the most effective space to analyse, attune information and refocus the supervisee's professional work. It allows the supervisee to develop a professional identity that demonstrates how and what occurs in the workplace, meet organisational requirements, feel supported as well as engage in ongoing growth and development (Harris, 2018).

3. The benefits of supervision

There are many benefits to having supervision. Supervision provides the opportunity to debrief with the purpose of minimising professional fatigue, stress and burnout. It enhances the supervisee's skills and knowledge, and assists them to be highly conscious of the intended outcomes in their role. It encourages supervisees to engage their professional practice framework in order to articulate the approaches they take in their work. Supervision also assists supervisees to maintain ethical practice (Milne, 2007).

4. Supervisor capability

Supervisors are required to attend credible training and demonstrate the transfer of knowledge and skills from the training into their supervisory practice. To perform their role at a required standard, supervisors are to engage in refresher training every two years and have their supervisory practice evaluated to demonstrate ongoing capability. Any evaluation process is to be supportive, positive and within a developmental framework. Supervisors are required to review their supervisory practice from the organisation's capability framework that includes the following categories: Skills, Tasks, Attributes and Knowledge (STAK). Where capability does meet the minimum requirements, supervisors are required to engage in further formal and informal development as well as demonstrate participation in their own executive (leadership) supervision using a relevant supervision model (Harris, 2017).

5. Components of supervision

There are four components in supervision identified by Harris (2018) that assist the supervisor to focus the supervision discussion with intention and purpose. The PASE™ model – Professional/Practice, Administration/Line Management, Support/Person and Educational/ Professional Development – is an evidence-informed supervision model that assists both parties to assess where the focus of the discussion has been throughout the supervision conversation. The four components of supervision are identified separately and are integrated as they relate to each other in the organisational context (outlined in Chapter 4).

6. Types of supervision

There are different types of supervision and often the type of supervision is determined by the organisation; however, the most common type is organisational or line management supervision. This is usually undertaken by the supervisee's line manager or supervisor and predominantly focuses on the non-negotiables and tasks of the role. The organisation may also have peer, collegial and/or group supervision. Whatever type of supervision provided is outlined in the guideline.

Professional supervision discussions focus on the professional aspects of the supervisee's role including professional identity, practices, client outcomes and reflection. It is common for supervisees to receive line management direction from their manager and professional supervision from another professional, either internal or external, to the organisation.

Group supervision is where a supervisor facilitates group discussion that focuses the agenda with contributions from all members of the group. It is a collaborative process whereby the members of the group seek to share their knowledge and engage in learning concurrently.

Formal supervision occurs where the supervisor engages a model such as the PASE model to focus on the discussion in an intentional, purposeful and meaningful way. The discussion is driven by an agenda, and the supervisee transfers discussion points into their practice and brings agenda items from their daily work routine.

Peer supervision takes place where a group of two or more professionals engage in a professional discussion about their role and practices in the role. It is focused and uses a model to guide the discussion allowing it to be productive and effective.

External supervision takes place between a supervisee and a professional who is external to the organisation. A formal contract is developed between the organisation and professional or where the supervisee pays for their own supervision, a formal agreement between both parties on expectations of supervision.

All types of supervision have strengths and limitations depending on a number of variables. It is important that all types of supervision are outlined in a supervision guideline, so supervisees understand the purpose and benefits.

7. Supervision process

The effectiveness of supervision is based on how the supervision process is developed and maintained. It is important that the supervision is premised on the basis of transparency, ethical practice and is provided in an environment where the supervisee feels valued. It is an environment that is meant to be supportive, developmental and dynamic. The supervisor is to be aware of the power dynamics in the hierarchical relationship and through the use of the PASE model any power differential is reduced as much as possible. For supervision to be effective, it is to be recognised within an ethical and industrial context and is appropriately documented where the supervisee understands the principles of informed consent. Supervision discussions are to be recorded on the appropriate documentation and reported in the context of the conversation using applied writing principles. The initial supervision meeting is to include an intake process where relevant questions are explored that allows a dynamic process to be set up and maintained for the duration of the supervisory relationship. Where there is a cultural context that needs to be respected, there may be reduced attention given to the amount of administration around supervision, i.e., reduction in documents and the supervisee sets up supervision in a mutually respected space.

8. Standards and indicators

Supervision guidelines need to include a set of outcome indicators that the supervisor and supervisee can clearly follow. They are to be clear, concise and relevant. The standards need to comprise upholding ethical standards, professional boundaries and the establishment of supervisory processes including minutes, agreements (where relevant), documentation and record keeping. Any guideline also outlines the use of external supervisors and ensures appropriate contracts are signed by the organisation and external provider. These contracts can include how supervision is reported, how it is evaluated, how external supervisors need to have been adequately trained, their level of experience, what resources they use, the supervision model used, the structure, format and if they are engaging in their own supervision (supervision of the supervisor). The contract also outlines how the supervisor has their own supervisory practice evaluated on a regular basis, i.e., every two years to demonstrate commitment to their own ongoing development (Harris, 2018).

Supervision Policy

Where there is no supervision guideline in place, at the very least a supervision policy is important given that supervision fits within an ethical and industrial context. A policy may not be as detailed as a guideline; however, it provides key information for both parties to follow. It acts as a reference point for both parties to come back to if issues arise in the supervisee's role or in the supervisory relationship.

The policy includes the following areas:

1. Introduction and purpose
2. Document scope
3. Key responsibilities
4. Definitions
5. Principles of supervision
6. Purpose and benefits of supervision
7. Types of supervision
8. Roles and responsibilities
9. Supervision timetable
10. Supervision meetings
11. Supervision environment
12. Professional conduct in supervision
13. Privacy and confidentiality
14. Performance concerns
15. Reference to organisational policies

Whether the organisation develops a supervision practice guideline or has a policy in place, it needs to integrate to other policies in the organisation such as any annual review policy, well-being and performance. Any performance issues identified are to be responded to in either line management supervision (if minor) or are dealt with outside of supervision in the organisation's performance policy.

Sample Supervision Policy Template

Supervision Policy

1. **Introduction and Purpose**

   (Organisation name) has a commitment to staff to ensure they are supported to undertake their role within the principles of high performance (positive mindset, professionality, have positive relationships, accountability, etc.). One of the most effective ways to do this is through line management and professional supervision. Supervision provides a reflective space and environment for staff to explore all aspects of their role, to feel valued and supported, and engage in ongoing professional development. It ensures that staff maintain a professional identity where they are conscious of how to maintain high performance in their role. Supervision is an integrated process that links to all other organisational performance areas including strategic plan, business framework, organisational and staff performance, the organisation's brand and services provided.

   The purpose of this policy is to describe the process by which supervision is provided and supports supervisors and leaders to perform their role within organisational requirements.

2. **Document Scope**

   This policy is intended for all managers, leaders, Board of Directors, CEOs, etc. who provide line management and professional supervision. It also provides guidance for all supervisees who receive supervision to ensure they use supervision effectively. All staff are required to positively engage and participate in supervision as the organisation values it as a way to support staff and meet requirements in their roles.

3. **Key Responsibilities**

   (Role) holds responsibility for review and monitoring of this policy, and supervisors and leaders (managers) are responsible for the implementation and interpretation of the policy detail. Staff are responsible for understanding their responsibilities in adhering to this policy.

4. **Definitions**

   Professional supervision is a professional conversation that takes place on a regular basis to ensure staff meet the requirements of their role. It is a collaborative and two-way process whereby the supervisor and supervisee discuss and monitor all aspects of the supervisee's role to ensure they perform within high-performance principles.

Supervision discussions focus on professional aspects of the supervisee's role, organisational requirements, supporting the supervisee and developing their practice. Professional supervision may be provided by the supervisee's line manager, another internal professional or someone external to the organisation or business.

Line management supervision is a professional conversation where the supervisee's direct line manager with the delegated authority monitors the supervisee's on-the-job performance, outputs and outcomes. Line management discussions focus on the tasks and processes of the supervisee's role, operational requirements and how the supervisee is meeting the requirements of their position description.

High performance: principles adopted in the organisation where all staff take a positive attitude, are conscious of their own beliefs and values that influence others, how they bring themselves to the role that supports others, ability to deal with change and commitment to their own professional identity.

5. **Principles of Supervision**

5.1. Supervision is a formal process that provides employees with clear direction and support to successfully perform their role in line with organisational policy and the supervisee's position description.

5.2. Supervision ensures employees feel supported, valued and encouraged in a positive and proactive way to perform their role with confidence.

5.3. Supervision is directly linked to any annual review process, and all documentation relates to each other to enable the transfer of information from supervision to the review process and vice versa.

5.4. Supervision is a two-way communication process in which open conversations (feedback) take place in order to maintain high performance in the role and ensure the supervisor has appropriate capability to perform the role.

5.5. Supervision ensures that the supervisee's work is planned and co-ordinated in a measured way, and workload and workflow are monitored and reviewed to ensure that any risk of fatigue and burnout is evaluated.

5.6. Supervision provides an environment and process in which supervisees can develop and maintain their professional framework, reflect, engage in self-awareness and have the skills to evaluate performance in their role.

6. **Purpose and Benefits of Supervision**

   6.1. Supervision is a positive mechanism that reduces the vicarious impacts of complex work. Having open discussions allows the supervisee to reflect and debrief in a supportive environment which can reduce the risks of burnout.

   6.2. Supervision is a positive process that assists supervisees to continue to hone and enhance skills and knowledge in their role. It assists the supervisee to be aware of what aspects of their role and practice need further development.

   6.3. Supervision is a process whereby the supervisee can be open about the things that are challenging them in their role and work with the supervisor to resolve any ethical dilemmas or challenges without concerns of being open.

7. **Types of Supervision**

   7.1. Face-to-face supervision: supervision conversations are generally held with both the supervisor and supervisee in the same space on a regular basis, i.e., monthly for full time staff. This may also take place via other mediums like social media mediums where both parties may be located in a different workplace, but still can have conversations remotely through technology.

   7.2. Observations: the supervisor may observe the supervisee in their role directly or indirectly. This may include using the supervisee's professional excellence framework to ask questions that allows them to know how the supervisee is undertaking their role. This may also take place through directly observing the supervisee to support them in a developmental process whereby the supervisor provides feedback through the supervisory process.

   7.3. Information supervision is often referred to as 'supervision on the run' whereby discussions take place in an informal context. Informal supervision takes place where the supervisee accesses the supervisor in between formal meetings or when required. This type of supervision provides the supervisee with an immediate response and only takes place where the supervisee needs a decision made that is outside of their delegated authority or where the supervisee is unsure of what action to take, etc. No formal agenda is developed, and the conversation may not be documented.

   7.4. Group supervision: this is where supervision occurs in a team environment and in conjunction with other team members. There is usually a formal agenda and regular time set aside for the group discussion. The supervisor or group members may rotate the facilitation role, or a line manager may facilitate the discussion. Supervision agenda and minutes are documented as part of the process. The group may also have guest speakers attend the meeting and often group supervision has an educational component where topics are developed in advance. Group supervision is highly effective in ensuring that group members learn from each other; however, it can be challenging when the group becomes too large as some members may over time feel the group process does not meet their supervisory needs where one-to-one supervision discussions would.

7.5. Peer supervision: peer supervision takes place where colleagues engage in professional discussion about their roles without a facilitator. An agenda is developed in each meeting, and discussion is informal in nature and may not follow an agenda or record minutes.

7.6. External supervision takes place with an experienced and suitably qualified supervisor external to the organisation. Supervision may take place with individual staff or in a group setting. Supervision can be provided within the workplace or off site. It is conducted on a regular or irregular basis with a formal agenda, and supervision minutes are recorded and signed off. Where external supervision is provided, there needs to be a contract in place so the external supervision understands the organisation's requirements, reporting processes and if the group will be open to staff coming in and out of the process or the group is closed with the same members regularly. The supervisor is usually aware of the objectives and aims of the employees' workplace and uses a formal framework.

8. **Roles and Responsibilities**

8.1. The two primary roles in supervision are the supervisor and supervisee. Both parties play an important role with particular functions and responsibilities to ensure supervision remains effective. One of the components to effective supervision is the development and maintenance of a positive and transparent relationship. The supervisor needs to understand the different developmental stages of each supervisee and in turn adjust their supervisory approach and discussion style to ensure they can progress the supervisee's capabilities over time.

8.2. Both parties are required to commit to supervision meetings on a regular basis and ensure appropriate processes are put into place to achieve key outcomes.

8.3. Both parties are responsible for
- working together in a positive, respectful, professional and collaborative manner;
- preparing for supervision meetings, any pre-preparation, research and completion of things in between meetings;
- engaging and participating positively in supervision;
- evaluating the effectiveness of supervision and
- raising and resolving issues without fear of the power differential.

8.4. Supervisor's responsibilities are to
- negotiate timing, venue and frequency of supervision sessions;
- use an evidence-informed supervision model, appropriate process and supervision framework;
- have their supervisory practice evaluated on an annual or bi-annual basis to ensure their supervisory practice is maintained;
- ensure supervision links to any annual review process;
- seek feedback to ensure their style of supervision meets the supervisee's needs;
- provide an environment of trust, transparency, ethical practice and positive support;
- provide direction, guidance, mentoring and coaching to the supervisee;
- recognise and celebrate the supervisee's achievements;
- use positive language that is supportive, and acknowledge the supervisee in good and challenging times;
- inspire the employee and coach the supervisee to be motivated in their role;
- ensure the supervisee has the appropriate skills and knowledge to perform their role as required;
- ensure the supervisee has the appropriate information to do their role well;
- provide supervision that engages the supervisee in an ongoing developmental process;
- understand what biases, beliefs and values that influence the supervisee's role;
- ensure that supervision is scheduled across the year with a minimum of 12 sessions a year where the supervisee is full time or relevant for part time and casual staff;

- supervision is to be provided in line with any professional association requirements;
- ensure the supervisee understands the supervisor's role, experience, training, background and qualifications to perform the supervisory role;
- complete relevant supervision documentation required, i.e., schedule, minutes, etc.;
- participate actively in their own supervision;
- ensure refresher training is attended bi-annually and there is evidence of what is transferred from the training back into the supervisory role and
- maintain the supervisee's supervision file with relevant documentation.

8.5. Supervisee's responsibilities are to
- participate in supervision in a positive and proactive way, be prepared and on time;
- contribute to the supervision agenda prior to supervisor or at the commencement of the supervision meeting;
- complete tasks and practices agreed on in between sessions;
- review the previous month's minutes in preparation for the next meeting;
- advise the supervisor if they are unable to attend a meeting and ensure the meeting is rescheduled;
- ensure minutes accurately reflect the supervision discussion;
- actively pursue a developmental learning agenda;
- take responsibility for supervision outcomes;
- discuss with the supervisor how to have open conversations where needs are not being met and
- build and maintain an open and positive relationship with the supervisor.

9. **Supervision Timetable**
   9.1. Ensure the organisation has a prescribed supervision timetable where employees engage in a formal face-to-face supervision in a consistent and regular manner depending on their role, i.e., full time, part time or casual.
   9.2. Full-time staff: participate in supervision in a formal setting on a monthly basis with their direct line supervisor and/or professional supervisor.

9.3. Part-time staff: participate in supervision in a formal setting on a six-weekly basis with their direct line supervisor and/or professional supervisor.

9.4. Casual staff: participate in supervision on a bi-monthly or quarterly basis individually or in a group setting where applicable.

9.5. All leaders and supervisors are required to attend their own supervision on a monthly basis and participate in bi-annual observations to assess their supervisory practice. Observations undertaken are to be conducted within a developmental process and a report completed to support further supervisory skills and knowledge.

10. **Supervision Meetings**

10.1. In initial supervision meetings, supervisors are required to complete the intake process and set up the supervisee's portfolio of documents including the organisations supervision policy or guideline, supervision agreement, supervision schedule record, agenda, minute template, intake questions, evaluation framework and copy of the supervision model used.

10.2. In the first meeting, the supervisor explains the relevant documents that are used in supervision and reviews the supervision policy and/or agreement. The supervisor and employee are both to sign the supervision agreement and a copy provided to the employee. The original copy is kept on the employee's supervision file, stored in a secure location.

10.3. A supervision agenda is developed in conjunction with the employee prior to the supervision meeting. Where this has not occurred, the agenda will be developed at the commencement of the supervision meeting. The agenda sets the format and direction of the discussion.

10.4. Supervision meetings will occur for a duration of 60 minutes. The focus of the supervision discussion is evaluated at the end of the meeting using the PASE or relevant model at the conclusion of the supervision meeting (see Chapter 4). Supervision minutes are documented in each meeting and signed off at the conclusion of the meeting with a copy being provided to the employee for their reference and file.

10.5. Professional supervision is not personal counselling, performance management or a disciplinary process.

10.6. Supervision discussions are guided by the PASE supervision model in which each quadrant includes prompt words that may assist to develop the supervision agenda.

- Professional/Practice (P): Professional practice framework, reflection, language, ethics/ethical dilemmas, case reviews, professional identity, professional beliefs and values, professional skills and knowledge, theories and evaluation.
- Administrative/Line Management (A): Policies, procedures, quality assurance, risk management, leave planning, timesheets, resourcing, workflow and workloads, time management, funding, budgets, systems, projects, client satisfaction, position description, planning, key performance indicators.
- Support/Person (S): Self-care, team functioning, morale, debriefing, stress, job and role satisfaction, work/life balance, health and well-being, workplace relationships, dynamics, refuelling, validation, personal beliefs and values, personal responsibility vs. professional accountability, encouragement, hope and courage.
- Educative/Professional Development (E): Professional excellence, training needs, transfer of learning from training and conferences into the role, competencies and skills, research, career planning, learning, growth and development, evidence base, coaching and mentoring.

11. **Supervision Environment**

11.1. Given the nature of supervision and to support the reflective process, supervision is to be provided free of distractions and interruptions.

11.2. Mobile phones are to be switched off or where appropriate turned on silent. This is to be negotiated with the other party prior to the commencement of supervision meetings.

12. **Professional Conduct in Supervision**

12.1. Supervision discussions are to be conducted with respect, within principles of confidentiality and both parties are to be professional at all times.

12.2. Supervision discussions are to be conducted in a supportive, positive, participatory and ethical manner.

12.3. Supervision is to be based on trust and positive relationship, and it promotes a desire to achieve.

12.4. Supervision is outcome focused in which discussions are reflective and solution focused.

13. **Privacy and Confidentiality**
    13.1. Information shared and disclosed in supervision is considered to be within the bounds of confidentiality. Limited confidentiality principles are to be discussed in the intake process of supervision.
    13.2. The supervisor meets relevant reporting requirements without breaching the employee's privacy or confidentiality.

14. **Performance Concerns**
    14.1. Where issues have been identified in supervision around per-formance, conduct or behaviour, support is to be provided that encourages the supervisee to make the required changes. Where changes do not occur, any performance discussion is to be taken out of the professional supervision space and a separate meeting is to be held in a line management conversation and the supervisor or line manager follows the appropriate policy.

15. **Reference to Organisational Policies**
    This section outlines any relevant organisational policies that relate to this supervision document, i.e., performance policy, well-being policy, code of conduct, code of ethics, etc.

Summary

This chapter has explored the importance of having an organisational supervision framework that overviews how supervision is to be provided. We have discussed the importance of having a supervision policy or guideline that supports supervision to remain effective. Consider the following reflective questions as a summary to this chapter:

What have been the key things you have gained from reading this chapter on organisational frameworks in supervision?
What have been your reflections about the importance of having an organisational framework for supervision?
List three things that you will take from this chapter to incorporate into your supervisory role.
What do you think will be useful to talk to your supervisee/s about regarding this chapter?

Chapter 2

Developing a Professional Excellence Framework

Key focus for this chapter

- Defining professional excellence frameworks
- Understanding your own professional excellence framework
- The importance of having a framework
- How to develop a professional excellence framework
- How to use your own professional excellence framework
- Understand how to maintain a framework in a professional role
- How to use the framework in supervision
- Evaluating the effectiveness of a professional excellence framework
- Developing your own supervisor leadership excellence framework

Introduction

Consider for a moment what conversations take place in supervision and where supervisees draw their skills and knowledge from to maintain performance and practice in their role? When thinking about your supervisor or leadership role, how do you use your leadership skills to demonstrate your supervision approach and style to ensure supervision meets the supervisee's needs? These are all useful questions to reflect on as we explore this chapter on what a professional excellence framework (PEF) is, how it is developed, how to maintain it and consider how you might get supervisees to evidence their PEF in their role (Davys & Beddoe, 2010).

As we explore this chapter, consider the following reflective questions as a supervisor and leader. These questions are helpful to ask your supervisees in supervision as they begin to develop their PEF. It assists supervisees to reflect more deeply on what their role is and how they undertake their practice. The questions can also be changed to suit the supervisee's role. Remember that as a leader and supervisor, it is equally as important to consider relevant questions yourself that demonstrate to your supervisees what you do and how you do it (Carroll, 2010).

Reflective questions:

- What do you base your ethical decisions on?
- What is included in your decision-making framework?
- What knowledge and skills do you draw from to evidence what you do in your role?
- What do you see as your professional identity?
- How does supervision support you to undertake your role more effectively?
- How do you regularly reflect on what you do in your work?
- What knowledge guides your work?
- What informs your professional knowledge?
- What supervision style suits your best?
- How do you actively engage your own self-care as a professional?
- How do you encourage supervisees to maintain self-care?
- What do you notice when you are stressed, fatigued or burnt out?
- How do you know any of your colleagues are stressed, fatigued or burnt out?
- What would others notice about yourself when you are stressed?
- What do you draw from in training and your qualifications that are evident in your practice?
- What beliefs and values influence you as a professional?
- How do you remain accountable in the role?
- How does the organisational structure inform your role?
- If you had a visual of your PEF, what would it look like?
- How do you evaluate the effectiveness of the supervision you provide?
- What reflective framework do you use to ensure supervisees analyse their role and practice?

These questions could be asked of you as a leader and supervisor, so consider them in relation to your own role.

What Is a PEF?

Having a PEF is an essential tool for maintaining performance in any role. As a supervisor a PEF is crucial to understand what supervisees are doing at any time in their role. Often referred to as a professional practice framework, it is a conceptual and visual representation that organises the supervisee's skills, knowledge and attributes. It arranges information in a formal way, so the supervisee can use it in their role to articulate and demonstrate what they are doing and why.

Having this framework provides the perfect platform for the supervisee to develop their professional identity and understand their personal and professional values. It shows how supervisees work holistically to engage professional practice in their role and it helps supervisees to articulate what they are doing in their role in all aspects of their work. A PEF is consistent with the purpose, standards and mission of the organisation and can change based on different roles or when the supervisee moves from one organisation to another.

A PEF

■ is a conceptual framework for analysing and understanding the supervisee's work;
■ is a visual way of organising key aspects of the supervisee's role;
■ provides guidance and direction for the supervisee in their role;
■ articulates evidence-based decision making in the role;
■ systematically orders the various approaches to practice relevant to the professional context;
■ provides a rationale for making professional judgements;
■ is a structure for communicating the supervisee's focus;
■ provides an avenue for reflection;
■ demonstrates professional identity;
■ provides guidance on what the organisation requires of the role and
■ is a professional way the supervisee can articulate and define what they do and why they do it.

In considering this, reflect on the following questions about your supervisees and their PEF. These questions are important to ask supervisees as it supports them to reflect at a deeper level the importance of having their own PEF in their role. It also provides supervisors with a useful way to begin discussions and explore with the supervisee different areas in the framework. As the supervisee starts developing their framework, it can form part of the

Table 2.1   Reflective Questions

Outline what you think a PEF is?	
What do you think is included into this type of framework?	
How might you work with supervisees to develop their framework in supervision?	
How would you ensure your supervisees review their framework through supervision?	
What role do you think it plays in the supervisee's role?	
As a supervisor, also consider how have you developed your own leadership excellence framework? What do you think has guided its development? How do you demonstrate it through your leadership role?	

supervision agenda on a regular basis. In Table 2.1, the reflective questions assist you as the supervisor to explore aspects of the PEF with the supervisee as they begin to develop their framework and demonstrate in practice.

PEF Components

There are six distinct areas in a PEF. Each area relates to the other and all are equally important. The six areas are as follows:

1. Professional/Practice Skills
2. Professional Knowledge
3. Approaches and Frameworks
4. Beliefs and Values
5. Professional Identity
6. Organisational/Business Context

1. **Professional/Practice Skills**
   The first area of the PEF outlines what professional and practice skills the supervisee uses in their role. The supervisee outlines the professional skills they have and how they demonstrate them in the work and practice context.
   Professional practice skills assist the supervisee to problem solve, make sound decisions and understand what they do in their role.

Table 2.2 Professional Practice Skills

Professional/ practice skills	How can supervisees demonstrate their practice skills in their role?

Articulating the professional practice skills that are used is integral to maintaining the requirements of the role. Skills are drawn from training; qualifications; attendance at conferences; professional development; peers and supervision conversations. Skills are practiced over time and are consistently honed and shaped to ensure the supervisee performs their skills competently in the role.

List the professional practice skills you think that the supervisees need to include in their PEF in Table 2.2. When supporting the supervisee to develop their PEF, this table can be used to explore each of the six areas.

2. **Professional Knowledge**

Drawing on professional knowledge is an important part of evidencing how the supervisee performs their role. Guiding staff about what knowledge they draw from to do their work promotes reflection and insight. Our professional knowledge is drawn from a number of areas including our qualifications, training, conferences, reading and in discussions with others. Enhancing knowledge is important for ongoing growth and development and it ensures that staff can articulate the knowledge base that guides them in their work. It is also important that supervisees know what transferrable knowledge they bring from other roles to their current one. List the body of knowledge that supervisees evidence in their role and where they draw their knowledge from in Table 2.3.

Table 2.3 Professional Knowledge

Professional Knowledge	How Do Supervisees Evidence Their Knowledge in Their Role?

3. **Approaches and Theories**

   Different approaches and frameworks inform professional knowledge and influence the practice skills that are used in the supervisee's role. Approaches and frameworks guide how we work with clients and provide confidence that the practice approach is appropriate for a particular client group. It can be challenging to keep up with the latest approaches and evidence base given the busy nature of the workplace; however, when staff use different approaches in their role, it helps others to see what evidence base the supervisee is working with (Harris, 2018). List the different approaches and theories that are important for the supervisee to demonstrate in Table 2.4.

4. **Beliefs and Values**

   Beliefs and values are shaped in childhood and through life experiences. They are an important part of who we are, and they influence our thinking, opinions and communication. We have many positive beliefs as well as conditional beliefs; therefore, it is important to ensure that the conditional beliefs are known to the supervisee and they do not impact negatively in the workplace. When we are aware of positive and conditional beliefs gained throughout life, it is easier to see how they impact our relationships and the professional role. Conditional beliefs are defined as I never get it right, I am not good enough, others see me as not good enough, etc. When we know what conditional beliefs interrupt professional thinking, it is easier to reframe them into

Table 2.4 Approaches and Theories

Approaches and Theories That Inform the Supervisee's Work	How Do Supervisees Evidence These?

Table 2.5 Beliefs and Values

Beliefs and Values That Inform the Role	How Do Supervisees Use These in Their Role?

being positive. List some beliefs and values that you have as a person and professional in Table 2.5. Try and list both positive and conditional beliefs that you have noticed at times.

5. **Professional Identity**

Our professional identity demonstrates to others how we see our professional self in relation to others and in our role. It is a way of telling others what our professional brand is. Our professional identity follows us throughout our career and defines others perceptions of us

Table 2.6 Professional Identity

Professional Identity Components	How Is This Evidenced in Practice?

in a professional context. It is influenced by our own and other's self-perception and changes over time depending on our role and where we are in our career. Professional identity can incorporate our job title and the type of organisation or business we work in. Being a member of a professional body or association also defines our professional identity through their standards and code of ethics. It is developed as we become aware of the various parts of our professional self and how reflective we are as a professional. Consider aspects of professional identity that are important for the supervisees to demonstrate and how you might see this evidenced in their role in Table 2.6.

There are various things that are included in a professional identity framework, including
 – Values and beliefs
 – Behaviour and conduct
 – Mindset
 – How we develop and end relationships
 – Attitude and attributes
 – The meaning we attach to different things like opinions
 – How we see particular issues and topics in relation to our work
 – Language framework
 – Decision making
 – Professional boundaries
 – Motivation
 – Ethics and morals
 – Language framework

Table 2.7   Organisational Context

What Do Supervisees Take from the Organisational Context to Inform Their Work?	How Does This Influence or Impact on Their Role?

6. **Organisational Context**

   The organisational environment is just as important in a PEF as the other areas. It is important to understand the organisational structure in which the supervisee's role sits and how the management and/or board structure influences decision making. In any organisation, policies and procedures guide supervisees in their work as does their position description and employment contract. Organisational culture also influences how supervisees engage in their work, work in teams and have professional relationships with others. Outline what aspects of the organisational context are vital for the supervisee to demonstrate in supervision in Table 2.7.

Developing a PEF

Now that we have discussed what a PEF is, the next step is to explore how to develop the framework. To assist supervisee's to develop their own framework, it is useful spend a whole supervision conversation discussing each of the areas shown in Visual 2.1. Exploring the six individual areas of the framework through a reflexive process allows the supervisee to reflectively explore where they draw from in each area and what they are, i.e., what their skills are, what knowledge they have, etc. It supports the supervisee to remain conscious in their role and reduces the risk of complacency.

The first part of developing a PEF is to ask where the supervisee draws each area from. For example, the question 'where do you draw your

Professional Skills	Professional Knowledge
Approaches & Theories	**Beliefs & Values**
Professional Identity	Organisational Context

Visual 2.1   Professional excellence framework.

professional skills from?' assists the supervisee to consider their professional practice skills and where they draw them from. A follow-on question in each of the next area is 'where do you draw your professional knowledge from that informs your work?', 'where do you draw relevant approaches and frameworks from?', 'where do you think you draw your beliefs and values from?', 'where do you draw aspects of your professional identity from?' and 'what do you draw from to maintain organisational requirements?'.

   '*Where do you draw from*' questions.

1. Where do you draw your professional practice skills from?
2. Where do you draw your professional knowledge from?

3. Where do you draw your approaches and frameworks from to inform your work?
4. Where do your beliefs and values come from that you see in your work?
5. Where do you draw your professional identity from?
6. Where do you draw from to consider organisational requirements?

If the supervisee has never engaged in this type of reflective process, it is important that the supervisor uses additional prompt questions to support the supervisee to open up the reflective process. Once the supervisee has explored all six areas of the framework and this is documented in the supervision minutes, the following question explores each of the areas in more detail – 'what are your professional practice skills?', 'what knowledge do you believe you have?', 'what approaches and theories would I see you use to inform your role?', 'what beliefs and values do you bring to your role?', 'what are the components of your professional identity?' and 'what things in the organisation do you use in your role (Harris, 2018). The 'what are the ...' questions allow the supervisee to critically analyse the skills and knowledge they use in their role, document them in the PEF and consciously demonstrate them in their work and discuss in supervision.

The 'what are the' questions.

1. What are your professional skills?
2. What is your professional knowledge base?
3. What approaches and theories do you use in your work?
4. What are the beliefs and values you bring to your role?
5. What do you see as your professional identity?
6. What things in the organisational context do you use as a professional?

The 'what are the' questions can be challenging for many supervisees given they are aimed at supervisees being able to clearly articulate what they use in their role. Supervisee responses are then detailed in supervision minutes for ongoing discussions.

Maintaining a PEF

Once the supervisee completes this process in supervision, they complete the excellence framework template (resource) that is included in this chapter. The supervisee starts to use the framework consciously in their role as a way to effectively demonstrate how they use any and all of the framework areas. In supervision meetings, the supervisee brings agenda topics from the framework, and this becomes part of the focus of the discussion on a regular basis. The supervisor also uses the framework to promote reflective discussion around the supervisee's work. This assists the supervisee to further develop and maintain all areas of their framework over time as well as encouraging the supervisee to maintain critical self-awareness in their daily practice and in between meetings.

As the PEF is explored in supervision, the supervisor gains an understanding of what the supervisee is doing in their role, how they are practicing and why they do what they do (Carroll, 2007). Having this information is nearly as useful as if the supervisor was directly observing the supervisee in their work. Through the process of questioning and critical reflection, both the supervisor and supervisee engage in a positive conversation process that explores all aspects of the supervisees work over time (Harris, 2018).

Questions in Table 2.8 align with the PEF and can be explored in supervision over time.

Table 2.8   PEF Questions

Professional Excellence Domain	Example Questions
Professional practice skills	What skills do you use when...? What practices did you engage with...? What would I have noticed about your practice when...? What practices were evident? How might you change your practice approach with? How did you use your communication skills? How important were your interpersonal skills? How did you undertake an assessment with...?
Professional knowledge	What knowledge base did you use? How did you know your knowledge in that situation was useful? What would I have noticed when you were focused on being strengths based? What do you know about being client centred? What approach do you think will work? How do you transfer your knowledge to others? How does your knowledge inform your practice? How do you know what you about...?

(Continued)

Table 2.8 (*Continued*)   PEF Questions

Professional Excellence Domain	*Example Questions*
Approaches and theories	What theory do you think is relevant? How might we include the theory on...? What approach applies to...? What do you consider when you think about a particular theory? How do you know that approach is relevant with...? What does that article say about...? What theories do you think apply? Are there any gaps in the current approach you are using?
Beliefs and values	What beliefs do you think surfaced? What impact did your belief have when...? How do you think empathy played a part in...? When do you think that belief came into play? How did your values around influence your decision? Why was that so important for you? What values are essential to you? How is your practice influenced by your beliefs and values?
Professional identity	What do you see as part of your professional identity? How is that relationship important to you as a professional? What might that tell you about your mindset at the time? How would others see your integrity? How does your thinking influence your approach with...? What would others say about your professional identity? How would I see your professional identity in your practice? How could your professional identity be further developed?
Organizational context	What policies do you think are important in this case? How does the management structure impact...? What do you think is important to consider in your role? What organizational requirements do you think are important? What organizational values are relevant to...? How do you align that policy with your practice? How do you demonstrate the requirements of your position description? How does that relate to the organization's purpose?

Evaluating a PEF

As the supervisee develops their PEF and begin to integrate it into their role, it is important for the supervisor to evaluate how it is effectively being used to demonstrate performance and practice. The question is, how do you evaluate that the framework is being used in the supervisee's role? The most effective way to do this is through the use of reflective questions in supervision or through the use of a more formal evaluation process. This can be undertaken through observing the supervisee in their work and reflective discussion to evaluate how it is being used. Table 2.9 overviews each of the professional excellence areas and useful questions to assess how it is being used.

Table 2.9   Evaluation Framework

PPEF Area	Evaluation Questions	Notes
Professional skills	• How have you evidenced the use of professional skills in your role? • What skills do you think have been important to use in your role since our last supervision? • What skills development would you see as important for the team? • How have you imparted your skills to others in the team? • What skills do you see that are crucial when working with clients?	
Professional knowledge	• How have you used your body of knowledge to inform how you work in your role? • How have you transferred your knowledge from your qualifications and other professional experiences into your role? • How have others benefited from your knowledge base? • What knowledge would you like to gain to inform your practice? • What knowledge have you found the most useful in your role over the last year?	

(Continued)

Table 2.9 (*Continued*) Evaluation Framework

PPEF Area	Evaluation Questions	Notes
Approaches and theories	• What theories do you incorporate into your practice? • What approaches are relevant with the clients you work with? • How have the theories you have used been useful in your work? • How do you remain conscious of the appropriate theories to use in your work? • How has research informed your practice?	
Beliefs and values	• What beliefs and values are important to you as a professional? • How have these influenced your work and role? • How have other's beliefs and values influenced you in your role? • What beliefs and values have not worked that well as a professional? • How have your beliefs and values influenced practice outcomes?	
Professional identity	• How would you describe your professional identity? • What makes up your professional identity? • How would others see what your professional identity is? • How does it influence you in your role and professional relationships in the workplace? • How important is your professional identity to you?	
Organisational context	• What things in the organisation influence how you do your role? • What is important for you to consider when working with clients? • How does the organisational structure impact your role? • What things do you find useful working in the organisation? • What practices does the organisation have that you use in your work?	

Leadership Excellence Framework

Whilst it is crucial that supervisees develop and evaluate their PEF, it is equally important that supervisors and leaders also develop their own framework. It demonstrates to supervisees that their leader is congruent in the use of their own framework and they evaluate their leadership practice on a regular basis.

Leadership Skills	Leadership Knowledge
Approaches & Theories	Beliefs & Values
Leadership Identity	Organisational Requirements

Visual 2.2 Leadership excellence framework.

The same principles apply to the leader's framework as does the supervisee's framework. The only difference is the language that is used in the framework. Visual 2.2 overviews the components of the supervisor's PEF. 'Where do you draw from' and 'what are the' questions are the same for the leader and they may respond to the questions in a self-reflection process or explore them with their own manager or supervisor. A visual is developed to demonstrate what is used in the leadership role, and it is useful to show the supervisee how they feel confident that their own supervisor/leader is serious about demonstrating their skills and abilities.

Summary

This chapter has explored the importance of reflecting on the different aspects of the supervisee's role through the development of a PEF. Consider the following questions to review what you have gained from this chapter.

What have been the key things you have gained from reading this chapter on PEFs?
What have been your reflections about this chapter regarding the importance of supervisees having a PEF?
List three things that you will take from this chapter to incorporate into your supervisory role.
What do you think will be useful to talk to your supervisee/s about regarding this chapter?
What steps are important to ensure supervisees develop their PEF?

Chapter 3

The Contextual Nature of Supervision

Key focus for this chapter

- Defining what supervision is
- Supervision as a practice
- Exploring the benefits of supervision
- Key roles and responsibilities
- Accessing quality training
- The supervisory alliance
- Learning styles
- Preparing for supervision
- Setting up the first and subsequent meetings
- The role of supervision agreements
- How to set an effective agenda
- Setting goals in supervision
- Closing supervision meetings
- External and internal supervision

Introduction

Since the nineteenth century, professional supervision and leadership have played an important role across various disciplines such as business, human resources, psychology, counselling, nursing and social work. Whilst there are limited references to professional supervision made in early journals and books, the context and purpose of supervision prior to the 1920s was different to how it has progressed in its definition, purpose and process. Moving from an administrative function where historically, the primary task of supervision was managing and distributing resources and ensuring the supervisee was accountable in their role; supervision and coaching have moved from being purely about accountability to being more about focusing on professional practices of the supervisee's role and supporting them to feel valued and appreciated (Carroll, 2007; Falender & Shafranske, 2017).

Since the 1970s, there has been more emphasis on the role and value of professional supervision as a professional activity, evidenced by the number of studies undertaken over the three decades (O'Donoghue & Tsui, 2017). It has been refashioned as a practice in its own right where supervisors require specific skills, knowledge and attributes to remain effective in the role. Whilst supervision has a heavy emphasis on accountability and meeting organisational objectives, it is also viewed through a contemporary lens that reflects on the supervisees practice to ensure high-performance outcomes.

In thinking about the importance of professional supervision, there are two well-known cases in the United Kingdom – Victoria Climbié aged eight who died in 2000 and 'Baby P' (Peter Connelly) who was seventeen months when he died in 2007. Both children fell victim to horrific abuse at the hands of their guardians and caregivers. When Victoria Climbié was found deceased, it was reported that she had sustained over 100 separate injuries. The week before Victoria died, her case had been closed after deciding she was not at risk of 'significant harm'. A public inquiry into Victoria's death found that there were twelve opportunities where local authorities could have responded differently. When the Baby P case was investigated, it was reported he had received sixty visits from a wide range of professionals. The Judge in the trial following Victoria's death described the practice of some of the professionals involved as engaging with 'blinding incompetence' (House of Commons, 2003).

Many of the professionals involved in both of these cases disclosed similar responses of feeling overwhelmed due to their high workloads; felt unsupported in the workplace; under-resourced and were ill-equipped to provide good practice outcomes due to lack of supervision and support. Like them, their supervisor and managers were equally stressed and probably did not have the support they needed in turn to provide quality supervision. These two cases are like many others; however, they provide valuable insight across all workplaces about how important professional supervision is. During the public inquiries into these two cases, it was found there was a limited communication between different disciplines, staff involved and supervision was not provided on a regular basis (House of Commons, 2003).

The House of Commons' Health Committee report on these two cases (2003) brings to light how professional supervision needs to be integral for all professionals in any workplace.

> The question of adequate training and supervision for staff working in all the relevant agencies was also an issue identified in the Inquiry. The provision of supervision may have looked good on paper 'but in practice it was woefully inadequate for many front-line staff'. (p. 13)

Redefining Supervision

Professional supervision is a forum in which the supervisee reviews their work in order to seek feedback, engage in further professional development, reflect-in-practice to ensure quality services are provided (Bogo & McKnight, 2005). Professional supervision is being redesigned in a number of ways. There is more quality training available, and supervision is now valued more as a professional practice in its own right. Many supervisors are required to take part in their own supervision, and given more professions are now registered; supervisors are required to evidence what occurs in supervision. Professionals who receive regular and formal supervision are more effective in their practice and are better equipped to manage workplace challenges and issues (Wyles, 2007). With the explosion of the literature around neurosocial science, there is also evidence that supervision is considered to be a 'brain-friendly activity' where supervision discussions promote well-being and better health outcomes at work. When supervisors are equipped with the right skills, knowledge and attributes, supervision can assist to reduce workplace fatigue, stress and burn-out (Egan et al., 2016; Farmer, 2009; Scott et al., 2000).

The following statements about supervision provide useful language and definitions that can support the development of a supervision policy framework:

> Professional supervision is a professional discussion with intention and outcome. It is a conversation held on a regular basis to provide relevant support, ensure standards in practice and maintain ethical practice outcomes. It is integral to quality practice and performance. It facilitates the process for competent/skills practice within a supportive process.

Professional supervision is a dynamic and intentional conversation between a supervisor and professional who meet regularly to critically reflect on professional practice in a supportive and positive environment.

Supervision is a formal process to support and influence ongoing professional outcomes. It is a tool and process to develop and maintain competency and best practice in a positive and supportive environment to ensure expectations in the role are balanced in conjunction with organisational requirements.

Supervision is an interactive process based on coaching principles that assists to maintain competence in professional and practice outcomes. The purpose of supervision is to engage in a professional discussion with an appropriately trained and experienced supervisor that ensures ongoing performance, growth support of the professional. Supervision is designed to uphold quality practice, maintain resilience in a professional practice setting, provide a professional space to articulate the use of key professional frameworks including critical reflection, ethical decision-making and a professional practice framework.

Supervision is a focused, reflective exploration of practice, personal and organizational issues within a supportive relationship. It occurs in a safe environment to facilitate continued development and best outcomes for clients, workers and the organization. It is a structured and interactive discussion that assists to maintain skills, competencies and capabilities within the supervisee's role.

Reflection in Focus

Think about your own experiences of professional supervision. If you have never engaged in professional supervision, consider what you would want it to be like, or if you are currently or about to become a supervisor consider the following.

1. I know I provide effective supervision because

_____

_____

_____

_____

2. I know my supervision process and style is effective because

_____

_____

_____

_____

3. The model of supervision I use is

_____

_____

_____

_____

4. The evaluation process or model I use is

_____

_____

_____

_____

5. I seek feedback on my supervision by

_____

_____

_____

_____

6. I know I receive effective supervision because

_____

_____

_____

_____

7. The style of supervision that I find works best for me is

_____

_____

_____

_____

8. I know supervision is effective when

_____

_____

_____

_____

9. I believe the skills and competencies/capabilities needed to provide effective supervision are

_____

_____

_____

_____

If you have never received professional supervision, consider the following in thinking about what your own effective/quality supervision may look like:

10. I know I would be receiving quality supervision because

_____

_____

_____

_____

11. I know my supervision would be effective if

_____

_____

_____

_____

12. I would like my supervisor's styles to be

_____

_____

_____

_____

13. I would like my supervisor to evaluate supervision through

_____

_____

_____

_____

14. I would like my supervisor to seek feedback through

_____

_____

_____

_____

15. The style of supervision that works best for me is

_____

_____

_____

_____

16. I believe the skills and competencies/capabilities that any supervisor needs to be effective are

_____

_____

_____

_____

17. I think the following things contribute to poor quality supervision:

_____

_____

_____

_____

Supervision Is a Practice

I have been very fortunate to have had enlightening discussions with the late Tony Morrison. Tony was one of the most respected and prominent professionals who pioneered advancements in quality supervision where his research and practice in professional supervision, particularly in the United Kingdom and Australia, has provided innovation and best practice globally. Our discussions included reflections on the difference between poor, good and quality supervision. I reflect on one conversation we had on a freezing cold winter's morning where we were waiting to go into a meeting with pen and paper in hand madly scratching notes. We laughed as we explored our experiences and thoughts. Our evaluation although not evidence based, but evidence informed, thought that about 10% of supervisors that provide poor supervision. We both looked at each other and laughed. We guessed that most people have had at least once bad experience of supervision through-out their career. No matter what training and coaching these supervisors have, professional supervision is just not their forte (Scott et al., 2000).

Tony and I then discussed the notion that perhaps 70% of profes-sional supervisors were well regarded and provided what we termed as 'good' supervision. So, what did 'good' mean to us? We discussed the fact that these supervisors usually prepare for supervisory discussions, they follow up when needed, engage the supervisee and develop a positive supervisory relationship. These supervisors document discussions, set a clear agenda and develop a positive relationship. The remaining 20% provide effective or high-performance supervision. These supervisors think differently where they have an attentional mindset, range of meta-skills and their approach to professional supervision is to provide an integrated approach to the rest of the organisational needs. They are consistent in their practice approach, well organised, highly reflective, have a clear framework and use a supervision model. These supervisors have been appropriately trained and engage in their own professional supervision. They have specific skills, competencies/capabilities and are accountable in their supervisory practice. They are open to having their supervisory practice evaluated and are keen to seek regular feedback (Morrison et al., 2009). They understand what it means to be attuned to the supervisee and engage articulate interpersonal and practice skills. They also know how to positively challenge, reality test, motivate, inspire and engage critical thinking (Falender & Shafranske, 2012).

The question that lingered for both of us at that time was, how do we move some of the 70% into the 20% zone? *The journey continues...*

Supervision as a Skilled Activity

Much of the literature on this topic posits the belief that effective supervision outcomes primarily come from having a positive relationship between the supervisor and supervisee. Clearly, a mutually positive supervisory alliance between the parties is paramount, however not the totality of defining its effectiveness. There remains a wide scope to continue to explore other key components of professional supervision that can be evaluated to ensure supervision is effective and purposeful (Carroll, 2007). For supervision to be respected as a practice in its own right, it needs to be valued in the workplace, supervisors require a specific knowledge base and set of technical skills and competencies to ensure it is effective and it has intended outcomes (Falender & Shafranske, 2012; Mullarkey et al., 2001; Wyles, 2007). Supervision is often discussed as a professional discussion that is simplistic in context. In reality, it is a complex set of activities that require supervisors to be trained prior to providing supervision, be committed to ongoing professional development and engage in their own supervision. With many supervisors not having attended training, they draw predominantly from their own supervision experiences, and as Cousins (2004) suggests, this does not necessarily mean the supervisor has the required skills to provide effective supervision. Whilst previous experiences are useful and provide a certain level of competence in supervisory practice, it does not necessarily translate to quality supervision (Barak et al., 2009; Cousins, 2004; Falender & Shafranske, 2012).

When supervision commences, enthusiasm and motivation dominate the initial stages of developing the supervisory alliance. Over time supervision can become boring and unproductive and becomes more of a general discussion or catch up. The task and process of supervision becomes more about a 'tick and flick' approach without real purpose and meaning. No matter how competent a professional may be, or how long the professional has been in the supervisor role, it is important that supervision remains current and dynamic. If professional supervision is to be regarded as a practice in itself, it is crucial that supervisors attend formal or accredited training in professional supervision. Supervisors can therefore feel confident alongside other disciplines when providing evidence of having attended training and other requirements to remain an accredited professional supervisor (Cousins, 2004; Falender & Shafranske, 2012). In Table 3.1, the context of supervision questions is helpful for the supervisor and supervisee to get to know each other and set up the context of supervision (Egan et al., 2016).

My appreciation of the importance of professional supervision as a skilled activity developed from my experience as a senior manager in a government department, leading a team that was considered to be the poorest performing team in that department. Underperformance issues, conflict in the team and a lack of respect towards the previous manager could all be attributed to a lack supervision and support. In fact, most of the team members had never experienced professional supervision and some staff were very resistant about having to engaging in such a process for fear of retribution.

Using a change management framework and a defined skill set to boost morale, reduce underperformance, increase better client outcomes and address the poor team dynamics took eighteen months of focused investment for the team to fully value and appreciate their professional supervision. The end result was that the team was recognised as the best

Table 3.1   The Context of Supervision Questions

How would you define what professional supervision is?	
What do you think ensures supervision remains effective?	
What do you see as the purpose of supervision?	
What are the benefits of receiving and providing supervision?	
What are the qualities/attributes of an effective supervisor?	
What expectations would you have of your supervisor?	
What types of things are discussed in supervision?	
Is there anything that is not usually discussed in supervision?	

performing team in the state. All staff were required to attend professional supervision monthly, and a clear process and framework was implemented.

The following questions around the context of supervision are explored in the first meeting of supervision. They provide valuable information to the supervisor about the supervisee's experience of supervision and their expectations. The responses are maintained on file and reviewed annually.

Benefits of Supervision

There are many benefits of receiving and providing supervision. The benefits are numerous for the supervisee, the supervisor, organisation and for the clients that services are provided to. When professionals engage in supervision, clients can be confident that the services they receive are effective and of quality. The supervisee can continue to grow as a professional, the supervisor engages effective skills and knowledge to maintain high-level supervisory practice and the organisation knows that both parties are effectively doing their roles. Table 3.2 provides an overview of the benefits of supervision.

Table 3.2   Benefits of Supervision

For You	Your Organisation	Clients
Maintain performance	Adhere to policies and procedures	Quality and effective outcomes
Maintain professionalism	Clearer communication	Good client/customer service
Clear professional excellence framework	Consistent work practices	Services better planned
Higher role satisfaction	Reduces risks	Regular audit and review of services
Role clarity	Lowers absenteeism and sick leave	Decreases power dynamics
Shares responsibilities	Sets clear expectations of the role	Maintain privacy and confidentiality
Feel more valued	Team cohesion	Ensures ethical excellence
Better decision making	Professional boundaries	Responsive services

Roles and Responsibilities

All parties have a specific role in the supervisory process. It is important that these roles are well defined and that all parties understand what their role and responsibilities are. It is equally important to include this information in the organisation's policy or practice guidelines on supervision. In Table 3.3, the responsibilities are defined for the supervisor, supervisee and the organisation.

Supervision Training

Whilst there is a large body of research that explores the importance of professional supervision, there is limited research and understanding about what embodies effective supervision training. There are very few published studies of what core competencies are required for a supervisor or how to ensure supervision is provided within a quality domain.

Table 3.3 Roles and Responsibilities

Supervisor	Supervisee	Organisation
Have been trained in supervision and leadership	Takes responsibility for own role and learning	Has a supervision evaluation framework to ensure it remains effective
Suitably qualified and experienced to perform the role	Shares the responsibility to ensure supervision is effective	Ensures supervisors attend reputable training prior to taking on the role
Committed and passionate in the role	Is prepared and engages positively at all times	Supervisors have access to high-quality supervision
Understands different theories such as adult learning theory, learning theory and how information transfers from the supervision discussion back into the supervisee's role	Seeks and provides useful feedback	Supervisor capability is supported and evaluated in a developmental framework
To be supportive, open and transparent	Seeks out guidance, direction and validation	Supervisors know what is expected from supervision
Can positively challenge the supervisee to continually grow and develop	Is fully present in the process	Provide the appropriate environment for supervision discussions to take place
Has a clear process and framework	Identifies areas for further growth and development	See supervision as valuable and a priority
Engages in their own supervision	Contributes to setting the agenda	Have the appropriate documents to be used in supervision
Balances the discussion using a supervision model	Assists to drive the process to achieve key outcomes	See supervision as a skilled professional practice
Celebrates good work	Knows how to use the supervision model	Understands the difference between line management and professional supervision

From both a training and practice perspective, training curricula needs to embody quality supervision skills and knowledge, incorporate a framework to evaluate outcomes and emphasise the instructional and methodological components to promote the vital role that professional supervision plays (Scott et al., 2000).

It is crucial for any professional supervisor to attend quality training. This raises the question... what is quality training? Drawing on the literature and my lengthy experience in providing supervision training and providing supervision to thousands of professionals throughout my career, quality supervision training incorporates the following:

■ The trainer needs to understand the transfer of knowledge process and adult learning principles;

■ A pre-engagement process to engage participants in the training (information about the training, presenter bio, pre-reading material, key questions to consider prior to the training, what the training will involve, what to bring to the training, etc.);

■ The training needs to incorporate an interesting training curriculum;

■ The trainer is interesting, motivating and inspiring with a sense of humour;

■ The trainer understands the art of attunement in a group setting (how to move with group needs, understands group processes and theories, knows how to engage all participants and how to manage challenges that arise);

■ The participants can transfer what has been discussed in the training back into their role;

■ Training information is developmental, and each topic or module area builds on the previous one as well as the next;

■ The training has a session plan that is flexible to meet group needs;

■ There is a follow-up evaluation process, not on the day of the training as participants will have executive brain fatigue, but follow-up is two weeks post the training;

■ The training materials incorporate a mix of learning styles and various personality types to meet the learning needs of participants;

■ Training content is well-researched, and evidence informed incorporating best practice principles;

■ Training materials incorporate a neuroscience approach to ensure the information delivered and the training process is 'brain friendly'. Facilitating training that is one or two days is not considered to be brain friendly, so providing participants with regular breaks throughout the day and having a mixed mode of training, i.e., small groups, large groups, online and in person all assist to be brain friendly and

■ The training incorporates a mixed mode presentation. This means there may be a practice manual, handouts, small and large group activities, video and audio presentations, examples of supervision documents, file content, etc.

The Supervisory Alliance

Building a positive supervisory alliance is important in supervision. This means there is a positive and productive professional relationship between the supervisor and professional. Research indicates that the supervision alliance is one of the most important elements for staff. A relationship where expectations are known by both parties, the supervision framework is clear and the supervisor understands the model they use as well as their style of supervision (Harris, 2018).

Things of importance to the supervisory relationship:

■ In the first supervision meeting, discuss the organisation's supervision policy, sign the supervision agreement/contract and set the supervision agenda. It is also helpful to have a theme to focus on when there is not a lot to discuss on the supervision agenda. Ensure that the supervision agenda maps to the model of supervision to ensure the discussion is meaningful.

■ The supervisory alliance is psychologically secure, positive and is conducted in a trusting environment where the supervisor values the supervisee.

■ Supervision is outcome focused and achieves regular results.

■ The supervisor knows the supervisee's learning and personality style to ensure that supervision is effective.

■ The process is transparent and open; the discussion is in the context of it being confidential but knowing that minutes and other documents can be called on as evidence. Both the supervisee and supervisor hold the supervision space as a privileged space and do not discuss elements of the discussion without permission from the other.

■ Supervision is a team approach where the supervisor and supervisee work together in a partnership approach.

- Whilst there is a power differential between the roles of supervisor/supervisee, this is discussed and minimised in the process as much as possible.
- Clarify the relationship typified in supervision and set clear expectations in the process.
- Set the framework; ensure that supervision is within a formal setting and context, yet flexible enough to meet the needs of the supervisee.
- Explore ways to discuss critical issues, performance, excellence in practice and issues when they arise.
- The supervisor has the appropriate communication and neuroscience skills to deal with resistance, reluctance and avoidance when it occurs.

Supervision Discussions

So now that we have looked at the purpose of supervision as well as the roles and responsibilities, the following overviews what might be discussed in supervision? Most things are up for discussion in supervision; however, in the intake process, there is a question that allows supervisees to advise what they would like to include in supervision discussions.

- Education, training and professional development needs.
- Integration of theories into practice.
- Understanding how the transfer of knowledge and learning occurs.
- Ethics, dilemmas, boundaries, cases, review of cases, approaches and models to work with the particular client group.
- Policies, procedures and guidelines.
- Professional standards.
- Successes and achievements.
- Stressors in the workplace, self, team, management, plans for taking leave, etc.
- Reflective practice.
- Any personal issues that may be impacting in the workplace or in the work/role.
- How beliefs and values impact in the workplace or with clients.
- Workload management.
- Changes in the organisation.
- Team dynamics and achievements.

Supervision is not counselling, performance management or disciplinary action. These things occur outside of the supervisory process and most organisations have relevant policies to guide the supervisor about how to respond to conduct, behaviour, ethical and performance issues. Where the supervisor has concerns regarding well-being of the supervisee, a referral may be made to the organisations EAP (employee assistance program) service.

Profile of an Effective Supervisor

Understanding what is needed from a supervisor enables the supervisee to ask for what they need in supervision to ensure it remains effective. Knowing what to look for in an effective supervisor also enables the supervisee to ask relevant questions about their background, experience and commitment to the supervisory relationship and process. Profiling a supervisor can be difficult without knowing what to look for, particularly if the supervisee has not had a lot of experience in receiving supervision. The following profile assists to not only find the right supervisor but also ask relevant questions to ensure the relationship starts well and both parties come to trust each other and the process:

- The supervisor is suitably qualified to provide supervision
- Is committed to the vision and mission of the organisation
- Understands learning theory, adult learning principles and the transfer of learning process
- Feels confident and comfortable in the role
- Is able to develop the skills and knowledge of the supervisee
- Is supportive, empathic, honest and transparent
- Understands ethical decision making
- Has their own professional excellence framework
- Engages in their own professional supervision
- Uses a clear supervision process
- Sets clear intentions and expectations
- Understand theoretical perspectives that enable the supervisee to reflect critically on their practice and role using synthesis, appreciative enquiry, different types of questions, attunement and clarification
- Knows how to get the best from the supervisee
- Deals with any issues or challenges positively
- Can articulate their qualities and attributes
- Is highly self-aware and has an articulate sense of self in the role

Learning Styles

Knowing how the supervisee learns can enhance quality supervision outcomes. One of the questions in a supervision intake and assessment process of supervision is to enquire how the supervisee learns best. Kolb's model is an easy framework to use and provides the opportunity for supervisory discussion on how to best meet the needs of the supervisee.

David Kolb and Roger Fry (1975) have developed an effective learning tool that encompasses four different learning styles – ***concrete experience (CE) abilities***, ***reflective observation (RO) abilities***, ***abstract conceptualisation (AC) abilities*** and ***active experimentation (AE) abilities***.

Those learners who are concrete (CE) and active (AE) will prefer to carry out tasks and work in a collaborative process rather than observe others at a distance. They will learn by reviewing what they have done. Those learners who are abstract (AC) and reflective (RO) may prefer to read something and discuss in the supervisory process and to conceptualise tasks before carrying them out. The principles of adult learning are also incorporated into the process as supervisees take an active role in their own learning through integration and practice in between supervision meetings. Visual 3.1 provides an overview of Kolb's learning styles framework.

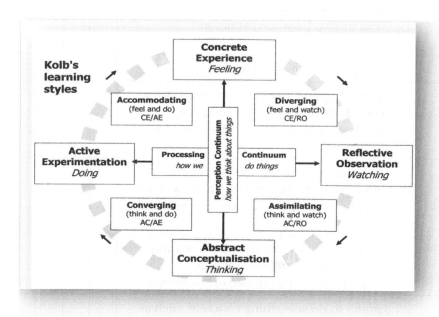

Visual 3.1   Kolb's learning styles. Adaptation and design Alan Chapman 2005–2006; www.businessballs.com.

Supervisees complete the questionnaire in Table 3.4. It is also useful if supervisors complete the questionnaire to assess their own learning style. This provides the perfect platform for how both parties can work effectively together in supervision. The statements below describes the different strategies of learning. Rate each statement from 0 to 4, with 4 representing the statement most accurate for you. Tick one box only for each statement.

Table 3.4 Learning Styles Questionnaire

	Learning Strategy	Statements	0	1	2	3	4
1	CE	I prefer to discuss my work with colleagues, because it helps me to think about what I'm doing.					
2	RO	I prefer to accurately recall a situation, such as observing someone else's work, but keep an open mind about what I heard or saw.					
3	AC	I prefer to logically reason out the relationship between events and experiences.					
4	AE	I prefer to test out my ideas.					
5	AE	I prefer to participate in group discussion, contribute my ideas, hear the group's reactions and reach consensus about what to do.					
6	CE	I prefer to develop my ideas through interaction, in everyday situations with lots of people, such as colleagues, friends and family.					
7	AC	I prefer to read textbooks or articles and arrive at the meaning for myself, responding to the intellectual challenge.					
8	CE	I prefer to do something concrete, such as conducting an interview, rather than read theory.					

(Continued)

Table 3.4 (*Continued*)   Learning Styles Questionnaire

	Learning Strategy	*Statements*	*0*	*1*	*2*	*3*	*4*
9	RO	I prefer to derive ideas through critical reflection on my past experience: for example, in my career or when I learnt the skills that I now use; or even refer to my past writing.					
10	AC	I prefer to derive my ideas and concepts from experts or use resource books prepared by qualified specialists.					
11	CE	I prefer to rely on my gut reaction to the overall picture (for example, a situation in my agency).					
12	AE	I prefer to learn by experimenting with new methods or ideas about practice.					
13	AC	I prefer to work from a set of principles or recognised theory as guidelines for my own practice and for supervision of students.					
14	RO	I prefer to observe impartially what happens in my own agency.					
15	RO	I prefer to work in groups in which I am expected to throw in ideas that may be creative or imaginative but may not be strictly logical.					
16	AE	I prefer to be challenged to explore new experiences and ideas or take on new roles despite the uncertainties and the possibility of criticism.					

Questionnaire Results

To identify your preferred learning strategy, add the scores that you assigned to each question in the groupings listed below. For example, if you scored 4, 3, 2 and 3 in questions 1, 6, 8 and 11, your result for '(CE) Concrete Experience' would be 12 out of a possible score of 16. Your dominant learning style is the one with the highest score. You may find that you have one or two dominant learning styles as outlined in Table 3.5. Transfer the results to the table to ascertain what your preferred learning style is.

Preparation prior to any supervision session is important and helps to enhance the supervision discussion and the supervisory alliance. On most occasions there may not be a lot to prepare from a practical sense. It may be more about psychologically and physiologically preparing for the supervision session ensuring you are focused on the process, and to minimise any potential distractions prior to attending supervision.

Table 3.5 Learning Styles Overview

Learning Characteristic	Total Score	Add Questions	Your Results
(CE) Concrete experience	16	1, 6, 8, 11	
(RO) Reflective observation	16	2, 9, 14,15	
(AC) Abstract conceptualisation	16	3, 7, 10, 13	
(AE) Active experimentation	16	4, 5, 12, 16	

Learning Style	Learning Characteristic	Description
Converger	AC+AE	• Strong practical application of ideas • Can use 'hypothesis testing' to solve problems • Unemotional in the learning process • Holds narrow interests
Diverger	CE+RO	• Strong in imaginative ability • Interested in people • Broad cultural interests • Good at generating ideas and seeing things from different perspectives
Assimilator	AC+RO	• Strong ability to create theoretical models • Excels in inductive reasoning (i.e., hypothesis formulation) • Concerned with abstract concepts rather than people
Accommodator	CE+AE	• Greatest strength is doing things • More of a risk taker • Solves problems intuitively • Performs well when required to react to immediate circumstances

(Continued)

Table 3.5 (*Continued*) Learning Styles Overview

Mode of Learning	Characteristics	Educational Method
CE *Feelings*	*Emphasises personal experience* • Uses the senses to actively participate in a situation • Develops emotional rapport with others • Uses intuition to explore a situation • Explores the here-and-now • Is concerned with practical outcomes	*Prefers:* • Individualised feedback • Sharing feelings about the subject • A collegial relationship *Potential constraint:* • Theoretical assignments
RO *Watching*	*Understands concepts* • Accurately recalls observations and perceptions about individuals, transactions • Distinguishes between essential and trivial information • Keeps an open mind and maintains impartiality in information gathering • Withholds judgement until all possible sources of data are accounted for • Emphasises reflection instead of action	*Prefers:* • Observation and appreciation • Expert interpretations • Guiding and limiting discussions with others • Performance to be judged by external criteria *Potential constraint:* • Task-oriented assignments
AC *Thinking*	*Prefers logical thinking* • Identifies relationships between concepts • Draws conclusions from analysis of data • Develops tentative explanations • Develops generalisations and principles from the information • Develops a plan or proposal to address the identified issues	*Prefers:* • Case studies • Thinking alone • Reading and discussing theory *Potential constraint:* • Group interaction, role simulations
AE *Doing*	*Applies knowledge and skills* • Tests ideas and concepts already developed • Attempts new activities in testing the ideas • Tests hypotheses by AE • Identifies outcomes that have immediate applications • Emphasises practical application instead of reflective understanding	*Prefers:* • Small group discussions • Projects • Peer feedback • Modelling by others *Potential constraint:* • Didactic presentations

The Initial Meeting

The first supervision session is all about developing the supervisory rela-tionship in a formal setting. It is about setting expectations, and important that the groundwork is done in this session as it sets the scaffolding for future supervision sessions. It is equally important to articulate what you believe you can offer the supervisee and what is expected from both parties. The first session is an honest and open discussion about whether you can both work together productively in this supervisory environment to achieve the agreed goals. In subsequent meetings you will find the discussion will flow more freely through the agenda topics. It is important to think about what you would like the supervisee to know about you, what they don't need to know, what you would like to know about the supervisee and what is not important to know. Where you feel as though you can share a little about yourself in the first supervision meeting it can act as an effective way to build rapport and find a connection with the other person. Encourage the supervisee to informally interview you to get to know you, your qualifica-tions, experience and expertise to provide quality supervision.

What Do I Need to Do to Prepare for Supervision?

A self-check may include

- Am I clear on the purpose, process and agenda?
- Am I clear on what my role is?
- What expectations do I have?
- How am I going to engage effectively?
- What are my energy levels like?
- The appropriate question to lead off with, i.e., 'what would you like to focus on today?' Try to avoid leading off with 'how are things today?' or 'how have you been lately?'
- How will I manage any distractions that may arise?

Other things to check in the preparation stage of supervision include

- A copy of the supervision policy to review (first meeting)
- Have a copy of the supervision agenda document
- Copy of the supervision agreement for review
- Understand the steps in the supervision process

- Be aware of the time
- Prepare the room to reduce or minimise – put voicemail on your phone
- If you are conducting supervision in another office/building, prepare with water, pen, paper, temperature, tissues and a welcoming environment

Formulate a set of questions that are useful to ask in the first supervision meeting.

Question 1:

_____

_____

_____

_____

_____

_____

Question 2:

_____

_____

_____

_____

_____

Question 3:

_____

_____

_____

_____

_____

Question 4:

_____

_____

_____

_____

_____

Question 5:

_____
_____
_____
_____
_____
_____

Gathering initial information about the supervisee, their expectations of the process and your expectations as the supervisor is sound professional practice. It is a great idea in getting to know the supervisee to see if they have had any other experiences of supervision. Include in your intake discussion what worked well for them regarding their experience of supervision, what could have worked better for them and explore their learning style. This will make it easier for you to match your supervision style with the supervisee and incorporate your model of supervision.

So, consider what you would like to know about your supervisee/s? What is important for you to know to develop a positive supervisory relationship, ensure you have a sound process and the right documents in place? Consider what is not important for you to know.

I would like to know the following about the supervisee.

_____
_____
_____
_____
_____

I would like the supervisee to know the following about me as a supervisor.

_____
_____
_____
_____
_____

Professional Supervision – First Meeting

Name: _____

Contact Number: _____

Date: _____

Organisation: _____

Qualifications: _____

Line Manager: _____

Internal Supervisor: _____

What have been your previous experiences of supervision? What type of supervision have you had previously?

_____
_____
_____
_____
_____

What are your expectations of me as your supervisor?

_____
_____
_____
_____
_____

What do you see as your learning style, so we can tailor supervision to how you learn best?

_____
_____
_____
_____
_____

What do you see as your role in supervision? What do you think my role is?

_____
_____
_____
_____
_____

What would you like to achieve out of your supervision?

_____

_____

_____

_____

_____

Supervision Agreement – What Is a Supervision Agreement?

An agreement needs to be written, agreed to and signed off between the supervisor and supervisee in the first or second meeting. Your organisation may have a layout that you can use which will include key areas that need to be discussed and agreed upon. This part of the supervision process is focused on reading through the supervision agreement, discussing its contents and signing off. It is important to work through each point of the supervision agreement to ensure the supervisee is aware of their responsibilities in the supervisory process. The agreement also sends staff the message that the organisation takes supervision seriously, and it is an opportunity to spend quality time in supervision to discuss a range of things as set in the agenda. Many organisations include in their job advert that states one of the benefits of the role is the inclusion of professional supervision. The supervision agreement also needs to incorporate aspects of the organisations code of conduct including professionalism, how to deal with any challenges and what the process of supervision will include.

Supervision Agreement:

■ The objectives of supervision including any learning objectives.
■ If you are available for informal supervision in between sessions.
■ Meeting structure.
■ Processes – where, when, how often, duration, what to do if supervision cannot be held, how to reschedule the next meeting, what form will supervision will take, e.g., who will be involved, what model will be used and what is the communication avenues in between sessions.
■ Responsibilities of each person.

- Location of meetings.
- Process for dealing with ethical dilemmas.
- Process for review and evaluation.
- How supervision will be assessed and evaluated, how will feedback occur and how often.
- Documenting discussions.
- Confidentiality issues.
- Recording keeping.
- Grievance processes for both parties.
- If supervision is voluntary or part of the role.
- What reporting does the organisation require.

Importance of Written Supervision Agreements

- A written supervision agreement represents and reflects the commitment of the organisation to staff supervision.
- Negotiating and recording a supervision agreement between the two parties, because of the difference in the power dynamics, provides positive role modelling of the partnership.
- A written agreement ensures staff are aware of their responsibilities and the role of supervision.
- It also ensures the supervisor is aware of their responsibility to the supervisee.
- A written agreement ensures that meeting minutes are recorded, and this provides a basis for review and developing goals. It also provides an opportunity for development of future professional goals.
- Develops boundaries within the supervisory alliance.
- Assists to develop a forum for continual review.
- Explores how the annual appraisal process links to supervision.
- Identifies the power differential.
- Sets up supervision as a professional activity.
- Supports the development of an open and trusting professional relationship to begin with.
- Encourages joint responsibility in the process.
- Helps to develop a more collaborative relationship.

Sample Supervision Agreement

Name:_____

Contact: _____

Role: _____

1. Frequency
2. Content of Sessions
3. Documentation
4. Supervision Environment
5. Conduct and Professionalism
6. Privacy and Confidentiality
7. Accountability
8. Review

We have read, understood and agree to work within the above supervision guidelines.

Signed: _____ Date: ____/____/____ (Supervisee)

Signed: _____ Date: ____/____/____ (Supervisor)

Setting the Agenda

The agenda provides a focus for supervision discussions. Having a framework to set the agenda ensures that both parties' expectations are clear. It is important to develop the agenda in line with the relevant Position Description and supervision policy to ensure that outcomes are met. Once the agenda is developed in each meeting and you have begun implementing it as a normal part of the supervisory process, the focus of discussions is easier in subsequent meetings, and tasks and practice outcomes can be identified. This promotes accountability and responsibility for both parties in the supervisory partnership. It also makes it much easier for you as a supervisor to deal with inaction or diminished performance. You have a robust and solid framework you can refer to and fall back on, given you have the contract that was agreed to in the first supervision session.

Sample Supervision Agenda

1. Reflections from previous supervision meeting
2. Topics for discussion (from both supervisor and supervisee)
3. Client cases
4. Operational discussion
   a. Organisational
   b. Client
   c. Staff
   d. Policy/Procedure
   e. Workload
   f. Achievements, challenges, goals
5. Professional development/training
6. Supervisee goals
7. Outcomes/actions/follow-up
8. Next meeting

Exploration/Goals Phase

This is where the key focus in supervision takes place. It is important to structure your supervision meetings to ensure that you do not run out of time and that adequate time is available to explore issues, ideas, future goal setting and reach outcomes. During the exploration phase in each discussion, you can use the supervision agenda as the guide in the process. Ensure that the supervision conversation is flexible enough to meet the supervisee's needs yet structured to achieve outcomes. Look over the supervision agenda and request any agenda items to be included on the agenda prior to the meeting or at the beginning of the conversation. It is important that staff take responsibility for their own supervision process and do not expect the supervisor to do the majority of the work. It can be challenging to know what to include in the agenda, so the supervisor can suggest items to go on the agenda where the supervisee is unable to identify anything to talk about. If the supervisor has a supervision model such as the PASE™ (Professional/Practice, Administrative/Line Management, Support/Person, Educative/Professional Development), LASE™ (Leadership/ Management, Administrative/Line Management, Support/Person, Educative/

Professional Development) or FASE™ (Frontline/Professional, Administrative/ Line Management, Support/Person, Educative/Professional Development) model, setting the agenda for each meeting will be simple and effective (Harris, 2018).

Are there any other topics you can think of to include on a supervision agenda?

_____

_____

_____

_____

Goal Visioning/Attention Planning

We traditionally set goals by saying 'I am going to lose weight this year', 'I am going to start reading that book next week' and 'This year I am going to learn how to play the piano'. When we set goals this way, a lot of the time we do not get around to reaching that goal, or do not make the commitment to put the timeframes into place to ensure we reach this goal. There is a far more positive and effective way of setting goals for yourself as a professional and also for setting visions with your staff in supervision. By forecasting the date or month and what is achieved or being worked on is a more effective way of setting goals or a focus. Try setting the focus for what to achieve and see how effective it is.

It is now the (date) _____ / _____ / _____; and I am/have _____

_____

_____

_____

It is now the (date) _____ / _____ / _____; and I am/have _____

_____

_____

_____

It is now the (date) _____ / _____ / _____; and I am/have _____

_____

_____

_____

Closing the Supervision Meeting

It is important to keep an eye on the time without interrupting the process. It is also important not to conclude the supervision conversation if there are any emotional responses occurring, however, to try and finish on time where possible. By setting the agenda and discussion, it is less likely you will need to introduce any new topics near the end of the supervision session, i.e., 55 minutes into the discussion. This will ensure that the supervision meeting will end on time. Always summarise what has been discussed and what was included in the minutes and outline what language and wording has been used. In situations where there is a need for more in-depth discussion that crosses into a therapeutic counselling situation, ensure you refer the supervisee to an EAP service. Where there is a staff conflict or conflict between two staff, it is more appropriate to refer this through dispute resolution processes. Do not feel as though you have to manage with this in supervision given the specialist skills required to resolve the conflict.

Self-Reflection Checklist

As the supervision meeting comes to an end, it is important for the supervisor to reflect on the discussion and how it went. Where there may be any issues, it is equally important for the supervisor to take this to their own supervision meeting to reflect, also being mindful of confidentiality and privacy.

1. Have I ensured the supervision discussion was balanced? If not, why not?
2. How did the supervisee respond to the supervision discussion?
3. Can I identify any areas that could have been different and why?
4. What strengths did I bring to the meeting?
5. How did I ensure the conversation was effective?
6. What did I use from my leadership excellence framework?
7. What elements of my professional identity were evident?
8. What other things do I need to be aware of?

Evaluating Supervision Discussions

Regular informal and formal review and evaluation of supervision is as important as the supervision meeting itself. But what do you evaluate?

Think of the key elements of supervision and using the following tool, evaluate your supervision sessions with staff. The following list of questions are a useful evaluation tool for supervisor's self-reflection. These questions are also useful to discuss with supervisees. A more formal evaluation framework is discussed in a later chapter.

1. **The supervision agreement**
   – Does the supervision agreement represent what the supervision process is achieving?
   – Is the frequency, timing, etc. still relevant at that point in time?
   – Has the supervision agreement been adhered to?
   – How does the workplace value supervision and the agreement?
2. **The supervision policy**
   – Is the supervision policy relevant for the workplace?
   – Does the supervision policy need reviewing or changing?
   – How are we working to the policy framework in supervision?
   – How have we effectively used the supervision policy?
3. **The supervision agenda**
   – Has our agenda been effective and aligned to discussions? What might we need to change?
   – Does the agenda map to the supervision model?
   – Has our agenda been balanced across the role, organisational requirements, supporting the supervisee and enhancing their development?
   – How have we kept the agenda dynamic and interesting?
4. **The supervisory alliance**
   – How has the relationship developed over time?
   – Has rapport been established and maintained?
   – How have we progressed the alliance over time to achieve key outcomes?
   – How have we managed any relationship conflicts or challenges?
5. **The supervision discussion and process**
   – Are discussions and the supervision process meeting the needs of the supervisee?
   – Are discussion topic/s relevant?
   – Is the supervisory space free of distractions?
   – Does the supervisee feel supported and valued?
   – How is the supervisee assisting to develop the agenda?

- Is the supervisee committed to supervision?
- Is the supervisee coming prepared for supervision?

6. **The style of the supervisor**
   - Is the style of the supervisor aligned to the supervisee's learning style?
   - Is the style of supervision flexible?
   - Is the supervisor aware of their own style of supervision?
   - How does the supervisor and supervisee adapt their styles for supervision to be effective?

7. **Tasks in between supervision sessions**
   - Are tasks in between sessions being completed?
   - Who is doing the follow-up?
   - Are the tasks adequate or relevant?

8. **Supervision model**
   - How is the supervision model being used effectively?
   - How is supervision evaluated using the model?
   - Is the model integrated to other aspects of the organisation?
   - Does the supervisee know how to use the model?

9. **Outcomes**
   - Do both parties provide feedback that meetings are positive and productive?
   - Are actions usually followed through?
   - Is there reflection time at the beginning of a new meeting?
   - Is the supervisor keeping the supervisee on track?
   - How is the supervisee taking responsibility?
   - Are supervision session discussions integrated with the annual appraisal documentation?

External Supervision

There are situations where staff may receive professional supervision from an external professional or provider and the organisation pays for them to attend on a monthly basis. External supervision is an effective way to ensure that staff feel supported and they can discuss things more openly, particularly where their line manager is also the professional supervisor. It is a difficult balance when the supervisor has a dual role of line manager and professional supervisor. It is crucial that the relationship is worked on regularly in case any difficult discussions need to occur where trust and credibility could be compromised. Where an external provider is engaged to provide supervision, it is important to have an agreement or formal contract in place. All too often no contract or agreement is in place to outline what is required of the supervisor or what the organisation's focus is for external supervision. The contract or agreement is to outline reporting requirements and links to the organisation's supervision policy or practice guideline.

Whilst the line manager holds decision-making authority, the external supervisor needs to be a positive influence in the supervisee's work. This collaboration ensures the supervisee is appropriately supported in their role to provide quality outcomes. The line manager holds responsibility

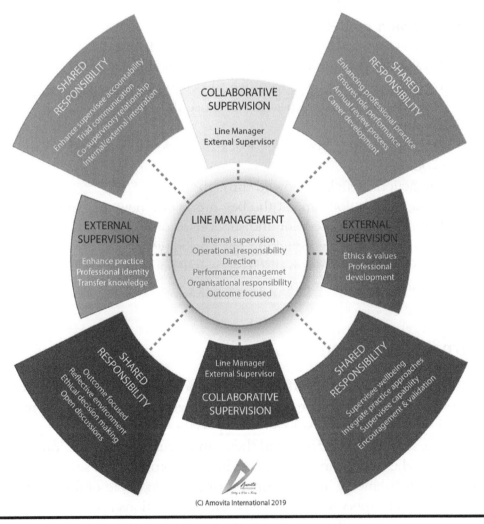

Visual 3.2   Collaborative supervision framework.

for internal line management supervision, operational requirements and provides performance management of the supervisee's work. The external supervisor is responsible for enhancing the supervisee's practice wisdom, assists the supervisee to develop and maintain their professional identity and transfer knowledge from supervision back into their role and vice versa. The external supervisor also supports the facilitation of reflective discussions to explore the impact on practice. Through the same supervision model, the line manager and external supervisor have shared responsibility for the supervisee engaging ethical practice, being outcome focused in order to achieve key results in the role, support the supervisee in their career development, maintain well-being, integrate practice approaches, develop capability and validate the supervisee's work. Visual 3.2 outlines the roles of both parties as they need to work together in a co-supervisory alliance, so the supervisee feels that both have their best interest at the forefront of the supervisory process.

Summary

This chapter has explored the context of supervision and the processes in setting up supervision so that it remains effective. Consider the following reflective questions as a summary to the chapter.

What have been the key things you have gained from reading this chapter on the context of supervision?
What have been your reflections about this chapter and the context of supervision?
List three things that you will take from this chapter to incorporate into your supervisory role.
What do you think will be useful to talk to your supervisee/s about regarding this chapter?

Chapter 4

The Importance of Supervision Models

Key focus for this chapter

- The importance of having a supervision model
- Different models of supervision
- Explore Amovita's suite of supervision models
- How to use a supervision model effectively
- The PASE™ supervision model in action
- Explore why an integrated supervision model is important

Introduction

Over the last few decades, there have been various supervision models that have evolved to enable effective supervisory discussions. A well-evidenced supervision model ensures the discussion is focused, intentional and meaningful. It encourages the supervisee to take the lead in the supervision process and assists the supervisor to reflect on how they maintain a high level of supervisory practice. Having a model also provides a common language framework for both the supervisor and supervisee to engage in conversation, maintain a positive relationship and deliver sound practice outcomes. Supervision models give a holistic approach to the supervision discussion by focusing on the supervisee's professional role and practices, organisational requirements and accountability, support of the supervisee in their role and the development of the supervisee (Falender & Shafranske, 2017; Harris, 2018; Milne, 2007).

Whilst there are many models of supervision in different industries, when taking a closer look at the literature they could be best described as an approach or framework for supervision, rather than a supervision model in their own right. Approaches in supervision are important to assist the supervisee to reflect on their practice; however, using an integrated supervision model is fundamental to developing an individualised approach for each supervisee based on their stage of development, professional experience and needs. A supervision model typically provides the supervisor with a systemised approach for integrating information in a way that continues to develop the supervisee in a facilitated learning environment. Models provide a coherent approach where both parties engage in the supervision process with purpose and meaning (Harris, 2018). Some of the better-known supervision models/approaches are outlined below.

Developmental Models

The underlying principle for developmental models of supervision is to engage the supervisee in the process of ongoing growth and development. The supervisor is committed to engage in their own development to remain competent in their role and demonstrate capability. Supervisors who use a developmental model incorporate adult learning principles into supervision discussions and adapt the supervision process to provide supervision that meets the developmental needs of the supervisee moving from beginner to advanced professional. Using a developmental model of supervision supports each stage of the supervisee's development and enhances their skills and knowledge (Falender & Shafranske, 2012).

When a supervisee commences their career or when they graduate, the supervisor takes on more of a guiding and teaching role. The supervisor has more of a hands-on approach to ensure the supervisee gains confidence in their role, is guided in their practice and makes sound decisions. Where a supervisee has had some experience and requires less guidance, they are able to demonstrate more independence in their role. The supervisor takes on more of a coaching and mentoring role to ensure the supervisee's skills and knowledge are implemented and evidenced in their practice. Where a supervisee has had extensive experience and has post-graduate study, the supervisor acts more in a collegial role to ensure the supervisee's advanced skills and knowledge are evidenced and maintained in their role (Falender & Shafranske, 2017; Harris, 2018).

Developmental models also assume that the supervisee will progress through the different developmental stages during their career. Each stage requires the supervisor to engage a different supervisory style and approach in supervision. Supervisors need to accurately assess the supervisee's developmental stage at a given point in time and know how to further develop the supervisee's skills and knowledge using various theoretical approaches and capability areas. As the supervisee transfers through each stage, they are supported to take prior knowledge and skills evidenced in deeper reflective critical thinking, analysis and attunement. When a supervisee is in the beginning developmental stage, they are predominantly focused on acquiring skills and knowledge. Advanced practice is about evidencing and attuning skills and knowledge in practice. Whilst advanced supervisees are autonomous in their practice, the supervisor's role is to further advance critical thinking and expand complex problem-solving skills (Stoltenberg, 1981).

Strength-Based and Person-Centred Supervision Models

Strength-based models of supervision focus on the supervision alliance and encourage both the supervisor and supervisee to engage in supervision around the process of reflection and curious inquiry. Strength-based questioning is the basis for this model of supervision, by understanding how the supervisee identifies and uses their strengths to focus on the core functions of their role. This approach suggests that there is little to no hierarchy in the supervisory relationship, but it is a relationship based on equality. The supervisor consciously seeks to identify the supervisee's strengths and sense of self in order to support their reflective practice and maintain resilience.

The supervisor is self-aware and consciously uses language to show appreciation of the supervisee and engage regular acknowledgement of their work. The supervisor does not seek to be highly directive but engages a reflective approach to encourage the supervisee to participate in the supervisory conversation through their own narrative style. As a result, the supervisee is able to reflect on their practice at a deeper level, allowing them to understand what beliefs and values may be influencing them in their work during the different stages of their career (Carroll, 2010).

Person-centred supervision models draw up the supervisee at any developmental stage and infers that no judgements are placed on the supervisee both as a person and professional. The supervisor uses an empathic approach in the supervision process, relationship and discussion to demonstrate their developmental supervisory style.

Structural Models

One of the better-known structural models of supervision is Holloway's (1995) Structural Approach to Supervision (SAS). It focuses on seven dimensions of the supervision process, including supervisor characteristics, the supervisory relationship, organisational context, client characteristics, supervisee characteristics, supervision tasks and the functions of supervision (Holloway, 1995). This structural model overviews different functions of supervision to suggest that it is the role of the supervisor to evaluate the effectiveness of supervision, to model good supervisory practice and share their practice wisdom. It also suggests there are different tasks that supervision needs to focus on, including ongoing development of the supervisee to maintain competence, acquisition of skills and client case conceptualisation, understanding the supervisee's professional role, self-awareness and an understanding of how the person intercepts in the professional space (Holloway, 1995).

Given these different models of supervision, consider for a moment ... as a leader or supervisor, what supervision model or approach do you use? Do you see your model as an approach, framework or model in itself, or do you see a model of supervision as something quite different?

_____

_____

_____

_____

Amovita's Suite of Supervision Models

In response to the limited number of supervision models available to supervisors and leaders, a suite of seven integrated supervision models have been developed by Amovita International in Australia to support different roles in any organisation or business. The models are integrative, meaning that they consider the relationship between supervision and other key areas within the supervisee's workplace. This includes the annual review framework, role functionality, strategic framework, reporting process, employee assistance program and governance of the organisation. When these components are intra-relational in and of each other, supervision models become a comprehensive ecosystem to focus the supervisee in their work and role, as they can see how supervision interfaces across all areas of the organisation. This not only enhances the supervisee's performance over time but also provides a common language framework to support higher performance in the organisational system (Harris, 2018).

Each of Amovita's supervision models outlined in Table 4.1 has been developed using four quadrants that focus on the professional's practices in their role, organisational requirements, support of the supervisee and how supervision can focus on ongoing development in the supervisee's role. The seven models also relate to each other in look and functionality, enabling any role to have a supervision model. The only quadrant that differs in each supervision model is the top left-hand side quadrant as each role incorporates different professional practices. The other three quadrants are similar in focus for the supervision discussion. The consistency of the quadrants across all roles ensures the model is highly effective in delivering key outcomes, making supervision far more productive.

The following overview provides a description of the model and what agenda items are typically discussed in each of the individual quadrants.

Table 4.1   The Seven Supervision Models

	Model	*Role Applicability*
1	PASE™ model	Practice and clinical roles
2	LASE™ model	Leaders, executives, CEOs, directors, business owners
3	FASE™ model	Operational, administrative and receptionist roles
4	MASE™ model	Coordinators, middle managers, project managers, IT, finance
5	VASE™ model	Volunteers
6	Yarn Up Time – CASE™ model	Aboriginal staff, cultural advisors
7	Basket of Knowledge – CASE model	Aboriginal staff, cultural advisors

1. **The PASE Supervision Model**

The PASE supervision model has been developed for professional and clinical staff in any community, allied health and human services setting. This model has been designed as a highly effective supervision tool to support professionals who are working with clients in a professional or clinical setting. The four quadrants contain words that form the supervision agenda. This assists supervisees to better focus supervision discussions and supports both parties to utilise supervision time effectively. Each quadrant includes the supervisor's style to enable the supervisor to be conscious of how they are facilitating and engaging in the discussion.

The four quadrants outlined in the PASE supervision model are *P: Professional/Practice*, *A: Administrative/Line Management*, *S: Support/Person* and *E: Educative/Professional Development*.

The *Practice/Professional* quadrant focuses the supervision discussion on ethics and the dilemmas faced in daily practice, use of professional language, critical analysis, case conceptualisation, skills enhancement, theories used for practice, professional identity and how the supervisee engages their professional excellence framework. The supervisor's style is reflective in this part of the supervision discussion, and the supervisor uses effective questioning to assess and evaluate professional aspects of the supervisee's work.

The *Administrative/Line Management* quadrant focuses discussion on the tasks and processes on the supervisee's role as well as organisational requirements. This part of the supervision discussion is all about the supervisee's performance in their role and usually occurs with the supervisee's line manager. If the supervisee engages in external supervision, discussion in this quadrant is limited, given the external supervisor does not have the delegated authority to make decisions on the supervisee's work and role. This part of the supervision discussion is outcome focused to ensure the supervisee is performing the role as required by the organisation. The agenda focuses on the organisation's strategic and operational processes, policies and procedures, performance, reporting and monitoring of the role, annual reviews, audits, compliance, etc.

The *Support/Person* quadrant focuses the supervisory discussion on the support aspects of the supervisee's role. Discussion includes any stressors that may be impacting on the supervisee, discussion about fatigue or burnout as well as any personal factors that may be influencing the supervisee's work. This part of the model ensures that discussion includes work–life balance, supervisee well-being, neuro self-care, team dynamics and role satisfaction. The aim of this quadrant is to ensure the supervisee feels supported, encouraged, validated and refuelled on a regular basis. In order to achieve this, the supervisor also needs to be congruent in their own self-care and well-being and needs to bring a high level of positive energy into the supervisory environment.

The ***Educative/Professional Development*** quadrant focuses on the supervisee's ongoing development as a professional. Supervision discussions may focus on career planning, the transfer of learning process from supervision back into the role and how the supervisee shares knowledge with their peers and colleagues. The educative/professional development discussion also focuses on how the supervisee evidences their knowledge into practice and how they maintain professional excellence.

Visual 4.1 outlines the words in each of the PASE model quadrants to assist the supervisor and supervisee in developing the discussion agenda. It also shows the blank PASE model which can be used to support the supervisee in setting their agenda for each meeting. The blank model is a useful minute template to document discussions.

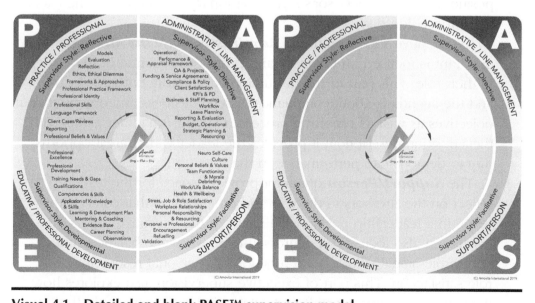

Visual 4.1   Detailed and blank PASE™ supervision model.

2. **The LASE™ Supervision Model**

The LASE supervision model has been designed as an executive supervision model for leaders, managers, CEOs, directors and business owners in any organisational or business context. The four quadrants assist the executive supervisor or leader to focus the discussion agenda on key aspects of the leadership role.

The four quadrants outlined in the model are *L: Leadership/ Management*, *A: Administrative/Line Management*, *S: Support/ Person* and *E: Educative/Professional Development*.

The L quadrant focuses on the leadership aspect of the role whilst the other three quadrants focus on what is required by the organisation or business, and ongoing growth and development in the leader's role. The A, S and E quadrants have similar words in them to focus the agenda. This makes it easy for common language to be used across the A, S and E quadrants in any role. As with all of the models, each quadrant suggests a supervisor style that ensures the supervisor is self-aware and conscious of how they are engaging in the discussion.

The *Leadership/Management* quadrant focuses the executive supervision discussion on the leadership aspects of the role. This includes leadership analysis and visioning, operational and strategic direction, political acumen, integrating leadership approaches and frameworks in the role, key partnerships and organisational growth and positioning. The supervisor's style is visionary in this part of the executive supervision discussion.

In executive supervision, the *Administrative/Line Management* quadrant is focused on the tasks and processes required of the leader in their role. This part of the discussion is primarily outcome focused, and the agenda is about compliance, assets, business and organisational objectives as well as reporting processes. As this quadrant aligns with their position description, it provides the leader with a great opportunity to demonstrate performance in the role.

The *Support/Person* quadrant provides space for the leader to reflect on the stressors in the role and other factors that come with being in a leadership position. This part of the executive supervision discussion also focuses on neuro self-care, work–life balance, motivation, professional values, team functioning, personal resourcing and role satisfaction. This part of executive supervision also explores how the leader is supporting staff and celebrating achievements in the workplace.

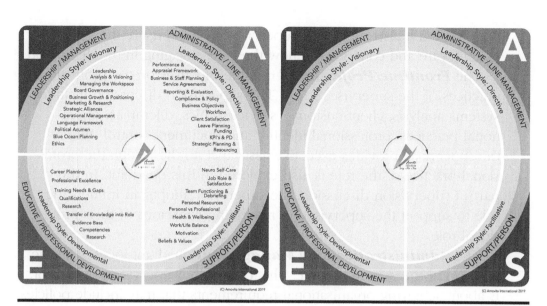

Visual 4.2   Detailed and blank LASE™ supervision model.

The ***Executive/Professional Development*** quadrant in executive supervision focuses the discussion on the developmental needs of the leader and how they transfer leadership practices and approaches to staff. The executive supervision agenda may also focus on career planning, qualifications, competencies evidenced in the role and how their leadership practice framework is maintained.

Visual 4.2 provides an overview of the agenda items within the LASE model of supervision, and a blank model that can be used for documenting the executive supervision discussion.

3. **The FASE Supervision Model**

The FASE supervision model is designed to support staff in frontline services. These staff are in roles including operational support, administration and reception services. Operational and administrative roles are often not provided with professional supervision. This model provides an effective framework for supervisors to understand the importance of engaging these staff in supervision to ensure they maintain high performance in their roles. The four quadrants assist both the supervisor and supervisee to focus the supervision discussion on key objectives in the role.

The four quadrants are ***F: Frontline/Professional***, ***A: Administrative/Organisational***, ***S: Support/Person*** and ***E: Educative/Professional Development***.

The four quadrants assist supervisees to focus their supervision discussion as outlined with key words in each of the quadrants.

Each quadrant also suggests a supervisor style to ensure the supervisor is self-aware and conscious of how they are engaging in the discussion.

The ***Frontline/Professional*** quadrant focuses on the professional practices of the supervisee's role. The supervision discussion includes systems analysis, client/customer service, ethics, dilemmas, operational practices, professional identity and document control. Where the supervisee provides executive assistance to the leader, the professional practice of the role is also explored in this quadrant. In this part of supervision discussion, the supervisor adopts an influencing role to support the supervisee in remaining conscious of their professional role.

The ***Administrative/Line Management*** quadrant focuses on the tasks and processes in the role. This part of the supervision discussion is about achieving organisational requirements that may include policies and procedures, role functionality, service agreements, client satisfaction, resourcing, business objectives, funding requirements, assets and workload management.

The ***Support/Person*** quadrant allows the supervision discussion to focus on self-care or anything that may be impacting the supervisee in their role. This quadrant explores how the supervisee maintains a work and life balance and team functioning. It assists the supervisee to maintain resilience, reduce vulnerabilities and feel valued in the role. This part of the supervision discussion is about acknowledging and valuing the work the supervisee does.

The ***Educative/Professional Development*** quadrant discussion focuses on the supervisee's training and professional development needs, the transfer of learning into their practice, career planning and the progress of the employee's annual learning and development plan. Agenda topics also centre on how the employee demonstrates skills and competencies, evidences professional practice and maintains professional excellence in their role.

Visual 4.3 provides an overview of the FASE model with words in each quadrant to assist in developing the meeting agenda. The blank FASE model assists the supervisee to set the agenda and focus the discussion in the various quadrants.

4. **The MASE™ Supervision Model**

The MASE supervision model has been designed for supervisors who may be in middle management roles and often juggle their role as a manager, coordinator, team leader, policy maker or project manager.

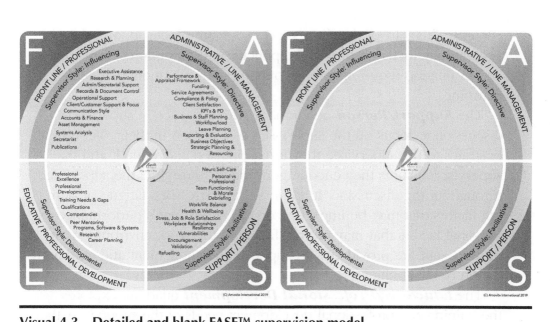

Visual 4.3   Detailed and blank FASE™ supervision model.

The M quadrant i the MASE supervision model has been developed to combine the P from the PASE model and the L from the LASE model. This also means that the agenda items in the M quadrant align to that of the P and L quadrants in the PASE and LASE models.

The four quadrants outlined in the MASE model are ***M: Managerial/ Coordinate***, ***A: Administrative/Organisational***, ***S: Support/Person*** and ***E: Educative/Professional Development***.

As with the other supervision models, the four quadrants assist supervisees to focus their supervision discussion and can assist to formulate the supervision agenda. Each quadrant also suggests a supervisor style to ensure the supervisor is self-aware and conscious of how they are leading the discussion.

The ***Managerial/Coordinate*** quadrant focuses the supervision agenda on managerial and coordination activities in the supervisee's role. Agenda items include ethics, professional reporting requirement, professional identity, operational requirements and any approaches or frameworks that the supervisee uses in their role. It also includes policy development, implementation, project management, professional language framework and any leadership activities that align with being a middle manager.

The ***Administrative/Line Management*** quadrant emphasises the tasks and processes required of the supervisee from an organisational context. This part of the discussion is outcome focused, and the agenda may focus on processes, policies and procedures, reporting and evaluation requirements, resourcing and operational/strategic planning.

The ***Support/Person*** quadrant provides a space in supervision discussion to focus on the supervisee as a person in their role. It demonstrates to the supervisee they are supported and valued, and the supervisor ensures they encourage, validate and refuel the supervisee throughout the discussion. It addresses any stressors, fatigue or burnout factors that may be impacting on the supervisee's performance or personal factors that may be interfacing in the work environment. It ensures staff are provided with support, encouragement and commendation of their achievements.

The ***Educative/Professional Development*** quadrant explores the training and professional development needs of the supervisee, the transfer of learning into their role, career planning and progress of the employee's learning and development plan. Supervision topics also centre on how the employee evidences their approaches in their work and how they demonstrate skills and competencies to be successful in the role.

Visual 4.4 provides an overview of the MASE model with words in each quadrant that assist in developing the meeting agenda. The blank MASE model helps the supervisee to set the agenda and focus the discussion in various quadrants.

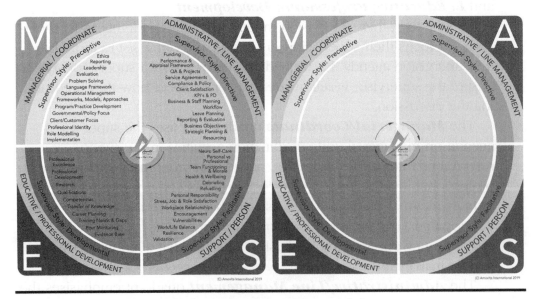

Visual 4.4   Detailed and blank MASE™ supervision model.

5. **The VASE™ Supervision Model**

Many organisations rely heavily on volunteers to support various operational aspects of the organisation. Whilst they are provided with guidance and direction, they are not often provided with professional supervision. Given the vital role volunteers play, providing professional supervision is crucial from both a professional and industrial perspective. As a result, the VASE supervision model has been specifically designed to support volunteers in their quasi-professional role.

The four quadrants are *V: Volunteer/Humanitarian*, *A: Administrative/Organisational*, *S: Support/Person* and *E: Educative/Professional Development*.

As with the other supervision models, the four quadrants have words included to assist the volunteer to focus the supervision discussion.

The *Volunteer/Humanitarian* quadrant focuses the supervision discussion on the quasi-professional aspects of their role. Agenda items may include engaging ethical practices, effective decision making, assessing situations with clients, privacy and confidentiality, operational support and effectively juggling the demands in the role.

The *Administrative/Line Management* quadrant in supervision focuses on the tasks and processes required from an organisational context. This part of the discussion is outcome focused, and the agenda may explore relevant policies and procedures, reporting and evaluation requirements and any professional documentation required in the volunteer's role.

The *Support/Person* quadrant focuses on any stressors, fatigue or burnout factors that may be impacting on the volunteer's performance. It also explores the personal interfacing in the work environment, the volunteer's work and life balance and acknowledgement of the quasi-professional role that they play.

The *Educative/Professional Development* quadrant explores the training and professional development needs of the volunteer, how they transfer learning and confidence into their role, and any training gaps and topics to engage the volunteer in a continuous learning process.

Visual 4.5 provides an overview of the VASE model with words in each quadrant to assist to the supervisor and volunteer to develop an agenda for the meeting. The blank VASE model assists the supervisee to set an agenda and focus the discussion from various quadrants.

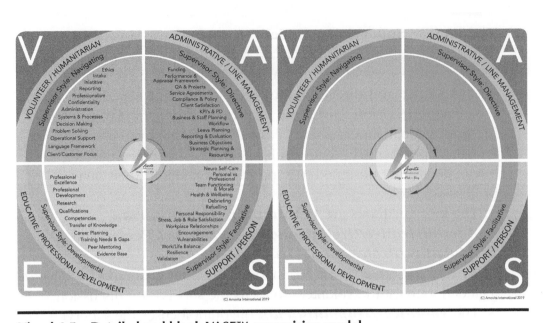

Visual 4.5   Detailed and blank VASE™ supervision model.

6. **The Yarn Up Time – CASE Supervision Model**

The sixth model in the suite of Amovita's supervision models is the Cultural Supervision Model (CASE). Titled 'Yarn Up Time', this model has been designed to support both Aboriginal and non-Aboriginal supervisors in providing supervision to Aboriginal staff in their role. Whilst many Aboriginal staff use the PASE supervision model, the aim of developing the CASE model was to provide staff with the choice between using a cultural supervision model or a more mainstream supervision model. The CASE model provides a useful platform for yarning to take place in supervision. Whilst staff may set an agenda, the supervisee can also use the symbols to engage in Yarn Up Time to have a supervision discussion. The model includes four quadrants as in the other models; however, the agenda items are illustrated as symbols and metaphors through the artwork in the CASE model.

The ***top left hand quadrant (C)*** in Yarn Up Time focuses supervision on the supervisee's professional practices, their client work and how they engage as a professional in their role. The circles in this quadrant connect with each other in perfect harmony to ensure that professionals work collaboratively together to achieve professional practice through ethical decision making in the organisational system.

The **top right hand quadrant (A)** represents the workplace as a well-organised system. Yarn Up Time discussion focuses on meeting the requirements of the role, workflow management, reporting, compliance and auditing. The smaller circles connect to the larger circles showing how they need to relate to each other to ensure outcomes are achieved.

The **bottom right hand quadrant (S)** focuses on the supervisee's connections to their cultural identity around sea, land, community, family and culture. This provides a space for the supervisor and supervisee to understand key cultural and community protocols the supervisee may have and it allows the Yarn Up Time supervisor to better understand the supervisee's cultural priorities and explore any supports they need in the role whilst meeting organisational outcomes. The symbols in this quadrant show smaller and larger circles that weave together in the journey of professional relationship.

The **bottom left hand quadrant (E)** focuses the supervision discussion on the developmental needs of the supervisee, how cultural stories are passed from one generation to the next through yarning and how this is transferred into the role. The smaller circles depict the importance of nurturing and how they grow into larger circles where knowledge is shared with others in the workplace. The circles flow between each other and are connected by direct lines of knowledge and information.

Visual 4.6 provides an overview of the CASE model with the artistic visual that assists supervisees to develop their yarning agenda for meetings.

7. **The Basket of Knowledge – CASE Supervision Model**

The other CASE supervision model is titled 'The Basket of Knowledge'. Based on the design of Amovita's suite of coaching and supervision models, the Basket of Knowledge illustrates 'the reeds' as the focal point of the visual model. Reeds are a useful metaphor for how roles must flow and be flexible to meet organisational needs. It shows how the reeds change with the flow of water over time and have flexibility through the main green, purple and orange colours. In the context of professional supervision and support, these elements are crucial to ensure that the outcomes of supervision are achievable and maintained.

The Basket of Knowledge 'twinning' flows through all four quadrants that allow the focus of the supervisory discussion to be around

Visual 4.6   Yarn Up Time – CASE™ supervision model.

the professional in their role and relationship to their community. The joining of the reeds is a useful metaphor as it holds all the quadrants together as a common theme and story as does a supervisory alliance. For supervision to be successful and for desired outcomes to be met, each of the quadrants need to relate to each other for the professional to be successful in their role. The twinning also supports ongoing growth and development of the supervisee, allows for 'self and culture' to be intertwined with each other for they cannot exist without each other. The outer layer of the design represents the natural river reeds and shows respect and protection of knowledge passed on in cultural communities through Elders and Aunties.

The colours in the model embody the knowledge that Aboriginal people bring to their role, the strength they bring to their role and how know ledge and wisdom is passed on. The colours of Tasmania's bull kelp in the model represents how strength is maintained through the power of resilience. Bull kelp is washed against rocks under the water that flow in rhythm with the fierce tides that are at the mercy of the weather.

The ***Practice/Professional*** quadrant shows an image of the eye that primarily focuses on the professional's story and the passing of knowledge through art as it has survived throughout the generations. In the eye, one sees the reflection of Country, Culture, Community, Land, Sea and how this is embodied into the professional role. Elders guide others in the community through the journey of belonging and this in turn provides an identity. Professional identity is transferred to the role as a way of relating to others, with others and for others.

The ***Administrative/Line Management*** quadrant is overviewed by cave and bark protective shelters. This metaphor represents the role of the organisation in providing shelter for staff for them to feel supported in their role, cope with the challenges that present and support the professional to achieve what is required in their role. For Aboriginal people, each family member has a role in the planning and building of Bark Shelters as they are designed and arranged to be strong for families and tribes to meet and 'yarn'. The strength in the organisational environment is then passed onto other professionals as they understand the shelter and the importance of its role in the workplace. The stars, sun and moon provide direction and guide stories in the organisational space. Animal tracks have been incorporated into the model to show the native Tasmanian emu.

The ***Support/Person*** quadrant provides the image of the body. The head shows the mind and support for mental well-being and the body represents physical and spiritual well-being. The reeds throughout the model provide a metaphor for the professionals' arms and legs flowing outwards in orange. The hands represent ongoing knowledge and learning in a professional and personal space. The interconnection of the white circles is about protecting the journey of the supervisee given their personal life story and the professional role. The rock petroglyphs show the impact of Aboriginal people's ancient beliefs and values as these are of high importance for Aboriginal people to be on country and connected with both the land and sea. This provides a place of energy, replenishment and healing to allow a space for balance between what the organisation requires and the supervisee's cultural and personal well-being.

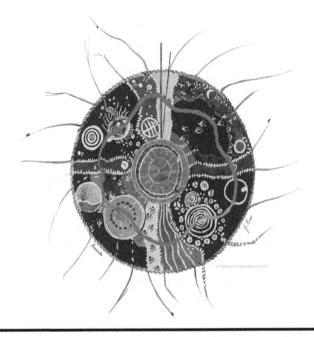

Visual 4.7   The Basket of Knowledge – CASE™ supervision model.

The ***Educational/Professional Development*** quadrant is represented by the small circle of grass root plants, showcasing how skills and knowledge are passed from each generation to the next. The grass roots are painted red symbolising how Community members share knowledge through strong blood lines with their Ancestors. Through education, development and learning, it takes time to earn respect and responsibilities that have come through teachers, Elders and Country. Yarning is how knowledge and skills are transferred so that responsibilities and obligations can be practiced. The tracking of animal prints is important with respect to Country and where the story of Aboriginal people have originated from.

Visual 4.7 provides an overview of the Basket of Knowledge – CASE model with the artistic visual that assists supervisees to develop their yarning agenda for meetings.

The Models in Action

Tables 4.2–4.7 provide an overview for each model, the focus of each quadrant and the style adopted by the supervisor in each part of the supervision conversation.

Table 4.2   PASE™ Supervision Model Focus and Supervisor Style

PASE	Focus	Supervisor Style
(P) Practice/ Professional	Discussion is focused on the *professional* in their role and practice context	**Reflective** Discussion is highly reflective and incorporates the supervisee's reflective capacity and key frameworks used in their role
(A) Administrative/ Line Management	Discussion is focused on the *organisation's* requirements within the context of the role	**Directive** Supervisor is outcome focused, providing guidance and direction. The supervisor is key in the decision-making process. External supervisor is a partner to the process but not a key decision maker
(S) Support/Person	Discussion is focused on the *person* as a professional, providing a platform for support, validation and encouragement in the role	**Facilitative** Supervisor provides the necessary space to guide the discussion that allows the supervisee to draw conclusions and decisions for self
(E) Educational/ Professional Development	Discussion is focused on *learning and professional development* of the professional in an ongoing capacity	**Developmental** Supervisor provides a developmental platform in which the supervisee can continually learn and grow, plan for the future and evidence their professional practice in the role

Table 4.3   LASE™ Supervision Model Focus and Supervisor Style

LASE	Focus	Supervisor Style
(L) Leadership/ Management	Discussion is focused on operational and *strategic acumen*, growth and positioning of the organisation/*leadership* area	**Visionary** Key frameworks include the supervision model, operational and strategic management
(A) Administrative/ Line Management	Discussion is focused on the *organisational* requirements within the context of the role	**Directive** Supervisor is outcome focused, providing guidance and direction. Supervisor is key in the decision-making process
(S) Support/Person	Discussion is focused on the *person* as a professional, providing a platform for support, validation and assurance in the role	**Facilitative** Supervisor provides the necessary space to guide the discussion that allows the professional to draw conclusions and decisions for self
(E) Educational/ Professional Development	Discussion is focused on *learning and professional development* of the professional	**Developmental** Supervisor provides a developmental platform in which the professional can learn and grow further in the role, plan for the future and evidence their professional practice

Table 4.4 FASE™ Supervision Model Focus and Supervisor Style

FASE	*Focus*	*Supervisor Style*
(F) Frontline/ Professional	Discussion is focused on client/customer focus, systems, operational and *professional practices*	**Influencing** Key frameworks include the supervision model, operational and strategic support as well as accounts, finance and HR support
(A) Administrative/ Line Management	Discussion is focused on the *organisational* requirements within the context of the role	**Directive** Supervisor is outcome focused, providing guidance and direction. Supervisor is key in the decision-making process
(S) Support/Person	Discussion is focused on the *person* as a professional, providing a platform for support, validation and assurance in the role	**Facilitative** Supervisor provides the necessary space to guide the discussion that allows the professional to draw conclusions and decisions for self
(E) Educational/ Professional Development	Discussion is focused on *learning and professional development* of the professional	**Developmental** Supervisor provides a developmental platform in which the professional can learn and grow further in the role, plan for the future and evidence their professional practice

Table 4.5 MASE™ Supervision Model Focus and Supervisor Style

MASE	*Focus*	*Supervisor Style*
(M) Managerial/ Coordinate	Discussion is focused on programme/*practice* development, policy focus, client/customer focus, professional identity	**Preceptive** Supervisor is insightful, is able to manage up and down given they may be in a middle manager role, leadership role in a program or policy area
(A) Administration/ Line Management	Discussion is focused on the *organisational* requirements within the context of the role	**Directive** Supervisor is outcome focused, providing guidance and direction. Supervisor is key in the decision-making process
(S) Support/Person	Discussion is focused on the *person* as a professional, providing a platform for support, validation and assurance in the role	**Facilitative** Supervisor provides the necessary space to guide the discussion that allows the professional to draw conclusions and decisions for self
(E) Educational/ Professional Development	Discussion is focused on *learning and professional development* of the professional	**Developmental** Supervisor provides a developmental platform in which the professional can learn and grow further in the role, plan for the future and evidence their professional practice

Table 4.6 VASE™ Supervision Model Focus and Supervisor Style

VASE	Focus	Supervisor Style
(V) Volunteer/ Humanitarian	Discussion is focused on the *volunteer* in their role and organisational practice	**Reflective** Discussion is highly reflective and incorporates the volunteer's reflective capacity in the role. Supervisor uses the volunteer's life and other experience to develop a quasi-professional perspective
(A) Administrative/ Line Management	Discussion is focused on *organisational* requirements within the context of the volunteer role	**Directive** Supervisor is outcome focused, providing guidance and direction. The supervisor is key in the volunteer's role
(S) Support/Person	Discussion is focused on the *person* as a quasi-professional, providing a platform for support, validation and encouragement in the role	**Facilitative** Supervisor provides the necessary space to guide the discussion that allows the volunteer to draw conclusions and decisions for self
(E) Educational/ Professional Development	Discussion is focused on *learning and professional development* of the professional in an ongoing capacity	**Developmental** Supervisor provides a developmental platform in which the supervisee can continually learn and grow, plan for the future and evidence their professional practice in the role

Table 4.7 Yarn Up Time and Basket of Knowledge – CASE™ Supervision Model Focus and Supervisor Style

Yarn Up Time CASE™	*Focus*	*Supervisor Style*
(P) Cultural/ Professional	Discussion is focused on the *professional* in their role and considers the cultural practice context	**Reflective** Discussion is highly reflective and incorporates the supervisees reflective capacity and key frameworks used in their role
(A) Administrative/ Line Management	Discussion is focused on the *organisations* requirements within the context of the role	**Directive** Supervisor is outcome focused, providing guidance and direction. The supervisor is key in the decision-making process
(S) Support/Person	Discussion is focused on the *person* as a professional, providing a platform for support, validation and encouragement in the role, considering cultural protocols and obligations	**Facilitative** Supervisor provides the necessary space to guide the discussion that allows the supervisee to draw conclusions and decisions for self
(E) Educational/ Professional Development	Discussion is focused on *learning and professional development* of the professional in an ongoing capacity	**Developmental** Supervisor provides a developmental platform in which the supervisee can continually learn and grow, plan for the future and evidence their professional practice in the role

Moving Around the Quadrants

All model quadrants include words that form agenda items that you would typically see in each of the respective quadrants. However, any agenda topic in the supervision discussion can be focused on from any quadrant. For example, if you are discussing leave planning – this would be typically discussed in supervision from the 'A' quadrant. You could talk about leave planning from the 'S' quadrant if they needed to debrief about getting their work caught up before going on leave, or you could talk about leave planning from a 'P' quadrant if the supervisee needed to discuss their client or customer work from a practice perspective.

The questions and statements outlined in Table 4.8 assist the supervisor to move around the different quadrants in the supervision models. This provides the supervisor with ideas of how to move around the quadrants as the supervision conversation shifts focus. There is no right or wrong way to engage the discussion from any of the quadrants, the only thing to remember is that agenda items can be discussed from any of the quadrants. The focus of the discussion shifts depending on the quadrant focus and the supervisor's style. Table 4.8 demonstrates the types of questions that are typical in each of the individual quadrants; however, they can be asked in any quadrant using different language and question types. The following provides examples of all supervision models and the types of questions that are relevant to each of the quadrant areas.

The questions in the LASE supervision model in Table 4.9 assist the leader or manager to move around the quadrants during the conversation. Each area demonstrates the types of questions and statements typical of each of the quadrants; however, they can be asked from any quadrant using different language and question types.

The questions and statements outlined in Table 4.10 assist the supervisor to move around the different quadrants in the FASE supervision model. Each area in this document demonstrates the types of questions and statements that are typical of each of the individual quadrants; however, they can be asked in any quadrant with different language and question types.

Table 4.11 overviews questions and statement to assist the supervisor to move around the different quadrants in the MASE supervision model. Each area in this document demonstrates the types of questions and statements that are typical of each of the individual quadrants; however, they can be asked in any quadrant with different language and question types.

Table 4.8 PASE™ Questioning Framework

P – Practice/Professional	Types of Questions and Statements to Use in the P Quadrant
• What do you think you did specifically in your practice that ensured that particular outcome? • What did you draw from in that situation to get the outcome with the client? • What were your reflections prior to that taking place? • What were you thinking and reflecting on whilst you were in that situation? • What were your reflections immediately after you…? • Tell me about how you reached that decision – what did you consider? • How do you consider that was the appropriate approach to use in that situation? • How did you determine that your approach would work? • What professional beliefs or values were influencing your practices at that time? • Tell me more about how you interpreted that as part of your ethical framework? • What else were you doing at that time that demonstrated 'good' practice? • How did you evaluate that situation? • Tell me about your professional practice framework? • What skills and knowledge were you focusing on…? • What practices did you notice others engaged in/doing? • How do you know your decision at the time was relevant for the situation?	
A – Administrative/Line Management	Types of Questions and Statements to Use in the A Quadrant
• What things do you see as important for the team agenda next week? • How are you going writing up those notes/report? • Let's have a look at the policy on this area and have a discussion about how you interpret that information? • Let's discuss the leave plan for the Christmas period • It would be useful to review that policy in line with what occurred last week • In reviewing the meeting minutes from the recent meeting, what did they include? • Can you please have that completed by Friday? • I am just checking about the detail of the report and what was written • I really need you to follow up, can you please check this for me by Friday • I know you are busy, however this really needs to be followed up • Remember to complete the form and include… • Your timesheet indicates… • Remember to include… • What things need to be included to follow compliance of…	

(Continued)

Table 4.8 (*Continued*)   PASE™ Questioning Framework

S – Support/Person	*Types of Questions and Statements to Use in the S Quadrant*
• How have the current issues in the team impacted on you? • What can I do as a supervisor/manager to support you in that process? • How can we adequately support you in your role? • It appears that impacted on you, let's discuss… • What current beliefs and values do you have in relation to… • How do you think we can work better to… • Do you need to take some time out for… • Tell me more about what happened when… • What things would enable us to… • That was really great work, I would like to acknowledge… • I really appreciated it when you… • I understand there were some issues the other day, what happened? • You seem to be a little distracted lately, what might be happening for you? • How are you managing your current workload? • I understand you have some concerns in relation to… • I was very impressed when you… • I have noticed that you have… • I would like to support you better by… • What key strategies are you engaging to ensure self-care? • What is included in your health care strategy?	
E – Educative/Professional Development	*Types of Questions and Statements to Use in the E Quadrant*
• When you read that article on XXXX what stood out for you? • Regarding that information I gave you last supervision, how have you incorporated… • Can you think back to what was included in that training you attended, what information and learning are you now using in your role? • What further training or professional development would assist you in your role? • You may like to consider integrating… • Let's review your current qualifications to support your career… • What other training do you think is important for the future? • What skills and experience do you think you bring to your role? • What evidence do you have to support that theory? • How are you consciously undertaking your role? • How can we develop XXXX further…? • What do we need to learn as a group for…? • Let's explore that part together in… • How do you see that you are maintaining professional excellence?	

Table 4.9 LASE™ Questioning Framework (L Quadrant)

L – Leadership/Visionary	Types of Questions and Statements to Use in the L Quadrant
• What leadership approach were you using when…? • How are you managing that situation? • What management framework is important in that circumstance? • What ethical stance do you think is important when…? • What do you consider as the important political consideration in that situation? • What position do you think this role needs to take? • Let's consider what strategic direction is important when… • What is your view in positioning… • How would you like me to manage…? • How would you like to manage and support…? • What operational framework are you going to use? • How are you integrating the strategic direction with support of…? • What integration framework will you use with…? • What language do you think is supportive in that situation? • Tell me about your leadership model in…? • What approach will you take when…? • What strategy do you think we need to take with…?	

Table 4.10 FASE™ Questioning Framework (F Quadrant)

F – Frontline/Professional	Types of Questions and Statements to Use in the F Quadrant
• What type of customer satisfaction practice do you think would be relevant? • What practices do we need to consider when doing our records management framework? • When we do our systems analysis what would you like us to consider? • Our newsletter publication might need to reflect…? • What influences do you think impacts on…? • What is your decision-making framework? • How has that situation impacted your thinking about? • What would you like to discuss regarding that ethical dilemma? • What professional approach do you think would be helpful if…? • How would you like us to communicate that? • The research approach we can look at might include… • What is your communication style in that situation? • What skills do you think you engaged with…? • How has the organisational approach…?	

Table 4.11   MASE™ Questioning Framework (M Quadrant)

M – Managerial/Coordinate	Types of Questions and Statements to Use in the M Quadrant
• Let's discuss what we need to include in that report • What form of evaluation are we going to use with… • What impact do you think that policy focus will have on… • As you developed the practice of… how did you actually do that? • When you talked to the client/customer the other day what approach did you take? • What technical communication skills did you engage when you were…? • In your coordination of that, what leadership skills did you use? • As a leader, what type of role modelling did you see that was important? • What was important to consider in the operational management approach you took? • What do you consider is important in your leadership model? • What skills did you use with…? • What are you doing to coordinate? • What professional beliefs and values did you see surface when…? • What were you reflecting on when…? • What evaluation process did you use with…?	

As outlined in Table 4.12, the questions and statements assist the supervisor to move around the different quadrants in the VASE supervision model. Each area in this document demonstrates the types of questions and statements that are typical of each of the individual quadrants; however, they can be asked in any quadrant with different language and question types.

Table 4.13 provides an overview of the types of questions and statements that assist the supervisor to move around the different quadrants in the CASE supervision models. Each area in this document demonstrates the types of questions and statements that are typical of each of the individual quadrants; however, they can be asked in any quadrant with different language and question types.

Questioning and Statement Framework Activity

Now that we have looked at all the different questions and statements in each of the seven supervision models, consider the following questions or statements in Table 4.14 and nominate which quadrant in the PASE model you think they fit.

Table 4.12   VASE™ Questioning Framework (V Quadrant)

V – Volunteer/Humanitarian	Types of Questions and Statements to Use in the V Quadrant
• What did you think occurred as a volunteer in that situation? • What did you draw from in that situation to get the outcome with the client? • What were your reflections prior to that taking place? • What were your reflections immediately after you…? • Tell me about how you reached that decision – what did you consider? • How do you consider that was the appropriate approach to use in that situation? • How did you determine that your approach would work? • What else were you doing at that time that demonstrated 'good' practices? • How did you evaluate that situation? • What skills were you focusing on…? • What things did you notice others engaged in/doing? • How do you know your decision at the time was relevant for the situation? • How did you resolve the problem you were experiencing with…? • How might confidentiality be important in this situation?	

Table 4.13   CASE™ Questioning Framework (C Quadrant)

C – Cultural Practice/Professional	Types of Questions and Statements to Use in the C Quadrant
• What professional and cultural practices did you use with…? • What did you draw from in that situation to get the outcome with the client? • What were your reflections prior to that taking place? • What were you thinking and reflecting on whilst you were in that situation? • Tell me about how you reached that decision – what did you consider? • How do you consider that was the appropriate approach to use in that situation? • How did you determine that your approach would work? • How did culture play a role in…? • How did your professional protocols influence…? • What beliefs or values were influencing your practices at that time? • What else were you doing at that time that demonstrated…? • How did you evaluate that situation? • Tell me about your cultural practice framework? • What skills and knowledge were you focusing on…? • What practices did you notice others engaged in/doing? • How do you know your decision at the time was relevant for the situation?	

Table 4.14 PASE™ Questions and Statements

Statement/Question	P, A, S, E
Let's talk about when your Learning Plan is due, have you considered what you would like to focus on?	
Let's discuss what supports we need to put in place?	
Talk me through what your decision-making process was with that client?	
What did you do specifically in your practice that ensured that particular outcome?	
Do we need to discuss the report that is due next week?	
How have the current issues in the team impacted on you?	
I could see you were concerned in the meeting yesterday, would you like to discuss…?	
When you read the article on XXXX what did you take from that to bring to your role?	
What was your assessment of that situation?	
Would it help if you worked from home next week to finish the report on time?	
What reflective processes were you engaging at that time?	
What else needs to be followed up regarding your work by Friday?	
How did your interactions with your colleague go and what do you need me to do as follow-up support?	
What did you pick up from the conference that can be integrated back into your work?	
When you tried that approach, what was the learning you gained?	
You seem to be a little distracted in the last couple of weeks, is there anything impacting on you that we can help you with?	
What do you see as the ethical dilemmas in that situation?	
If I was observing, you in your role and practice, what would I notice you doing?	

Evaluating the Focus of Supervision Meetings

Having a robust evaluation framework is crucial to understanding the effectiveness of supervision. Evaluating supervision is the only way to understand what is being transferred from discussions back into the supervisee's role. Whilst we will talk about formal evaluations and supervision capability frameworks in Chapter 8, it is crucial to consider how you know supervision is achieving its desired outcomes on a regular basis, rather than just in the annual formal evaluation process. It is common for supervisees to provide verbal feedback to their supervisor about how supervision is going; however, feedback may not be reliable given the automatic hierarchy between the roles of supervisor and supervisee. This means it can be difficult for some staff to provide feedback for fear of being too open about the different aspects of supervision.

To reduce the imbalance between the two roles, each of the seven supervision models has an inbuilt evaluation process that can be undertaken at the end of the supervision meeting to see if both parties believed that they had a similar focus in the discussion. This provides the supervisor with a clear indication if they are meeting the needs of the supervisee, and if the supervisee is meeting the requirements of the role. Evaluating the focus of the discussion also ensures the supervisor is consciously present in the meeting and not distracted by other factors. Evaluating the focus of the discussion at the end of the meeting takes approximately 1 minute, and signals that it is the end of the meeting and no new agenda items can be brought into the discussion at that point.

In the evaluation process, the supervisor asks the supervisee using the relevant model: 'In thinking about our discussion in supervision how would you evaluate the focus of our discussion in the P quadrant 0–10? 0 represents no focus and 10 represents high focus on the discussion area'. Each quadrant in the model is represented by 10 and all quadrants stand alone, meaning that the scores do not need to add up to a whole number for the four quadrant areas. The evaluation framework is subjective and allows the supervisee to fully engage in the process without concern about evaluating the supervisor's performance given it is only about the focus of the discussion. The supervisee may be tempted to evaluate the S quadrant higher in the first few meetings as they will want to provide feedback that the supervisor is supportive. If this occurs, it is important to guide the supervisee, so they do not feel pressured to give a high evaluation in that quadrant. Remember to advise that it is about the focus of the discussion and not how much the

Table 4.15 PASE™ Evaluation

	Model Quadrants	*Supervisor/10*	*Supervisee/10*
P	Practice/Professional		
A	Administrative/Organisational		
S	Support/Person		
E	Educative/Professional Development		

supervisor is supportive. It is important to have a regular conversation in the S quadrant because supervision is meant to be a highly supportive process where the supervisee feels acknowledged and valued in their role.

The supervisor and supervisee explore each of the quadrants evaluating the supervision meeting through the following questions.

Using the PASE supervision model:

■ In thinking about our discussion today, how much of focus do you think we had on the Practice/Professional area of supervision?

■ In looking at our discussions on Administration/Organisation, where would you evaluate our focus out of 10?

■ In reflecting on the discussion in the Support/Person quadrant, how would you see the focus of that discussion, if any?

■ How would you evaluate the focus of our discussion in the Educative/Professional Development part of supervision?

This evaluation process applies to any model that is used. Table 4.15 demonstrates how the evaluation process is documented in each of the model quadrants. Each of the models can be evaluated in the same way at the conclusion of the supervision meeting.

Visual 4.8 provides an example of how the evaluation scores may look in each of the supervision models.

The Supervision Pipeline

Supervision is more effective when the supervisor has a clear process and framework to choose relevant supervision theories and a relevant supervision model. It also helps to clarify the function and purpose of supervision, what outcomes need to be achieved, choice of supervisor style that meets

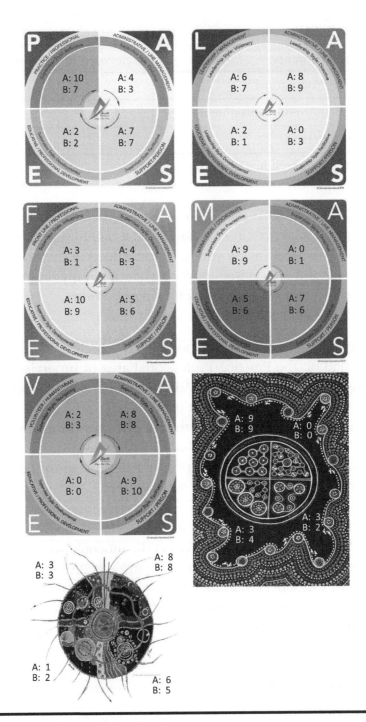

Visual 4.8　Supervision model evaluations.

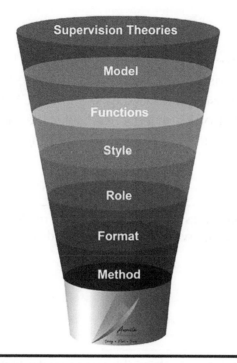

Visual 4.9 The supervision pipeline.

the supervisee's needs and how the supervisor understands the role. The supervisor works closely with the supervisee to adopt a format that engages appropriate methods and techniques to maximise supervision outcomes. When this combination is right, it forms a pipeline that enables supervision to be highly effective. Supervisors need to be highly skilled, have a body of knowledge and engage a range of qualities and attributes to support the pipeline over time (Shelley, 2003). Visual 4.9 outlines key areas for supervisors to enable effective supervision.

Summary

In this chapter, we have discussed the importance of having an integrated supervision model to ensure supervision remains. We have explored Amovita's seven supervision models, i.e., the PASE, LASE, FASE, MASE, VASE, CASE and Basket of Knowledge. Consider the following reflective questions as a summary to the chapter outlining the importance of supervision models.

What have been the key things you have gained from reading this chapter on the importance of having a supervision model to guide discussions in supervision?
What have been your reflections about this chapter regarding the importance of having a supervision model?
List three things that you will take from this chapter to incorporate into your supervisory role.
What do you think will be useful to talk to your supervisee/s about regarding this chapter?

Chapter 5

The Ethical and Industrial Context of Supervision

Key focus for this chapter

- Developing an ethical decision-making framework
- Understanding the ethical decision-making process
- Incorporating ethical discussions in supervision
- Moral reasoning
- Quality ethical questioning
- Ethical considerations as a supervisor
- Industrial imperatives in the supervisory context
- Understanding an ethical process for effective outcomes

Being a line manager and providing professional supervision fit within an ethical and industrial context. Supervision documents can be called upon in organisational and client review processes and documents can be sub-poenaed as part of an industrial tribunal process. Therefore, it is important to consider the process and documents required to be completed and held on file. As a supervisor or leader, it is important to have clear, relevant and ethical practices in place to set the foundation and expectations of supervision and how supervision conversations are conducted.

Ethics refers to how we make informed decisions in our work and how we embed professional standards of behaviour and conduct in a systematic way that is consistent over time. Ethics is the process of knowing right from wrong, having care and respect for others and understanding the importance of taking a moral stance on issues. As professionals, we make assumptions all the time based on our training, experience, values and beliefs. Even when we may be sure we have undertaken a full analysis of a situation and considered our own moral reasoning and value base on the topic, it can be difficult to know how we engage our decision-making process. As described by Carroll (2010), hindsight and retrospective reflection bring positive ruminations as a way to ensure we remain conscious in our ethical decision-making process (Carroll & Shaw, 2012).

Our brain processes anywhere between 50,000 and 60,000 thoughts a day. We make decisions between 0.3 and 0.5 seconds. Why is this important? It is important because we make many decisions on a daily basis and don't often reflect consciously on the decision-making process (Harris, 2018). We often see ethical decision making or ethical reflection remaining in the background of our work, only to surface when something happens or something is questioned (Carroll & Shaw, 2012). Sadly, at many times ethical reflection and sound decision making come too late. We get too busy to stop and reflect on how we make decisions and test the validity of our decisions. Supervision is fundamental to assist supervisees to take time out to reflect on all aspects of their work, refocus and go back into their role with clarity (Harris, 2018; Pillay, 2011).

So … it is important to reflect on the following questions:

■ What do you think the word 'ethics' means?
■ How do you see that supervision sits within an industrial process?
■ How do you engage ethical excellence as a supervisor and leader?
■ How do you make ethical decisions?
■ What is your ethical decision-making process?
■ What does your ethical decision-making framework look like?
■ How would others know what your ethical decision process is?
■ How do you know what your supervisee's decision-making framework is?
■ Why do unethical behaviour and decisions occur?

Consider the following questions as we start to explore the industrial and ethical contexts in which supervision fits.

1. Why is it important to consider industrial and/or ethical issues in professional supervision?

_____

_____

_____

_____

_____

2. What might be the implications or concerns for an organisation/business where this is not considered important?

_____

_____

_____

_____

_____

3. What terms, phrases, words or language might you hear in supervision that may be of concern and highlight there could be an industrial imperative?

_____

_____

_____

_____

_____

4. What do you see as the difference between ethical and industrial issues in supervision – is there a difference?

_____

_____

_____

_____

_____

5. What do you think organisations need to have in place to ensure that ethical and industrial considerations are ensured as part of professional supervision and line management?

_____

_____

_____

_____

6. What things does your organisation already have in place? What might you need to consider?

_____

_____

_____

_____

_____

Reflecting About Ethics

As a professional, think about a time when you had to make an ethical decision and it resulted in you engaging in unethical practice. It could have been something minor or a big ethical issue you were facing. You could have told a white lie or felt you took advantage of a situation. Sitting in a positive and curious space, think about the ethical issue, your decision making and how it turned out:

What would it take for you to cross the line?

What might someone else do, to take you across the line?

1. What do you think was unethical about what you decided to do?
2. Did others know about this? Did you tell them at the time or after? Why or why not?
3. What process did you go through prior to making your decision, and then whilst you were making the decision?
4. What did others notice about you during or after?
5. What role did your emotions play?
6. What was your learning from the incident and process?
7. Did you feel you needed to defend your position with others? If so, how did you do that?

In thinking about the reverse, reflect on the following.

Now as a professional think about a time when you had to make an ethical decision and the result was highly ethical. You felt great about your decision and it resulted in a great outcome.

Again, sitting in a curious space in your thinking, consider the following:

1. What do you think was ethical about what you did?
2. Did others know about this? Did you tell them at the time or after? Why or why not?
3. What process did you go through prior to making your decision, and then whilst you were making the decision?
4. What did others notice about you during or after?
5. What role did your emotions play?
6. What was your learning from the incident and process?
7. Did you feel you needed to defend your position with others? Why or why not?

These are all really useful questions to reflect on in supervision. We all make decisions at times that may not go that well or have felt we have had to make an ethical decision that resulted in unethical practice. I remember one professional some years ago who was working with children. One particular day she was working with a little child and he was very distressed as his mum had to leave him to go to work. At the centre where she worked, staff were not allowed to hug the children, and on this particular day she decided to give him a hug to let him know she was there to comfort him. She said to me that she felt guilty as she had not followed the organisation's policy; however, when she showed him warmth through her hug, he stopped crying and was able to join the other children and went to play.

All of the questions outlined are very helpful to use in supervision conversations. They are thought evoking and provide supervisees with challenging questions to consider how they view ethics in their work and life. Most people do not want to think they have done anything unethical; however, life and work throws us challenges and there will be times when we wished we had made a better decision.

What drives people to be unethical when they are appropriately trained, have relevant qualifications and have a clear set of guidelines and code of ethics to follow?

Under what circumstances is it ok to cross the line?

Some of the answers are with us in our brains. Our limbic system is a collection of structures that include the hippocampus, amygdala, anterior thalamic nuclei and fomix. This part of our brain supports emotion, behaviour and long-term memory. Whilst we have the capacity to do harm, our limbic brain structure has inbuilt instinctual inclination to hold decency

(Ray, 2018; Rock, 2009). When we hold respect for self and others, our decision making is more thoughtful and considered due to our ethics and moral reasoning. When difficult decisions have to be made, we can be compromised in our ethics. We can also find it hard to make decisions when under stress or in duress. Stress, burnout, self-talk and thinking biases all have a significant impact on decision making. When our brain is under a stress load, we have a reduced capacity to think clearly, and making informed decisions is significantly impaired. We are in the fastest moving time in our history, and it is difficult for our brain to process the amount of information it has to on a daily basis. It is no wonder that people are often overwhelmed, stressed and vulnerable. When vulnerability is high our resilience is compromised, and when resilience is high our vulnerability is lower. All of these factors impact how we make decisions and engage in ethical conduct. In the workplace, unethical behaviour can come in the form of continual justification or denial of behaviour and thoughts. Where a supervisee may continually blame others, be avoidant or engage in continual denial it is worth exploring if this is in the context of ethical decision making (Carroll & Shaw, 2012).

Other factors can influence how we make informed decisions that often leads to unethical behaviour or conduct:

■ Lack of self-awareness and self-regulation in emotions.
■ Being insensitive to the needs of others and only focusing on self all of the time.
■ Not seeing others as equals but holding a higher perspective of self over others.
■ Having regular impulsive behaviours.
■ Continual negative thoughts about others.
■ Holding inappropriate power and misusing it.
■ Flying under the radar at work.
■ Taking advantage of situations.
■ Ongoing conflicts with others.

Unethical conduct can also come from people being in denial in the workplace. Have you ever come across someone that no matter what you say to them they deny everything? Have you met someone that justifies or avoids responsibility a lot? Do you know anyone that blames everyone else and again don't take responsibility? Consider the following denial descriptions and statements in Table 5.1. When we relate denial in the supervisory

Table 5.1 Denial Statements (Carroll & Shaw 2012)

Denial Descriptive	*Statement*
Outright denial	This person will deny the facts even when you think they may have been involved in a situation. They are not concerned about any denial statements and believe their own story even if they were involved. They make statements such as 'I didn't do it, I was not involved, It never happened, I didn't see it happen'.
Denial of the consequences of the action	This denial is usually associated with the person engaging in particular actions and does not see anything wrong with their decision making. They are not concerned about the consequences and can be surprised when there is one directed at them. They make statements, such as 'Don't worry, I can handle it, I know what I am doing, you can leave it with me'.
Denial of own and other's feelings	This denial is about dismissing other's feelings or how something may impact. They also do not consider their own feelings in the process. Statements may be made, such as 'So, what, they will get over it, Do I look bothered by this, Why would they feel that way'.
Denial of the need to make changes	This person does not reflect that well and do not see that changes are necessary. They are often ok with the status quo and are dismissive of others' feedback about the required changes. Statements may be made, such as 'That's not for me, I don't need to change, Why would I ever consider that change, Why would I bother about that'.
Denial in reappraisal	This denial is about the lack of awareness and emotion of the impact of something done or said on another person. Statements such as 'I was only talking to her, I was only challenging them, They need to get over it, honestly what is wrong with them'.
Denial in holding responsibility	This denial is all about having any responsibility for anything. Even if the person knows they have done something that could impact others, they never hold any part of the responsibility or will pass it off onto others using statements such as 'I don't remember that, that's not how it happened, totally their doing, if they had only done … it would not have happened'.
Denial in invoking harm or injury	Whilst this person may not intentionally think about doing harm to another person, this denial can be about doing minimal harm such as emotionally and then justifying their actions through language such as 'It was an accident, come on that didn't hurt them that much, they are over reacting, they need to get over it'.

Table 5.2 Ethical Decision-Making Questions

Self-Reflective Question	Response
Does this have the potential to hurt anyone else?	
Would I recommend this action to another person?	
What would I say to someone else in this situation?	
How might others see what I am about to do?	
Are there any areas of denial that I need to reflect on in my thinking?	
Am I being mainstream or fundamental in my actions?	
What might be an opposing view?	
What is my intention in this decision?	
What does my own behaviour/conduct tell me? What beliefs do I hold?	

context, these are triggers for the supervisor to consider as there could be unethical conduct occurring, or at the very least a lack of awareness of how the person engages in the work and with others. Being in denial limits awareness of one's professional identity and how the person holds positive relationships in the work environment (Carroll & Shaw, 2012).

The questions in Table 5.2 are useful to consider when making ethical decisions and developing an ethical framework.

Carroll and Shaw's (2012) steps in ethical decision making:

1. Be aware of your own ethical radar. Understanding how intuition, self-talk and beliefs influence our decision making to ensure professional decisions are conscious and clear steps are followed in the decision-making process.

2. Be aware of how ethical decisions are made. Ethical decisions are part of daily work practices; however, when we are asked what our framework is, it is more difficult to answer. Being clear on what your framework is assists others to know how ethical decisions are made.
   - The next stage is to implement ethical decisions. Weigh up the options by understanding the impact of the decision, consider what information is required to make the decision and what supports may be needed before putting the decision into action. Being able to live with the decision is an important part of putting the decision into place.
   - Being able to articulate the why, what and how is also an important part of decision making. Being able to reflect beyond the surface assists to make better decisions. Being able to provide a rationale, justify and explain clearly to others what and how the decision was made is crucial in professional practice. This also means being able to back up the decision from a professional viewpoint.

3. Feeling good with your decision is important. Ask yourself reflective questions such as Can I live with the decision? Can others live with it? Consider what consequences may be in play and if the decision needs to be reconsidered.

4. Being able to test and experience the decision-making process is important as well. When we understand our decision-making process, we consider moral reasoning and the values we believe are important. Over time this increases ethical wisdom. Part of holding ethical maturity is about knowing what you have learned or are currently learning in the process of decision making.

5. The supervisor's role is to
   - Be aware of one's own personal values and beliefs and the impacts they have as a supervisor.
   - Adhere to the organisation's policies and processes.
   - Be aware of what professional boundaries are and relay these to the supervisee.
   - Know what an ethical decision-making framework is and show the supervisee how to embed it in their role.
   - Ensure the supervisee has access to supervision regularly.
   - Being aware of what an ethical dilemma is.
   - Know the process of inference and how perceptions form decision making.

Ethical Decision-Making Framework (*Adapted from McAuliffe–Chenoweth Framework*)

The ethical decision-making framework developed by McAuliffe and Chenoweth (2008) is based on four key principles:

1. Accountability
2. Consultation
3. Cultural Sensitivity
4. Critical Reflection

The four principles are underpinned by five steps to ensure sound professional decision making as a professional. This framework assists supervisors to have ethics and ethical decision making as part of the supervisory discussion on a regular basis. Is also supports supervisees to engage in clear decision making in their role. The principles are followed to evaluate decision making and then (re) evaluated again in case something different needs to occur in the process.

1. **(Re) Define the ethical dilemma**
   - Define competing ethical principles as they present.
   - Explore if there are any cultural considerations that need to be made.
   - Who has the decision-making accountability? Who are the influencers and decision makers?
   - What past experiences need to be considered? Is new knowledge needed to make an informed decision?
   - Is this a single incident or part of a larger picture?
   - Are there any historical things that need to be considered?
   - How is the dilemma conceptualised?
2. **(Re) Mapping legitimacy**
   - Consider legitimacy – who has it? Who needs to be included or not involved? Is the dilemma real or perceived?
   - Are there any factors around inference that need to be considered?
   - What is the appropriateness of sharing and consulting with others?
3. **(Re) Gathering information**
   - Consider guidance from professional codes of ethics, policies or legal consideration.
   - Are there any areas of conflict between personal, professional and organisational contexts?

- Are other resources or consultations required?
- What information needs to be gathered and contextualised?

4. **Alternate (re) approaches and action**
   - Consider available and alternative courses of action.
   - What cultural considerations need to be made?
   - Who is involved? Who is not involved?
   - How can all parties live with the decision?
   - Implementing and documenting the decision.
   - Have all options and consequences been considered?
   - Any other possible courses of action to take?
   - Is there resistance to any approach and/or action?
   - What support strategies may be necessary?

5. **Critical (re) analysis and (re) evaluation**
   - Work though any resistance from others or self.
   - Re-evaluate the decision being made.
   - Accept the outcome of the decision made.

The ethical navigation process in Visual 5.1 provides an alternative framework for supervisors to use in supervision. It provides a clear roadmap about the decision-making process and can be used by supervisees to articulate how they make decisions. Developed by Harris (2018), Phase 1 of the navigation process maps the dilemma and reflects on what has occurred. This phase questions if the dilemma is real or perceived and allows the supervisee to reflect on aspects of the dilemma and the context in which it has occurred. Phase 2 seeks to understand what has occurred by gathering relevant information from appropriate sources in a relevant time frame. Phase 3 considers what supports are needed prior to a decision being made and how long support is required. Phase 4 in the framework considers the

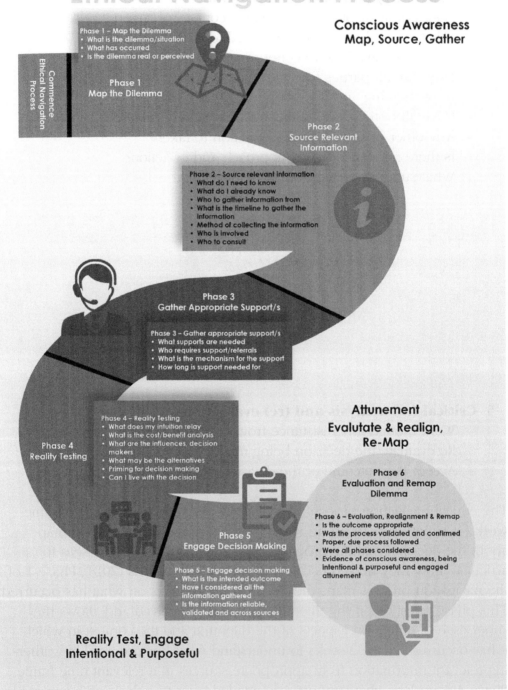

Visual 5.1   Ethical navigation process.

intuitive lens by which the decision is made. Are there alternatives that need consideration and how does the supervisee prepare for the decision to be made? Phase 5 is about engaging the decision, ensuring that all information has been examined. It also confirms the information is reliable and validated from a number of sources. Phase 6 is about actually making the decision and ensuring that the decision maker was conscious and intentional in the process. This also allows the person to re-evaluate the decision made and to see if they need to redress any of the phases along the way.

Table 5.3 provides reflective questions for the supervisee to consider in the decision-making process as outlined in the Ethical Navigation Process.

Whilst it is key to have an ethical navigation process, it is as equally critical to have an ethical decision-making framework that is clear to follow. The framework outlined in Visual 5.2 is an ethical decision-making framework used to guide the supervisor and supervisee of the areas that need to be discussed and considered in the decision-making process. The key areas of the framework include the consideration of internal and external stakeholders; the role of moral reasoning, values, beliefs and intuition; the intersection of the supervisee's professional practice framework in the decision-making process; considerations of power, culture and religion; the language framework used; any organisational impacts; influences on self and others; and the consideration of legal imperatives (such as legislative requirements, informed consent, privacy, confidentiality, code of ethics and professional association requirements). Each of the areas includes reflective questions to guide the process and allow the supervisee to feel confident in making decisions from a professional perspective. Where supervisees do not have an ethical decision-making framework or are not guided in how to make clear decisions, they often have to rely on personal beliefs and values which may be biased in the process (Table 5.4).

Supervision provides the perfect platform to understand how the process of reflection takes place. Most professionals are time poor and engaging in critical thinking and reflection can be somewhat of a luxury. Supervision allows both parties to stop and reflect, enhancing well-being through acknowledgement and validation of the supervisee. This can increase dopamine and act as a reward to the supervisee feeling better supported and valued. Stopping to reflect also assists the supervisee's brain to engage its braking system and slow things down. This is particularly useful when feeling stressed or fatigued (Farmer, 2009).

Whilst it is important to reflect during our work on a daily basis, it is also important to get some space to critically reflect on aspects of practice and the

Table 5.3 Reflective Questions for Ethical Decision Making

Phase 1 Map the dilemma	• What is the dilemma/situation? • What has occurred? • Is the dilemma real or perceived? • What is my mapping tool?
Phase 2 Source information	• What do I need to know? • What do I already know? • Who do I need to gather information from? • What is the timeline to gather the information? • What method of collection will I use? • Who is involved?
Phase 3 Gather appropriate support/s	• What supports are needed? • Who requires support/referral? • What is the mechanism for the support? • How long is support required?
Phase 4 Reality testing	• What does my intuition relay? • What is the cost/benefit analysis? • What are the influences? • What may be the alternatives? • Priming needed for the decision-making process • Can I live with the decision being made? • Will others be able to live with the decision? • What are the consequences and impacts? • Analyse the information carefully • Have any personal beliefs and values come into play?
Phase 5 Engage decision making	• What is the intended outcome? • Have I considered all the information gathered? • Is the evidence/information conclusive? • Is the information reliable, validated and from a number of sources?

Phase 6
Evaluate and re-align,
  map to ethical map
	• Is the outcome appropriate?
	• Was the process validated and confirmed?
	• Was proper and due process followed?
	• Was an ethical decision-making model used?
	• Is there evidence of conscious awareness, being
	  intentional and purposeful and attunement in place?

role more broadly. Reflection requires us to engage in asking ourselves the right questions. Knowing the types of questions that elicit deeper reflection assists us to make better decisions. Part of making sound decisions is being able to identify any personal beliefs and values that may intersect in the professional space and be able to defuse any decision-making biases that are evident. Visual 5.3 provides a stepped reflection process for sound decision making.

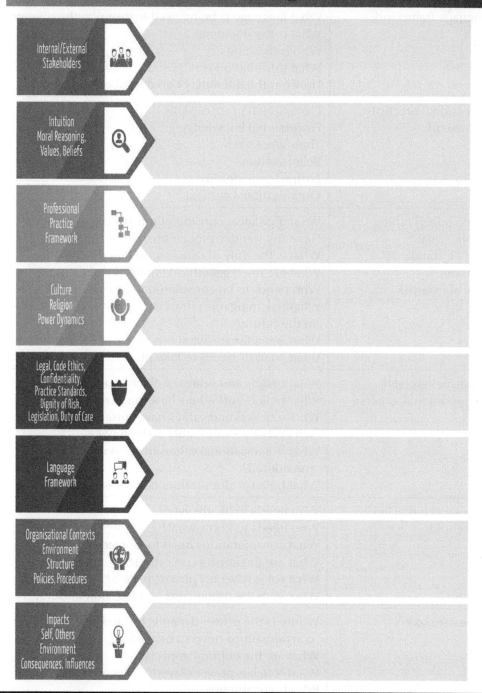

Visual 5.2 Ethical decision-making framework.

Table 5.4   Ethical Decision-Making Framework: Reflective Questions

Ethical Decision-Making Framework Focus	Reflective Questioning
Language framework	What language is being used to describe the dilemma? What is the dilemma? Who is defining it? What information is required? How has the dilemma been described/explained?
Professional practice framework	Professional/practice skills Professional knowledge Theory/research Beliefs/values Professional identity Organisational context
Legal/code of ethics/ confidentiality Practice standards/ legislation Duty of care/risk	What legislative considerations need to be made? Have any standards been breached? What is the duty of care required in this situation? What are the legal/ethical implications? Who needs to be considered in this situation? What risk mitigation strategy needs to be considered in the future? What is legitimate, what is not? What analysis needs to take place?
Values/beliefs (self, organisational, others)	What beliefs and values come into play? What beliefs and values have surfaced? Whose beliefs and values have surfaced? What were self and other's thoughts at the time? What organisational values/mission need to be considered? What beliefs/values influenced the situation?
Internal/external key stakeholders	Who needs to be involved? Who needs to know what? What considerations need to be made? What are the impacts on others? What roles have key players played? Who were the influencers and decision makers?
Culture/power	Where is the power dynamic located? What cultural considerations need to be made? What are the cultural impacts? What role has power played? Who holds the power?

(*Continued*)

Table 5.4 (*Continued*)   Ethical Decision-Making Framework: Reflective Questions

Ethical Decision-Making Framework Focus	Reflective Questioning
Professional boundaries	What boundaries have been crossed? How strong were the boundaries? What are the boundaries in this situation? What role did ethical conduct play? What were the professional frameworks?
Impacts/self and others	What are the consequences of what has occurred? What might be the impact/stress on self or others? Is anyone vulnerable in this situation? Who needs to be consulted? What is the rationale?

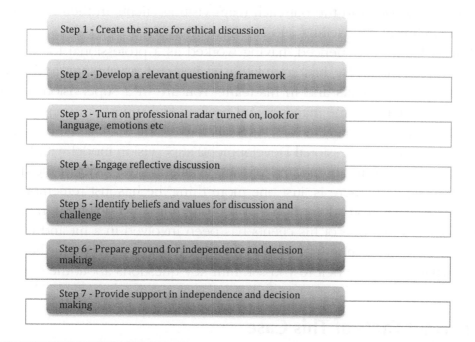

Step 1 - Create the space for ethical discussion

Step 2 - Develop a relevant questioning framework

Step 3 - Turn on professional radar turned on, look for language, emotions etc

Step 4 - Engage reflective discussion

Step 5 - Identify beliefs and values for discussion and challenge

Step 6 - Prepare ground for independence and decision making

Step 7 - Provide support in independence and decision making

Visual 5.3   The reflective process.

The following case study is useful to explore in supervision, as it allows the supervisor to see how the supervisee engages their decision-making process. In exploring the case about Tom, it is important for the supervisee to identify the key areas of their decision-making framework and describe what their ethical framework looks like. You will want to see most of the ethical framework aspects covered in this chapter. This case study is also useful when providing group supervision. When you use this case study with supervisees, ask them to consider what goes through their mind initially. This gives you an idea of where their mind goes to and how they make decisions. As the supervisor, where do you go to in your own thinking in a case like this, and why?

Case Study

You are a line manager and professional supervisor in a human services organisation that provides various clinical health services to clients who have mental health concerns. The organisation is located in a general practitioner clinic and offers clinical and outreach support to clients with complex health issues. One of your staff, Tom, has been in the role of senior practitioner for thirteen years. He is in the outreach team visiting clients in their own home providing clinical counselling and support services.

Tom is highly experienced, having worked as a professional for approximately fifteen years. He has completed bachelor of psychology and is well respected by his clients and in his team. You are in a supervision meeting with Tom, and as his line manager and professional supervisor you are using the PASE™ (Professional/Practice, Administrative/Line Management/Support/Person, Educative/Professional Development) supervision model with him. As the meeting comes to an end and you are evaluating the focus of the discussion, Tom suggests there is 'just one more thing' he has just remembered to talk to you about. You advise him that you only have a couple of minutes and Tom discloses that one of his clients has been involved in a hit and run that took place about six months ago. Tom then proceeds to give you further detail about what took place before you ask him key questions about the case.

Important Facts of This Case

- Tom has known about this incident for two months.
- Tom has not disclosed this information to anyone in his organisation (including yourself) prior to this supervision conversation.
- Upon being told this information from the client, Tom reported the matter to the police as he felt compelled to advise the police of what he knew.
- The person died at the scene of the hit and run.
- The client and two other people in the car tampered with the body and removed it from the scene of the accident.

- Tom continues to report information to the police on a semi-regular basis.
- The police have questioned Tom and directed him not to discuss the case with anyone or he would be 'in contempt' when this case goes to court.
- The police have advised Tom he will be their 'key witness' in court.
- The client is not aware Tom is providing information to the police.
- Tom has been seeing the client for eight months.
- The client has been diagnosed with anxiety and a complex trauma condition so has a high mistrust of people but trusts Tom.
- Tom has discussed the matter with some members of his family.
- Tom is a member of his Professional Association.
- Tom was of the view that supervision was the best place to discuss the matter, knowing he would have the bounds of confidentiality in which to disclose.
- Tom is not aware of any ethical dilemma he may have placed himself in, the organisation, the client or you as the line manager and supervisor.
- Tom is not recording much information disclosed by the client in his case notes.

What initially went through your mind when reading this case study? Where did your thinking start? This provides some hints about your decision-making process and why it is important to see where your supervisee begins their decision making. Consider the following reflective questions as you work through the case study in supervision and ensure that the supervisee can use the ethical framework in this chapter in their role.

1. What might be the initial thoughts that went through the professional supervisor's mind?
2. What are the presenting issues in this scenario?
3. What do you need to consider in this scenario as the professional supervisor?
4. What else do you need to know as the professional supervisor?
5. What information do you not have in this scenario?
6. What are the ethical dilemmas?
7. Outline the steps in your ethical decision-making framework
8. What would you do if you were the professional supervisor in this scenario?
9. What are the ethical implications in this matter?
10. Consider how you would use the ethical decision-making framework that is included in this chapter.

Summary

We have discussed the importance of having an ethical decision-making framework to support supervisees in making key decisions in their role. In this chapter, we have included various tools to support the decision-making process. Consider the following reflective questions as a summary to the chapter about ethical decision making.

What have been the key things you have gained from reading this chapter on the importance of having an ethical decision-making framework?
What have been your reflections about this chapter?
List three things that you will take from this chapter to incorporate into your supervisory role.
What do you think will be useful to talk to your supervisee/s about regarding this chapter?

Chapter 6

The Art of Reflection in Supervision

Key focus for this chapter

- Developing a framework for critical reflection as a professional
- Engaging staff in reflection
- What the role of reflection in supervisory practice is
- How to be a reflective supervisor
- How we engage inference
- Engaging a range of reflective frameworks

Reflection in Our Work

Our thoughts occupy our day-to-day work. Whilst we are cognitively aware of what we are doing, so often we do not regularly reflect more deeply on things given the busy lives we lead. We are very outcome focused which takes our thinking process to the very task in front of us and therefore the more critical reflective thinking is often thought to be something that takes us away from what we are doing. When we engage in deeper reflective thinking, it evokes us to be connected to our environment and self; therefore, we feel more content and happier. This tells our brain that we are not stressed and in a coping space, therefore is good for health and well-being outcomes (Farmer, 2009). The benefits of thinking reflectively provide better performance, have a sense of purpose and meaning and our relationships are more meaningful. It is important to take time out of the busy daily grind to be with yourself and think about many things; however, being connected to yourself in a reflective and mindful way whilst you are going about your daily activities is critically important.

When we relate this to a professional role, reflection assists us to understand the context in which we operate and helps us to remain conscious of how we engage our professional identity, be fully present in our work and understand the personal and professional beliefs and values that influence what we do. Thinking about what is important for you, why it is important and how you want to connect to what you are doing each day is crucial for remaining healthy and well. Unfortunately, many professionals that I work with reflect just beyond the surface as it is thought that we need to stop and sit quietly for the reflective process to take place. Deeper reflection is necessary to remain effective as a professional.

Let's Go on a Journey of Self-Reflection

Reflect on the following statements about what is important for you:

I really enjoy

_____
_____
_____

I could really do with

_____
_____
_____

I know I would rather

_____
_____
_____

My real desire is to

_____
_____
_____
_____

I often think about

_____

_____

_____

_____

I don't like to

_____

_____

_____

_____

Other people see

_____

_____

_____

_____

I would like them to see

_____

_____

_____

_____

I am stuck in

_____

_____

_____

_____

I believe I am

_____

_____

_____

_____

I need to think about

_____

_____

_____

I am going to

_____

_____

_____

_____

When I ask professionals these questions, most professionals advise they take them to a deeper reflective space. It helps to consider what is important in different situations. When we connect to our true sense of self through our enteric brain 'gut brain', we connect to our inner self and have a better understanding of how we reflect what is important. So now let's apply this concept to the professional environment. What is meant by reflection or reflective practice in supervision.

> Reflection is a critical thinking process by which we are conscious about what we are doing, how we do it and why we are do it. It is a highly attuned process by which we use attentional intelligence that neurologically connects our cognitive, heart and enteric brains. Reflection is the way in which we connect to our purpose, values and the meaning of how we work and assists to keep us motivated and inspired to engage best practice and relate to others in a meaningful way.
>
> **Harris (2018)**

Reflection assists us to consider what approach to use in your work?
- Reflection is the search for approaches as they relate to what you do in your role.
- It is about critiquing and analysing actions, attitudes and behaviours in all areas of your practice.
- Reflection is about how we see ourselves in relation to what we do and remaining aware of how we connect to others and our work as a professional.

Refection provides a framework in which to examine practice?
- It is the process of understanding what knowledge and perspectives influence the professional role.
- It assists to understand the elements in a professional excellence framework and what is relevant to use in the workplace.

- Reflection reminds us to examine and analyse what occurs in practice.
- It assists to ask relevant questions that guide how we practice.

Reflection provides a framework about what you reflect on?
- Reflection enables us to accurately engage in reflection prior to, during and after an interaction.
- It assists us to locate and consider our thoughts, feelings and actions in any situation.
- Reflection also enables us to consider the impact of our interactions, beliefs, values, thoughts, etc. on others.
- It ensures we keep in touch with our consciousness and maintain awareness, therefore avoiding complacency.
- It gives us the opportunity to be retrospective.
- Understand the process by which we make decisions.

One of the leading thinkers on reflective practice is Donald Schon (1983). His work on this area has played a major role in assisting professionals to be more reflective in their work. Schon (1983) suggests that just because one draws upon their own knowledge in practice, for example having knowledge of leadership, it does not necessarily mean that person knows how to lead. The professional still needs training, professional development and supervision to enhance their capability over time.

Schon (1983) suggests there are three key elements of reflection necessary for high performance:

1. Reflection-for-Action
2. Reflection-in-Action
3. Reflection-post-Action

1. **Reflection-for-Action**
   This is a process in which to prepare us to think about what we do before we do it. This part of the reflective process prepares our executive thinking function to engage with the interaction or activity we are about to do. At this beginning phase of reflection, there are important reflective questions to consider. The questions are predominantly future focused prior to stepping into the situation.
   1. What am I trying to achieve? Identify the aims and objectives of what you are doing, this comes more from a model of goal setting.
   2. What do I want to achieve, what is my intended purpose?

3. How will I achieve what I am setting out to do? What processes do I need to put into place to get you from point A to B?

4. What do I need to consider before I engage?

2. **Reflection-in-Action**

This phase of the reflection process considers how we evaluate, question and respond whilst in the action. In any situation, it is all too easy to concentrate on one aspect of the action, rather than integrate various aspects into the one reflective space. Again, you can ask yourself a series of questions that ensure you consider what you are doing in that given moment.

– Am I in a conscious space at the moment?
– What other options are present at this time?
– What am I thinking right now?
– What thoughts am I experiencing?
– Do they align with what I am doing?

These questions can assist to clarify our thinking and what feelings may be influencing the situation. It also provides the space to feel confident in any decision-making process.

3. **Reflection-Post-Action**

This part of the reflective process involves thinking back over what has occurred and is more than recollection; it is also analysing the recollection. In this process, a range of questions are asked to consider what took place. To analyse something, whether an object, a set of ideas or a situation, is to undertake a detailed examination of the structure or constituent parts of elements and ask questions about them in order to more fully understand their nature and how the parts relate to and influence each other (Schon, 1983). The term 'critical' introduces a further dimension in the reflective process, in that judgements are made about the strengths and weaknesses of the different parts as well as of the whole.

Having a framework to question in the reflective process is important.

■ 'What' questions – This requires us to formulate a definition or picture of what has happened – For example, What happened today? What happened when I…

■ 'So what' questions – This invites reflection and analysis of that event or issue.

■ 'Now what' questions – A prompt to formulate an action plan or perhaps outline learning needed.

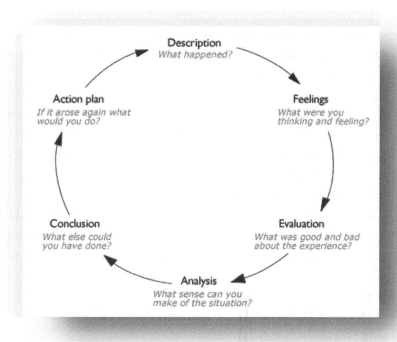

Visual 6.1   Gibbs reflective learning cycle.

- ■ 'Why' questions – Why did I … What made me think that way…
- ■ Reflective questions and prompting to support the staff member to reflect beyond the surface.
- ■ Exploring discrepancies between theory and practice.
- ■ Before, during and after questions.
- ■ Observational questions, recalling observations and professional opinions.

Reflective mind mapping techniques using the reflective learning cycle can also assist in the reflection process and lead to deeper questioning that continues the reflective process (Visual 6.1).

The Ladder of Inference

Another useful framework to use in the reflective process is the Ladder of Inference as it encourages reflection in a stepped process as part of decision making (Argyris, 1970, 2010). We are often under pressure to act now rather than engage reflection and reason in the decision-making process. It can challenge perceptions and assumptions that underlie thought processes and encourages analysis and synthesis of information in decision making. The ladder espouses six steps in the reflective process (Visual 6.2).

Step 1: When we are in a conversation or are making observations, we take on information that we need to both interpret and select information to take forward in the reflective process. We ask ourselves relevant questions that allow relevant data and information to be selected from the interaction or observation. We then overlay the context of the situation and pick up information that is important removing what is not.

Step 2: In this part of the reflective process, we consider what stood out in the interaction or observation. Once we select the relevant information, we then move to the next step around what meaning we derive from the situation.

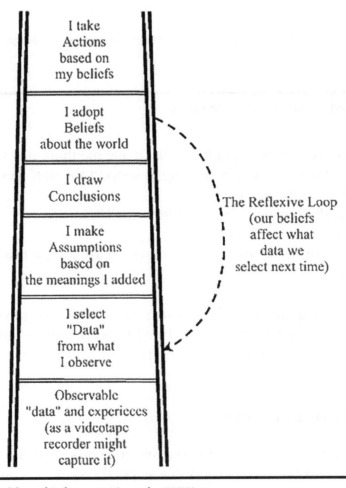

Visual 6.2   Ladder of Inference (Argyris, 1970).

Step 3: One of the most important steps in the Ladder of Inference is about how we derive or interpret meaning from what the other person says. We take the information and then attach a meaning depending on how the message is conveyed, what is spoken about and the purpose of the discussion. We also interpret the meaning based on our own experiences.

Step 4: When interpretations are made, we then make assumptions based on the meaning we have derived. We reflect on the assumptions made and if those assumptions are correct, it informs how we assess what decision is made.

Step 5: The next step in the Ladder of Inference then progresses towards the decision-making process. In this step the supervisee concludes what is occurring and what needs to happen. The supervisee overlays relevant beliefs that may inform their decision and checks what biases may influence the outcome.

Step 6: Once all the steps have been considered, the supervisee progresses towards making a decision. All of the steps are reflected on once more and the decision is then made.

Reflection Discussion Framework

When reflecting it is also important to consider what key areas to reflect on. As outlined in Chapter 1, Professional Excellence Frameworks, it may be relevant to reflect on the supervisee's professional skills, knowledge, beliefs and values, professional identity and the organisational context. As outlined in Chapter 4, the four areas in the PASE™ (Professional/Practice, Administrative/Line Management, Support/Person, Educative/Professional Development) supervision model may provide appropriate areas to reflect on, i.e., aspects of the supervisee's professional practice, the organisational context, the supervisee or their development. Whatever the framework or model by which to reflect, the process of reflection is critical in providing best practice outcomes. The following areas with a set of reflective questions can also assist the supervisee to reflect on their work.

Decision Making
■ Am I confident in the decision I am making?
■ What options do I consider appropriate?
■ What was my decision based on?
■ Was my decision based on the evidence I have?

- What informed my decision?
- What beliefs/values are at play in my decision-making process?
- Was that decision based on previous experiences?
- What steps do I need to take prior to making that decision?
- What is my decision-making process/framework?

Professional Boundaries

- What boundaries need to be considered?
- How does that fit into my role?
- What ethical considerations need to be made?
- What is the boundary of my role?
- How did my actions align with my professional identity?
- What would my Professional Association say about this?
- What do my actions say in this situation?
- What influence do my beliefs have?
- What beliefs/values influenced/impacted the decision?

Purpose/Outcomes

- What is the intended outcome?
- How will others see the outcome?
- Do I have a clear outcome in mind?
- Can I live with the outcome?
- What is a priority?
- What steps need to be in place to achieve the outcome?
- What might be the consequence if the outcome is not achieved?

Ethical

- What is my duty of care in this situation?
- What are the legal/industrial implications?
- What would you consider as reasonable in the situation?
- What needs to be considered in the ethical decision-making framework?
- What would I notice myself doing in making that decision?
- What ethical dilemmas are evident?
- What do I see as the ethical implications in this situation?
- What do I consider as ethical excellence?
- What does this decision look like from a professional perspective?
- What responsibility do I have in this?

Beliefs/Values

■ How might my beliefs and values impact/influence this?
■ How have my beliefs influenced my decision?
■ What values inform that decision?
■ How do the organisational values fit with my own values/beliefs?
■ What value do I place on...?

Professional Identity

■ What is my mindset around this?
■ What role did I play?
■ What did I notice about others?
■ What does this say about my professional identity?
■ What was my engagement style?
■ How does my professional identity inform this?
■ How do others see me in the workplace?
■ How did I influence the situation?
■ How do others see me in...?
■ What level of insight do I have...?
■ What is currently challenging my professional identity?
■ How am I a positive team member?

Professional Assumptions

■ What assumptions did I make at the time?
■ What assumptions do I need to consider?
■ Where do my assumptions come from?
■ What meaning have I attached to...?
■ What do I conclude from this?
■ What does this mean for me?
■ What do I need to reflect on?
■ What patterns are important to consider?
■ What beliefs/values validate or challenge my assumptions?
■ Have my assumptions been founded?
■ What role have my assumptions played?

It is important to not only reflect whilst going about our daily practice but also build in thinking and reflecting time on a regular basis. We maintain professional well-being, good practice and positive relationships when we consciously reflect using some of the frameworks discussed in this chapter.

Reflection can happen when we are in professional discussions, client or team meetings and supervision meetings. It is equally important to work in an environment where you are encouraged to stop and reflect. When time is spent in reflection you will save time, be more focused and declutter the white noise that builds up in our mind. For reflection to be effective, it needs to be valued.

In Table 6.1, **the process of reflection** is a framework that incorporates six elements that are important to reflect onto maintain quality social work practice. Reflecting on all aspects of the social worker's professional excellence framework: professional/practice skills, professional knowledge, approaches and frameworks, beliefs and values, professional identity and the organisational context. There are a number of prompt questions that assist the supervisee to reflect in each area.

For reflection to be impactful, it is important to step out of the situation in order for the reflective process to take place. It can be difficult to reflect if there is a lot of noise or distraction. The next step is to prepare to step into a reflective mindset and consider the appropriate reflective questions and think about what assessment process to use in order to

Table 6.1 Professional Practice Reflective Framework

PROFESSIONAL/Practice Skills	PROFESSIONAL Knowledge
• As a professional what practice skills/ expertise did I engage? • If your supervisor was observing your practice, what key professional/practice skills would they notice? • What skills do you think are relevant in a given situation? • What theoretical approach did you engage...? • What did you reflect on at the time? • What key skills would your supervisor see you using? 	• What ethical decision-making process did you consider? • What knowledge guided you in your practice? • What is the relevant knowledge base to think about? • How did you transfer information from ... into your work? • What knowledge base did you draw that from? • What knowledge can you impart to others? • How does your knowledge influence the practice outcome?

(Continued)

Table 6.1 (*Continued*) Professional Practice Reflective Framework

APPROACHES/Theories	BELIEFS/Values
• What theories inform your practice? • What does the evidence base say in that situation? • How would you link the theory into practice? • What does the literature say? • What theory applies in this context? • Does that approach fit that client context? • Is that the most effective approach in that client case? • How does that theory influence that outcome? 	• What beliefs or values were at play when…? • How were you challenged in that situation? • What values • What conflicted with your own personal beliefs? • What conflicted with your professional beliefs/values? • What beliefs impacted/influenced that decision/outcome? • What ethical decision-making process did you engage? • How did you engage reasoning in that situation?
PROFESSIONAL Identity	**ORGANISATIONAL Context**
• What role does your professional identity play? • How much of a role do you think your professional identity played? • How has your professional identity shaped your practice? • If you developed a professional identity – what would that look like? • What do you see as the role of professional identity? • What are the key aspects of your professional identity framework? 	• What policies or guidelines were important? • What organisational values do you think were relevant in that situation? • What organisational processes were considered? • What legislation guided you? • Did the structure impact on…? • How do you see the change in this situation? • What role did culture play? • How can you negotiate the system in that situation?

reflect on the right things. Reflection is effective when you externalise what has or is occurring to another person. Talking things through with someone else asking questions assists to engage in the deconstructive process. Unpacking and deconstructing the story and meaning is helpful to make sense of things and reduces the threat of the fight or flight process taking place unnecessarily where the supervisee is under stress. The process also considers what the evaluation process is in order to consider what is an appropriate course of action. Having a plan with appropriate actions supports the supervisee to feel as though they are moving forward. Seek any support, further information, knowledge or further time out to reflect and then the process ends with moving towards an action or in action. Visual 6.3 provides an overview of the reflective process steps.

Take a *step back* in order to prepare to reflect

Step into the reflective space

Commence the *assessment* process

Externalise what has occured

Deconstruct the events that have occured

Make an *evaluation* of what needs to occur

Reconstruct and prepare to plan and *strategise*

Step into *action*

Visual 6.3   The process of reflection.

The supervision models outlined in Chapter 4 can also be used as a reflection tool in supervision. Each of the four quadrants *Practice/ Professional (P)*, *Administrative/Line Management (A)*, *Support/Person (S)* and *Educative/Professional Development (E)* quadrants include reflective questions that relate to that aspect of the supervisee's practice and role. Having the questions posed in the supervision model encourages the supervisee to reflect on each of the areas in their work regularly. Visual 6.4 outlines the questions in the PASE supervision model, and Visual 6.5 includes reflective questions in the LASE™ (Leadership/Management, Administrative/Line Management, Support/Person, Educative/Professional Development) model.

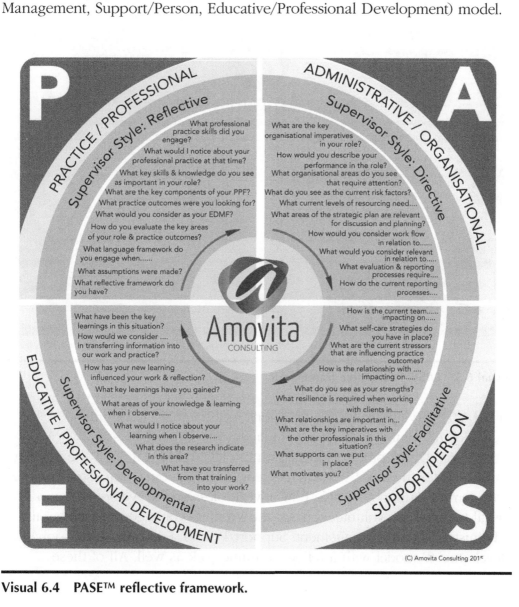

(C) Amovita Consulting 2015

Visual 6.4   PASE™ reflective framework.

Visual 6.5 LASE™ reflective framework.

Visual 6.6 overviews reflective questions in the FASE™ (Frontline/
Professional, Administrative/Line Management, Support/Person, Educative/
Professional Development) supervision model, and Visual 6.7 is the reflective
framework for the MASE™ (Management/Coordination, Administrative/Line
Management, Support/Person, Educative/Professional Development) model.
Visual 6.8 provides volunteers using the VASE™ (Volunteer/Humanitarian,
Administrative/Line Management, Support/Person, Educative/Professional
Development) model with a reflective framework as well. All of these

Visual 6.6 FASE™ reflective framework.

frameworks show some consistency in three of the quadrants, whilst the equivalent quadrant to the *Practice/Professional* (P) in the PASE supervision model has targeted questions to the relevant role.

The final reflective framework in this chapter that can be used in supervision has been adapted Chapman's (2005) work on Learning Styles Inventory. Abbey et al. (1985) suggest there are four different learning styles that we have: Concrete Experience, Reflective Observation, Abstract

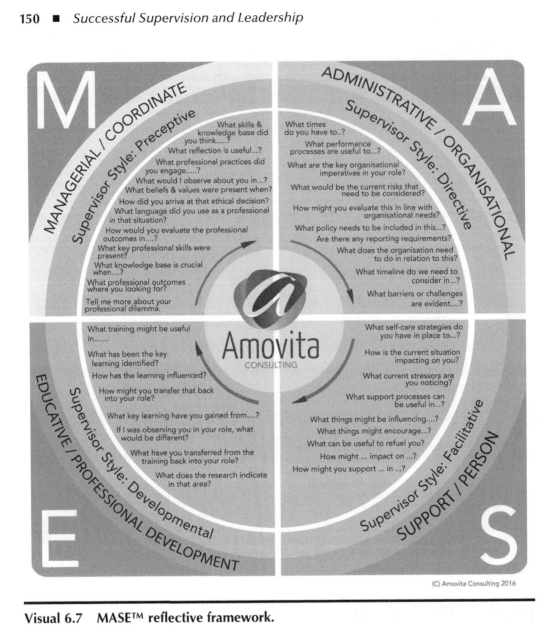

Visual 6.7   MASE™ reflective framework.

Conceptualisation and Active Experimentation. In adapting this inventory, reflective questions have been included in each of the four learning types inviting the supervisee to consider their practice from different learning perspectives. When the supervisee engages reflection after they have experienced something, the supervisee reflects on the experience

Visual 6.8   VASE™ reflective framework.

from a concrete or tangible perspective, what they observed about what happened, abstract aspects of the experience asking theoretical questions about what if and actively reality test what occurred as outlined in Table 6.2.

Table 6.2 Reflective Practice Tool

Reflective Area	Reflective Description
Concrete Contextual Experience *What do I notice about my practice?* *What do I sense about my experience of the practice?* *What is the context of the experience I had?* *What is the environment like, what does that tell me?*	
Critical Reflective Observation *What were my observations prior to, during and after the experience?* *What was I thinking/experiencing at the time?* *What did I observe about myself?* *What critical reflective thinking did I engage?*	
Reflective Conceptualisation Abstract *What would have been useful to know at the time?* *How did I conceptualise my experience?* *What was obvious now reflecting back?* *What would have been useful to know reflecting back?* *How conscious was I at the time?* *What do I now know about what happened?*	
Active Reality Testing *What will I consider next time?* *How might I respond in a similar situation?* *What did this experience tell me?* *What things do I need to review or reality check?*	

Summary

We have discussed the importance of engaging in reflection as part of maintaining best practice. Supervision is one of the best places to have reflective discussion. In this chapter, we have explored what reflection is, the process of reflection and how the supervision models can be used to be reflective as well. Consider the following reflective questions as a summary to the chapter about ethical decision making.

What have been the key things you have gained from reading this chapter on the importance of reflection in supervision?
What have been your reflections about this chapter?
List three things that you will take from this chapter to incorporate into your supervisory role.
What do you think will be useful to talk to your supervisee/s about regarding this chapter?

Chapter 7

The Neuroscience of Supervision

Key focus for this chapter

- Stress and its cumulative impact
- How mindset influences the supervisory environment
- Maintaining resilience and reducing vulnerability
- Understand how beliefs and values impact professional identity
- The important role that neurosocial science plays in supervisory practice
- Why self-care and well-being is so important in a professional role
- How our thoughts impact our performance

Stress Impacts

Over the last ten years, there has been a significant increase in information about brain functionality and its impact on behaviour and emotion. We know much more about how the brain is impacted by stress, fatigue, burnout and traumatic events than decades before. We know the importance of the first 3,000 days of a child's life for the future development of the brain, and we know that due to the brain's plasticity, it has an amazing ability to repair and recover from challenging situations (Rock, 2009). In this chapter, there are some simple facts about the brain that assist supervisors to know how to have open discussions in supervision, provide feedback and understand the impact of cumulative stress and burnout on the brain. It also assists to know how to support staff in the workplace when they may have a mental health challenge. This chapter also explores the importance of self-care, the impact of our memory, cognitive and behavioural biases and how the brain looks for patterns as part of making decisions. With more information known about the brain, it can better inform supervisors on how to provide supervision and evaluate its effectiveness (Pillay, 2011; Rock, 2009; Tversky & Kahneman, 1974).

Our mindset creates our performance

Our thinking patterns create how we feel about ourselves and others

Every year there is an increase in the number of supervisees and leaders we work with at Amovita who are stressed, fatigued, exhausted or burnout. There are many professionals who are just putting one foot in front of the other to get to work each day and feel as though there is no way out of the rut they are in. Most professionals will experience burnout at least once in their career, 82% feel high levels of stress regularly and 40% feel exhausted most of the time (Rock, 2009). Many of the thousands of professionals I work with in supervision are not that clear about what burnout is, what the symptoms are or how to fix it (Bunting, 2016). Let me provide an example.

In supervision I have been working with Max. He is thirty-six years old and has been in his current management role for five years. Max is a leader of a team of ten staff that provide education and support to parents. When Max came to supervision, it was immediately evident that he was burnt out. Max had no idea that he was, he just thought he was exhausted and fed up with his role. Some of his symptoms included:

- Feeling highly negative about his work and his team
- He found it hard to get out of bed each day
- Max found it hard to go to sleep then stay asleep
- He continued to be exhausted on a daily basis
- He did not feel like doing any exercise at all
- Max did not feel good about himself, how he looked, presented or engaged at work
- He was experiencing physiological impacts such as dry hair and skin
- He was drinking too much alcohol
- Very little enjoyment out of life

- Was shutting himself off from his partner and friends
- Could not see that much hope for the future
- Very emotional and was teary a lot of the time throughout discussions
- He was sensitive to light and noise

From this we get some idea of what was happening to Max. He could have been easily diagnosed with stress, anxiety or even depression. We talked about him visiting his general practitioner and naturopath to start the recovery process that would allow his nervous system to take a break.

When we are under prolonged stress, the cumulative impacts are real and it can take a long time to recover if things are really bad. One of the things I discussed with Max in supervision under the S (Support/Person) quadrant was about developing a clear well-being strategy as a professional to allow his brain and body to start recovering. Part of any recovery process when we are exhausted is to stop. Once the brain and body know it has stopped, it can pick up a new predictive loop (brain pattern) that says something is different. If Max continued to do what he was doing, things would only get worse and he would start to experience worse symptoms over time to the point where would not be able to go to work due to panic attacks, etc. Luckily, when Max started supervision, we picked this up straight away and he went to get help. In supervision, we explored his personal self-talk and the beliefs and values that were impacting him at work. Max identified that as a professional he knew he needed to do something different but did not want to talk to anyone about it as he did not know how he was going to fix it. His beliefs and values were impacting him at work, and he was not performing well in his role, felt agitated and anxious most of the time and knew it was only a matter of time before his line manager wanted to discuss his work (Farmer, 2009).

Whilst it can take up to twenty-four months to completely recover fully from serious stress impacts, through the development of his well-being plan in supervision in the S (Support/Person) quadrant, Max recovered within twelve months. The important part of his recovery was to be consistent each day and develop rituals. Rituals give the brain a message to look for different patterns and over time, they form positive habits that can assist the body and brain to increase resilience and decrease vulnerabilities. If Max is ever burnt out again he now has a clear plan of how to recover more quickly and he has a well-being plan that can easily be executed.

Stress Test

Think of a time when you have experienced a stressful event or have been stressed or burnt out for a prolonged period of time. What did you notice about yourself, your health, your body and mind? What did you consciously and unconsciously do to recover? How long did it take?

What usually happens to you in the following areas when under stress? What do you notice physiologically, emotionally, cognitively and behaviourally?

Physiologically (aches and pains, joint pain, soreness, stiffness, etc.)

_____

_____

_____

_____

_____

Emotionally (teary, reduced tolerance, little enjoyment in life and work, impact on relationships)

_____

_____

_____

_____

_____

Cognitively (negative thoughts about self and others, disrupted thinking, ruminations)

_____

_____

_____

_____

_____

Behavioural (agitated, isolates self from others, withdrawal, etc.)

_____

_____

_____

_____

_____

What Is Stress?

Stress is something that we live with each day. We need some level of stress to be motivated and this is often referred to as 'good stress'. Good stress motivates and inspires us to be driven to achieve the things we need to. It is only when we have too much stress in our lives that it impacts negatively. It is important that we understand what stress is so that we can pick it up in others and clearly explain what it is and what it does.

Stress is a physiological, psychological and emotional response that occurs when the body and mind has sustained a negative event or incident that is single or cumulative over time. Holding onto stress over a prolonged period of time results in loss of sleep, poor concentration, reduced ability to make sound decisions and disrupted bounceability and exhaustion. If you have had stress responses in your body and mind for some time, this causes burn out. Your body has to work harder at maintaining normal functioning and will increase the likelihood of remaining in survival mode. When your body and mind have to find ways to cope better, energy is diverted to organs and muscles to ensure the body maintains itself. Stress affects digestion, delays response times and hinders our capacity to respond in given situations. This impact often presents as reduced performance in the workplace, lack of professional boundaries and poor decision making. If not responded to, the workplace may only see the behavioural and performance impacts and therefore will treat it as a performance issue when it is about health and well-being concerns (Farmer, 2009; Rock, 2009).

Stress is an oversupply of cortisol (stress hormone) that stays in our body if we remain in a hypervigilant state. Over time, if cortisol is not released from the body, it stays trapped in our muscles and results in adrenal burnout. Stress impacts physical and mental health, the immune system and our emotions. Cortisol is released into the body when it perceives there is a threat, or we are unsafe. It keeps us alert to what is around us and assists to provide adrenalin to mobilise us if needed. When burnout is present, the brain may perceive a false imminent threat and release cortisol to maintain high alert. If too much cortisol is present over time, it is inevitable that the burnout will accumulate. Understanding the impact of stress can support the recovery process and have a well-being plan in place that reduces the impact of stress. We all respond to and deal with stress in different ways. Knowing what to look for and understand the types of stress that present in the workplace is crucial in providing positive health and well-being outcomes in the long term (Rock, 2009).

Types of Stress

- Environmental stress
- Locational stress
- Cognitive, emotional, physical, behavioural
- Relationship and performance stress
- Inter- and intra-stress

Stress can occur in a particular environment, where we are at a particular point in time, within ourselves, in relationships with others and in a team. It can also occur outside of ourselves but within the organisational system. It is important to assess where the stress is located in order to know how to appropriately respond to it.

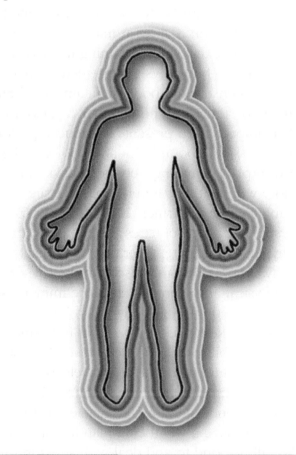

Visual 7.1   Blank body.

Where Do You Hold Stress?

In thinking about where you hold stress, reflect on the blank body in Visual 7.1 and mark where on it where you generally carry stress in your body. What do you think are the impacts on you when stress is present? How does your body respond in stressful situations?

Visual 7.2 overviews some of the cumulative impacts of stress on the body.

If you know someone is experiencing stress you may notice the following and support may be required:
■ Anxiety, irritability, easily distracted, feeling unsafe for no reason
■ Trouble getting to and staying asleep
■ Ongoing increased heart rate
■ Avoidance, withdrawal from others
■ Negative a lot of the time
■ Isolating others and self
■ Regular mistakes, loss of sense of humour, loss of motivation and energy
■ Excessive blaming of others
■ Lack of self-responsibility
■ Bottling up of emotions
■ Excessive complaining about self and others
■ Compulsive behaviours
■ Lack of self-care
■ Relationship issues
■ Apathy
■ Life is generally not pleasurable
■ Prolonged sadness
■ Increased feelings of anger and/or fear
■ Prolonged tiredness
■ Conflict with others
■ Reduced capacity to communicate with others positively
■ Reluctance to change
■ Lack of self-respect
■ Lack of visioning for the future
■ Broken connections

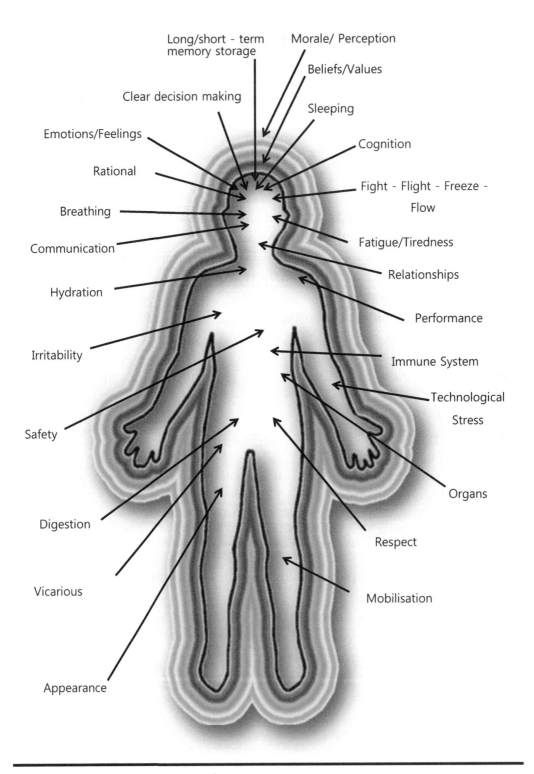

Visual 7.2 Cumulative impacts of stress.

There are a number of protective factors that assist to reduce and minimise stress over time. We are often aware that stress is present; however, there are many times when we are not aware of just how stressed or burnt out we are. The following protective factors assist to remain well.

- Regular supervision and debriefing
- Reflective writing
- Positive relationships
- Alignment of personal beliefs and values
- Moderate any negative impacts
- Plenty of rest and time out
- Solitude and being with self
- Exercise and plenty of water
- Being by the sea regulates brain waves
- Creative activities
- Be around colours
- Be in a problem-solving space
- Increase focus on self-care
- Reduce vulnerabilities and maintain resilience
- Connection to others
- Be in a curious space
- Build in rituals every day
- Reduce time at work

Neuroscience and Self-Care

The research into neuroscience has progressed significantly over the last two decades. It has provided neuroscientists and allied care professions with valuable information and insights into the connection between human behaviour, emotions and the brain. Whilst there has been a dramatic increase in the information readily available, much more needs to be done to understand the relationship between neuroscience and how it influences high performance in the workplace (Egan et al., 2016). When we understand the basics of brain functionality and the relationship between the right and left side of the brain, it provides useful insights as to how we lead and provide professional supervision. Right-side brain functionality includes creativity, working with colour, being insightful and its where our imaginative thinking and holistic thought patterning occurs. Our left-side functionality includes the use of language, numbers and logic thought processing (Rock, 2009).

Neuroscience is the scientific study of the nervous system. It provides an understanding on how the brain functions and its relationship to thought, behaviour and emotion. Study of the brain dates as far back as 4000 BC (Pillay, 2011), and since that time the study of neurosocial science has provided much needed insights as to how humans think, receive feedback and engage with each other. The body contains around 100 billion neurons (nerve cells), which describe the functional units of the nervous system. Neurons are highly specialised in processing and transmitting information in the body and brain and are transported by minute electrical signals. The connections known as synapses transmit the signals that are vital for functioning and relating to others (Rock, 2009).

Whilst our brain is a highly complex organ, only about 10% is utilised or engaged at any one time. The prefrontal cortex is the conscious or executive part of the brain region reflecting 17% of our total brain mass (Neurocapability, 2012). Our amygdala which is the flight, fight, freeze centre of the brain can pick up stimuli before we consciously know it, and understands what is needed to reduce our threat state by releasing cortisol into the body. All of this information is enlightening, telling us that the brain is complex and needs nurturing on a daily basis. No wonder we get tired on a daily, weekly, monthly and yearly basis. We often ignore the signs of fatigue and when we consider the above statistics, it is important to understand how the brain needs to be cared for (Visual 7.3).

Advances in neuroscience research and practice have also provided valuable information for leaders and supervisors on how to lead teams and engage supervisees in the feedback process, so that the brain is open to hearing. Through patterning, our brain is on the lookout for negative things meaning we tend to look for the threat first, then the positive. This also provides supervisors with knowledge on how to use a neurosocial and developmental approach in supervision that helps the brain see a positive (Collins, 2001; Farmer, 2009).

Now let's look some interesting brain facts that assist supervisors to provide effective supervision and have open conversations.

1. The brain is a social organ and therefore is all about connecting with others. Having a sense of belonging and connection to others in the workplace is important. Supervision needs to be a place where

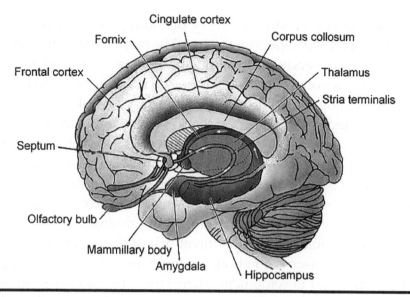

Visual 7.3   Brain overview.

connections in the supervisory relationship are positive and meaningful. It is important to make supervision conversations intentional, so the supervisee sees the value in engaging in the process.

2. Subtle autonomy in the workplace acts as a reward response to the brain, reducing the risk of the brain being in a threat state and releasing cortisol. The more the supervisors show their supervisees their trust and belief, the more the supervisee will get a sense of feeling appreciated and valued.

3. Having a positive language framework also acts as a reward response to the brain. The brain is more likely to release dopamine (our happy hormone) when feedback is useful and constructive, even if it is in challenging conversations. Supervisors need to be skilled to provide feedback in a way that the supervisee's brain can see that it has meaning and is not delivered in a way that is unhelpful. Remember, you may not know what limiting or conditional beliefs and self-talk the supervisee has, so it is equally important to understand how they like to receive feedback, so it is heard.

4. If the supervisee is fatigued, exhausted, stressed or burnt out, this automatically tells the supervisor that feedback may not be received in a positive way. When someone is fatigued, there is a risk that they will only pick up every fourth word mostly in the negative. This tells the supervisor that having open conversations needs to be done using appropriate language.

5. When having open conversations or providing constructive feedback, it is crucial that the supervisor 'primes' or prepares the supervisee's brain for the conversation. It is unhelpful to say … 'I need to give you some feedback about how you did not do ….' It is more brain friendly to say something like …' In supervision today I would like to put on the agenda under the S (Support/Person) quadrant some issues around how … did not occur'. It will be a positive, useful and open conversation under the S (Support/Person) quadrant. It is critical that supervisors know how to have conversations that the other person's brain can hear. If the supervisee is burnt out then having constructive open discussions need to be done carefully and with lots of priming.

6. Because the brain looks for the threat first, if the supervisor needs to have a negative discussion about anything, prime the supervisee first using positive and developmental language. This can assist the supervisee to engage their braking system first and therefore reduce the amount of cortisol that is released into the blood stream.

7. We lead very busy lives and it is now common for people not to have quality sleep on a regular basis. Many people have their smartphones in their bedroom, check emails, social media and the like during the night. This reduces the opportunity for our rapid eye movement cycles to be engaged at a deeper level, meaning we often sleep lightly and at the top of the REM cycle. This increases the risk of fatigue and a reduced capacity for quality decision making. It is important that supervisors are aware of this, as sleep alone can impact the quality of our work.

8. In line with this, many people in the workplace are now overusing technology, i.e., smartphones during a 24-hour period. It creates a world that is removed from reality and increases the opportunity to withdraw from others, reduces direct communication and enables us to be more individualised rather than part of a group. I have many experiences when facilitating presentations and training, where professionals advise that they find it hard now to go about their daily lives without their mobile phone nearby. One participant told me he could no longer operate during the day without knowing and feeling his mobile phone was in his pocket. He also experienced anxiety if he could not feel it.

9. When we experience a challenge and move towards resolving it, the brain sees this as a towards response and reduces the release of cortisol. When we take what is called an avoid response, it increases

the likelihood of the brain seeing this as a threat and releases cortisol to keep us safe.

10. Our neural connections are fragile, so integrating new information and practicing it muscle up the neural connections for more stickability. If you gain new learning by going to training and do not use the information in the first four weeks after the training, then the decay of stickability starts to occur. Repeated behaviours become hardwired in the brain.

11. We have approximately eight memory biases, thirty-five probability/belief biases and forty-two decision-making biases. This is particularly useful for supervisors to know when providing feedback. As we have many biases, the brain looks for patterns to determine what thinking, behavioural and emotional process is engaged. Using language to assist the supervisee to see the discussion as positive supports the brain to minimise or neutralise the biases present for the other person.

12. More information is being understood about the myth of multi-tasking. When multi-tasking is engaged, it is likely that somewhere productivity between 48% and 51% is lost when you return to the first task. This tells us that chunking our time from task to task is more productive. We can usually manage up to four tasks, chunking one at a time. For example, spending time on emails, then moving to something else and then something else again instead of tasking between each intermittently.

13. Dopamine needs to be present to maximise learning. If a supervisee attends training when and they are stressed, exhausted or highly fatigued, it is likely they will not retain a lot of information.

14. We mostly use computers to write and communicate in our world; however, if you can get supervisee's to write by hand from time to time, this is a very brain friendly activity as it engages both sides of the brain and the person will have a different experience in what they are doing.

15. One of the most important things we can do for our well-being is to have quiet time, down time or solitude. When we have quiet time, it increases opportunity for deeper reflection and generates new thought processes and feelings. Given we are so busy, reflective time and better-informed decision making are reduced. Supervision is one of the most brain friendly activities in the workplace, as it creates a space for stillness, deep listening and a positive relational experience (Dimitriadis & Psychogios, 2016; Ray, 2018).

Let's take a moment to reflect on some of these brain facts.

What comes to mind when you think about the facts above?

_____
_____
_____
_____
_____

How can this information assist you as a supervisor or leader?

_____
_____
_____
_____
_____

How does this information guide how you provide feedback or have open discussions in supervision?

_____
_____
_____
_____
_____

How can you support supervisees more effectively?

_____
_____
_____
_____
_____

How can supervisees use this information to get the best out of supervision?

_____
_____
_____
_____
_____

Our Biases

As outlined above, we have different biases that influence our thinking process. Cognitive biases were first introduced by Tversky and Kahneman (1974). Their research found that through rational choice theory, humans demonstrate repetition in the way that judgements and decisions are made. They explained the differences through heuristics, the rules by which the brain computes systematic errors or patterns. Tversky and Kahneman's (1974) work on biases is very useful for supervisors and leaders, as it informs how supervisees make decisions and how we can engage supervisees in supervision conversations more productively. Biases also inform supervisors about how to provide intentional and meaningful feedback. Visual 7.4 provides an overview of the Memory Biases we can display, Visual 7.5 outlines the Belief Biases, and Visual 7.6 overviews the Decision-Making Biases.

Our biases are the systematic patterns we display which deviate from what we might call 'normality' in the rational thinking process, decision

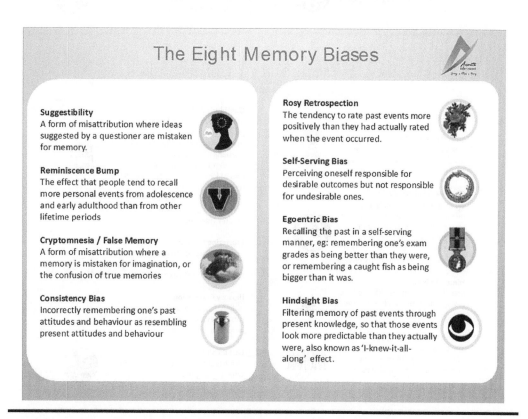

Visual 7.4 Memory biases.

The 35 Probability / Belief Biases

Positive Outcome Bias
The tendency to overestimate the probability of good things happening to them (see also wishful thinking, optimism bias and valence effect).

Telescoping Effect
The effect that recent events appear to have occurred more remotely and remote events appear to have occurred more recently.

Survivorship Bias
The tendency to concentrate on the people or things that 'survived' some process and ignoring those that didn't or arguing that a strategy is effective given the winners, while ignoring the large amount of losers.

Selection Bias
A distortion of evidence or data that arises from the way that the data is collected.

Texas Sharpshooter Fallacy
The fallacy of selecting or adjusting a hypothesis after data is collected, making it impossible to test the hypothesis fairly. Refers to the concept of firing shorts at a barn door, drawing a circle around the best group and declaring that to be the target.

Pareidolia
A vague and random stimulus, often an image or sound, is perceived as significant. Eg: seeing images of animals or faces in clouds, the man in the moon and hearing hidden messages on records played in reverse.

Outcome Bias
The tendency to judge a decision by its eventful outcome instead of based on the quality of the decision at the time it was made.

Disregard of Regression Toward the Mean
The tendency to expect extreme performance to continue.

The 35 Probability / Belief Biases

Overconfidence Effect
Excessive confidence in one's own answers to questions. Eg: for certain types of questions, answer that people rate as '99% certain' turn out to be wrong 40% of the time.

Observer-Expectancy Effect
When a research expects a given result and therefore unconsciously manipulates an experiment or manipulates an experiment or misinterprets data in order to find it (see also subject expectancy effect).

Hindsight Bias
Sometimes called the 'I-knew-it-all-along' effect, the tendency to see past events as being predictable.

Hawthorne Effect
The tendency to perform or perceive differently when one knows they are being observed.

Gambler's Fallacy
The tendency to think that future probabilities are altered by past events, when in reality they are unchanged. Results form an enormous conceptualisation of the Law of large numbers. Eg: 'I've flipped heads with this coin five times consecutively, so the chance of tails coming out on the sixth flip is much greater than heads'.

Clustering Illusion
The tendency to see patterns where actually none exist. Glovich example: 'OXXXOXXXOXXOOOXOOXXOO'

Illusory Correlation
Beliefs that inaccurately suppose a relationship between a certain type action and an effect.

Last Illusion
The belief that someone must know what is going on.

Visual 7.5   Belief biases.

(Continued)

The 35 Probability / Belief Biases

Availability Heuristic
Estimating what is more likely by what is more available in memory, which is biased toward vivid, unusual or emotionally charged examples.

Belief Bias
An effect where someone's evaluation of the logical strength of an argument is biased by the believability of the conclusion.

Ostrich Effect
Ignoring an obvious, negative, situation.

Attentional Bias
The tendency to neglect relevant data making judgements of a correlation or association.

Disposition Effect
The tendency to sell assets that have increased in value but hold assets that have decreased in value.

Availability Casade
A self-reinforcing process in which a collective belief gains more and more plausibility through its increasing repetition in public discourse (or 'repeat something long enough and it will become true').

Conjunction Fallacy
The tendency to assume that specific conditions are more probably than general ones.

Ambiguity Effect
The tendency to avoid options for which missing information makes the probability seem 'unknown'.

Capability Bias
The tendency to believe that the closer average performance is to a target, the tighter the distribution of the data set.

Authority Bias
The tendency to value an ambiguous stimulus, like an art performance, according to the opinion of someone who is seen as an authority on the topic.

The 35 Probability / Belief Biases

Sterotyping
Expecting a member of a group to have certain characteristics without having actual information about that individual.

Subjective Validation
Perception that something is true if a subject's belief demands it to be true. Also assigns perceived connections between coincidences.

Subadditivity Effect
The tendency to judge probably of the whole to be less than the probabilities of the parts.

Well Travelled Road Effect
Underestimation of the duration taken to traverse off traveled routes and over-estimate the duration taken to traverse less familiar routes.

Anchoring Effect
The tendency to rely too heavily or 'anchor' on a past reference or on one trait or piece of information when making decisions (also called 'insufficient adjustment').

Recency Effect / Peak-End Rule
The tendency to weigh recent events more than earlier events.

Primary Effect
The tendency to weigh initial events more than subsequent events.

Optimism Bias
The tendency to be over optimistic about the outcome of planned actions.

Neglect of Prior Base Rates Effect
The tendency to neglect known odds when re-evaluating odds in light of week evidence.

Visual 7.5 (*Continued*)   Belief biases.

The 42 Decision-Making Biases

Hyberbolic Discounting
The tendency for people to have a stronger preference for more immediate payoffs relative to later payoffs, where the tendency increases the closer to the present both payoffs are.

Irrational Escalation
The tendency to make irrational decisions based upon rational decisions in the past or to justify actions already taken.

Omission Bias
The tendency to judge harmful actions as worse, or less moral, than equally harmful omissions.

Mere Exposure Effect
The tendency for people to express undue liking for things merely because they are familiar with them.

Negativity Bias
Phenomenon by which humans pay more attention to and give more with to negative than positive experiences or other kinds of information.

Interloper Effect / Consultation Paradox
The tendency to value third party consultation as objective, confirming and without motive. Also consultation paradox, the conclusion that solutions proposed by existing personnel within an organisation are less likely to receive support from those recruited for that purpose.

Normalcy Bias
The refusal to plan for, or react to, a disaster which has never happened before.

Neglect of Probability
The tendency to completely disregard probability when making a decision under certainty.

The 42 Decision-Making Biases

Focusing Effect
Prediction bias occurring when people place too much importance on an event; causes error in accurately predicting the utility of a future outcome.

Illusion of Control
The tendency for human beings to believe they can control or at least influence outcomes that they clearly cannot.

Outcome Bias
The tendency to judge a decision by its eventual outcome instead of based on the quality of the decision at the time it was made.

Post-Purchase Rationalisation
The tendency to persuade oneself through rational argument that a purchase was good value.

Framing
Using an approach or description of the situation or issue that is too narrow. Also framing effect – drawing on difference conclusions based on how data is presented

Experimenter's or Expectation Bias
The tendency for experimenters to believe, certify and publish data that agrees with their expectations for the outcome of an experiment and to disbelieve, discard or downgrade the corresponding weightings for data that appears to conflict with those expectations.

Information Bias
The tendency to seek information even when it cannot affect action.

Extraordinarily Bias
The tendency to value an object more than others in the same category as a result of an extraordinarily of that object that does not, in itself, change the value.

Visual 7.6   Decision-making biases.

(Continued)

The 42 Decision-Making Biases

Planning Fallacy
The tendency to underestimate task completion times.

Deformation Professionnelle
The tendency to look at things according to the conventions of one's own profession, forgetting any broader point of view.

Impact Bias
The tendency for people to overestimate the length or the intensity of the impact of future feeling states.

Bias Blind Spot
The tendency not to compensate for one's own cognitive biases.

Semmelweis Reflex
The tendency to reject new evidence that contradicts an establish paradigm.

Not Invented Here
The tendency to ignore that a product or solution already exists because its source is seen as an 'enemy' or as 'inferior'.

Moral Credential Effect
The tendency of a track record of non-prejudice to increase subsequent prejudice.

Base Rate Fallacy
Ignoring available statistical data in favour of particulars.

The 42 Decision-Making Biases

Confirmation Bias
The tendency to search for or interpret information in a way that confirms one's preconceptions

Choice-Supportive Bias
The tendency to remember one's choices as better than they actually were.

Endowment Effect/Loss Aversion
The fact that people often demand much more to give up an object than they would be willing to pay to acquire it. (See also sunk cost effects).

Congruence Bias
The tendency to test hypotheses exclusively through direct testing in contrast to tests to possible alternative hypotheses.

Distinction Bias
The tendency to view two options as more dissimilar when evaluating them simultaneously than when evaluating them separately.

Contrast Effect
The enhancement or diminishing of a weight of other measurement when compared with a recently observed contrasting object.

Bandwagon Effect
The tendency to do, or believe, things because many other people do or believe, the same. Related to groupthink and herd behaviour.

Denomination Effect
The tendency to spend more money when its dominated in small amounts (eg: coins) rather than large amounts (eg: notes).

Visual 7.6 (*Continued*) Decision-making biases.

(Continued)

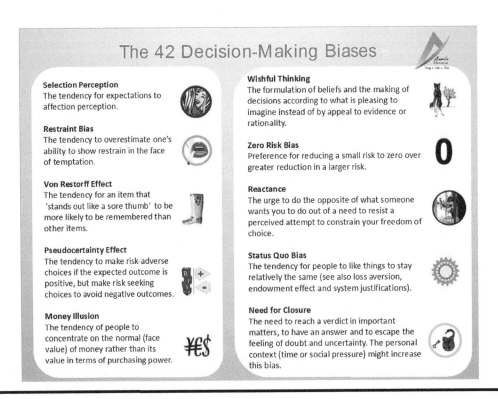

Visual 7.6 (*Continued*)   Decision-making biases.

making and judgement. For example, think about getting to know someone new. You might ask them particular questions that assist you to form a picture of what that person is like and how they engage in a particular situation. You may make particular biases in relation to the person that will validate your assumptions about them. Therefore, we can take a biased view on different aspects of how we operate as a supervisor or leader.

Through the process of inference, we make decisions and judgements based on previous experiences. Our brain takes in information from our interactions, conversations and observations. As we collect information, we select the relevant data and discard information that does not fit what we need. We then add meaning to the information based on what fits our thinking, making assumptions that align to our biases. We draw particular conclusions from our beliefs and values to make an informed decision. So, our biases can influence or interrupt what we think, feel and decide. It is important as a supervisor to understand the inference process and how it informs the supervision process (Argyris, 1970).

Self-Care & Well-Being

An important part of supervision is ensuring that supervisees are engaging self-care regularly. In supervision I often hear professionals say they have good self-care and when we get more into the detail of what this means, it is evident that the self-care plan could do with some more work. In this chapter, we have explored the impact of cumulative stress and the time it takes to recover from burnout. So, looking at the importance of self-care in supervision assists supervisees to remain well. When self-care is not included on the supervision agenda on a regular basis, inevitably self-care is left unchecked and supervisees have to grapple with fatigue and stressors on their own. One of the most important parts of self-care and supervision is having the space and time to debrief things. It assists the supervisee to deconstruct, clarify and declutter their brain. When this occurs on a regular basis, the supervisee feels valued and appreciated. When positive language, reflection and elements of self-care are included in the supervisory discussion, it contributes to the maintenance of well-being in the workplace. When there is a focus on well-being and self-care, the supervisee's performance is enhanced (Harris, 2018).

When we connect to nature, have reflective discussions, release things that are impacting our thinking and write reflectively, we are engaging in self-care. It is common for self-care goals to be developed in supervision; however, they are often not implemented or can be viewed as more work to put into place. For example, a self-care goal may be to stop and have lunch during the working day (we have all probably had this as a goal at some stage). Setting a goal like this means it is often not met. When we set goals around self-care in a different way, we are more likely to achieve them and feel great about it. Using language such as … it is now (date/year) and I have had lunch each day … or, I am achieving having lunch each day … is more brain friendly and it is likely that the goal will be achieved. The other thing to remember about setting self-care goals is to not feel burdened to achieve the goal. It is rather a sense of success or fulfilment when the goal has been achieved. In Table 7.1, the example self-care plan outlines how the goals are documented down the left-hand side, and when the activity or goal is achieved, the date is put in the relevant month. If you achieve a goal like exercising on a regular basis, you can see that this has been achieved based on the number of ticks in the month. Table 7.2 is the same self-care document ready for you to use for your own self-care planning. I keep mine with me most days as I go about my work to review how I am going. I have

Table 7.1 Example of Self-Care Plan

Self-Care Objectives	Jan	Feb	Mar	Apr	May	Jun	Jul	Aug	Sep	Oct	Nov	Dec
Walking												
Lunch break												
Cycling	4/1 10/1											
Haircut												
Massage		24/2										
Naturopath												
Friends/family												
Movies				1/4								
Kayaking		4/1							9/9			
Reading			22/3									
Holiday							2/7	3/8				
Cooking				10/4	8/5		29/7	4/8				
Dancing												
Swimming												
Vision board	10/1											
Time out/solitude												
Physio/chiropractor												

Table 7.2 Self-Care Plan

Name:

Self-Care Objectives	Year											
	Jan	Feb	Mar	Apr	May	Jun	Jul	Aug	Sep	Oct	Nov	Dec

used this template for some years now and feel a great sense of achievement when I get dates in the months to show when I have completed a self-care exercise. My brain sees this as an accomplishment, rather than feeling pressure when I have not completed something.

As a professional supervisor, I work with supervisees to develop their self-care plan and include it as a regular supervision agenda item under the S (Support/Person) quadrant of the PASE™ model (or relevant model to their role). I find that supervisees see the real difference in the way that the plan is developed and self-care achieved. So, for many professionals this particular way of setting self-care goals is really effective. Visual 7.7 is the Neuro Attento Wheel that provides a visual of the different areas in self-care to

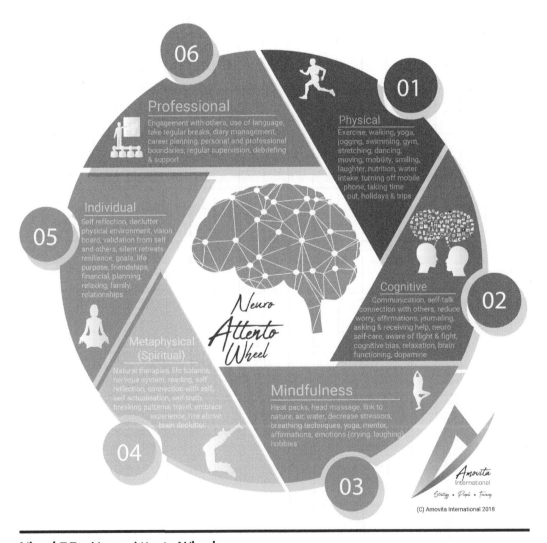

Visual 7.7   Neuro Attento Wheel.

Table 7.3 Self-Care Planner

Remove	Increase
Reduce	Begin/create

focus on. This includes physical activities and the importance of moving our bodies; cognitive self-care through communication and positive thinking; mindfulness and connection to the environment around us; metaphysical and how we make meaning of our lives; individual and how we self-reflect and enjoy being with ourselves; and the professional about how we engage with others in the workplace and go about our roles.

The final planning tool in this chapter is the Self-Care Planner. The four areas assist supervisees to explore elements that need to be increased, reduced, created or eliminated in relation to self-care. As the supervisor, you may notice things that the supervisee can remove in the workplace to reduce fatigue or stress. You may see something they could begin or create that would support self-care. This tool is a useful reminder of what can be planned to better support self-care in the work environment (Table 7.3).

Summary

In this chapter, we have discussed the importance of focusing on self-care as a professional. We also explored what stress is and the impacts on our health if it accumulates. Consider the following reflective questions as a summary to the chapter about the neuroscience of self-care.

What have been the key things you have gained from reading this chapter on the neuroscience of self-care?
What have been your reflections about this chapter?
List three things that you will take from this chapter to incorporate into your supervisory role.
What do you think will be useful to talk to your supervisee/s about regarding this chapter?

Chapter 8

Evaluating Supervision for Effective Outcomes

Key focus for this chapter

- Why evaluate supervision to ensure it is effective?
- What is evaluation in supervision?
- How to evaluate that supervision is effective?
- Different evaluation frameworks
- Annual review processes – are they effective?
- Tools to evaluate the effectiveness of supervision
- Understanding supervisor capability
- Who evaluates supervision?
- How often to evaluate supervision?

Evaluating Supervision

Supervision is often provided without any type of formal or informal evaluation to ensure it is effective. Many line managers and supervisors provide supervision without having been trained prior to being in the role, or engaging in supervision themselves (Harris, 2018). Knowing what skills are required to provide effective supervision is crucial to ensuring that supervision remains effective over time. The question is – why is it important to evaluate supervision? Supervisors often tell me they evaluate supervision, and when I ask how they do that, the answer is usually asking the supervisee how supervision is going?

Due to the power differential between the supervisor and supervisee, this type of information evaluation can put pressure on the supervisee to provide positive feedback. Information feedback can be useful at times, but often not reliable for this reason. When I observe supervisors providing supervision, both parties are asked particular questions at the end of the conversation, and invariably the supervisee always responds that the supervision was useful, helpful and they found the supervision discussion effective. When I meet with both parties separately, often the supervisee will provide other information about what they would have preferred to be different. Why is it that supervisees often feel they cannot provide authentic feedback? It can be because of the power difference in the roles, and too often supervisors do not have formal mechanisms for feedback that provides reliable information.

For supervision to be effective over time, it is critical that the supervisor uses various methods of evaluation. As mentioned above, this can be informal through direct feedback from the supervisee. Evaluation can occur through more formal methods, such as having an evidence-informed evaluation tool or instrument with relevant questions. It may also be through evaluation of the focus of the discussion using the PASE™ (Professional/ Practice, Administrative/Line Management, Support/Person, Educative/ Professional Development) model as outlined in Chapter 4. So, what does it mean to evaluate supervision? The purpose of evaluating supervision is to find out how effective the process, framework and conversations are over time. This chapter outlines the different tools that can be used to evaluate supervision to ensure it remains effective. If supervision is only informally evaluated, it is advisable that a formal evaluation of supervision is conducted on an annual basis (Wonnacott, 2012).

Where a formal evaluation process is conducted, it is important to take the information gathered and feed it back into the supervision process. Equally, discussions from supervision can form part of the formal evaluation, as they both need to align to each other.

The SaV-NAV (Supervision Navigation) Evaluation Tool

The first evaluation tool outlined in this chapter is called the SaV-NAV Evaluation Tool. The SaV-NAV is a supervision navigation tool that allows both parties to formally evaluate each other's engagement and practice in supervision. There is a separate SaV-NAV that both parties evaluate aspects of the supervisor's practice, and the other explores various aspects of the supervisee's engagement and participation. The two tools allow both parties to track different aspects of supervision on a regular basis to see how effective supervision is for both parties. It provides a picture of how supervision is going at a given point in time. This evaluation tool is useful for supervisors as it encourages supervisees to provide authentic and relevant feedback that assists supervision to remain effective. When supervision practice is evaluated, it allows the supervisor to reflect on what capabilities and competencies may need further development in their supervisory practice (Milne, 2010). Equally, supervisors can also better understand what they need to do in supervision to assist in measuring the effectiveness of supervisory outcomes. It encourages a reflective discussion without the supervisee feeling uncomfortable about providing feedback around what aspects of supervision that need realigning. Each time the SaV-NAV is used to evaluate supervision, a copy is kept on file as a record to show what is occurring in supervision at a given point in time. It can also be used in the supervisee's annual review process to look at the different aspects of their role (Harris, 2018).

The tool can be used in the following way:

■ By supervisors to evaluate student field placement supervision;
■ By supervisors to evaluate how a supervisee is engaging and participating in supervision at different points of time;
■ By supervisees to evaluate the effectiveness of their supervision and
■ By supervisors to evaluate their level of capability and competency as a supervisor.

Given that both parties have a different role and responsibility in supervision, the supervisor and supervisee have different criteria on the bottom axis for evaluating supervision, as outlined in Table 8.1. The criteria on the X axis can be changed to what aspects of supervision both parties would like to evaluate. The tool is based on two axes, the Y and X axis. We first explore the supervisor's SaV-NAV.

Supervisor's SaV-NAV

Y Axis: The Y axis (vertical) is represented by low (1), medium (5) and high (10); with 1 being the lowest and 10 being the highest. This axis depicts if both parties evaluate, the X axis criterion is evaluated as low, medium or high by both parties.

X Axis: The X axis (horizontal) outlines relevant criterion required to ensure supervision remains effective. Criterion may include

- Techniques used by the supervisor such as questioning framework, interpersonal skills, analysis, how to explore ethical dilemmas, etc.;
- Quality of the supervision provided;
- The supervisor's knowledge of supervision;
- Supervision skills such as listening, how supervision is set up, how to set the agenda, follow up in between meetings, how the supervisor develops the supervisee's practice, etc.;
- Use of supervision documents such as overview of the policy, practice guidelines, minutes, agreement, etc.;
- Use of supervision in a framework, i.e. how the process of supervision is undertaken for example how often supervision is provided, location and environment, duration of meetings, etc.;
- The use of a supervision model such as the PASE model discussed in Chapter 4;
- How supervision is evaluated either formally or informally, how often, what is documented, how the supervisor continues to enhance their supervision knowledge and skills, etc.;
- How the supervisor continues to maintain best practice through research and reading and
- How the supervisor conducts the intake and assessment process (as outlined in Chapter 4).

Both parties explore the criterion together, then evaluate where each of them are at in relation to low, medium and high. A comparative analysis is undertaken in supervision in a reflective process to understand what aspects of supervision are being maintained at a high level and what aspects of supervision need more focus. Visual 8.1 provides an example of the supervisor's SaV-NAV and how both the supervisor and supervisee evaluated different aspects of supervision.

Supervisee's SaV-NAV

Y Axis: The Y axis (vertical) is represented by low (1), medium (5) and high (10); with 1 being the lowest and 10 being the highest. This axis depicts if both parties evaluate, the X axis criterion as low, medium or high.

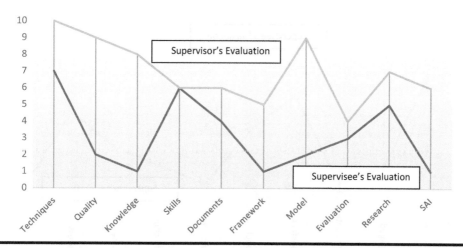

Visual 8.1   Example Supervisor's SaV-NAV.

X Axis: The X axis (horizontal) outlines relevant criterion to evaluate the supervisee's engagement in supervision, to ensure they are getting the best out of discussions and the process for supervision to be effective. Criterion may include the following:

- The supervisee is prepared for discussions;
- The supervisee is effectively engaged in the process;
- The supervisee participates fully in discussions and does not avoid supervision;
- The supervisee successfully transfers what is discussed and learned in supervision back into their role;
- The PASE supervision model is used effectively by the supervisee, and they know how to use it well, move around the quadrants, how to evaluate the focus of discussions and set the supervision agenda;
- The supervisee is consistent in their approach in supervision, how to have meaningful and purposeful discussions and they attend supervision regularly;
- The use of reflection is evident in discussions and in between meetings. The supervisee uses a reflective framework to analyse, critique and explore aspects of their practice and role;
- Follow up from decisions made and work to be completed between meetings is evident and
- The supervisee engages in effective evaluation of the supervision process, capability of the supervisor and how supervision progresses on what is agreed upon by both parties (Visual 8.2).

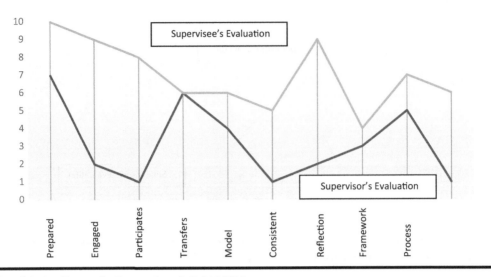

Visual 8.2   Example Supervisee's SaV-NAV.

The second tool that can be used to evaluate supervision is the Supervision Capability Framework in Table 8.1. This framework has a number of criteria with an explanation of what each criterion is, and how the supervisor evidences their skill level in relation to the criterion on a Likert scale 0–7. 0 is for no skill level, 3.5 adequate skill level to 7 as high skill level. The framework can be used by the supervisor to undertake a self-assessment, or the evaluation can be used by both supervisor and supervisee to explore aspects of the supervisor's capability together. This framework is used more effectively where there is a high level of engagement by the supervisee in supervision, where the supervisor is confident to have the supervisee assess their supervisory practice and where the supervisee also feels confident to provide feedback. The limitations of this framework are the supervisee feeling they have to provide a high evaluation in any of the criterion because of the power difference in the relationship. Therefore, it is important that the supervisor has a strong professional identity that invites an open discussion to elicit authentic responses from the supervisee.

Table 8.1 Supervision Capability Framework

#	Criteria	Evidence of Competency Skill Level	1	2	3	4	5	6	7
1	Discipline/ area of work knowledge (P)	Supervisor has knowledge of the supervisee's discipline or work undertaken, including • Professional standards and guidelines • Relevant approaches, frameworks, theories and models used in the role • Knowledge relevant to the supervisee's discipline area • Has some level of knowledge relevant to provide supervision in the area							
2	Ethical and industrial contexts (P)	Supervisor understands the legal and ethical framework in which to provide supervision. • Understands industrial legislative platforms in which the supervisee operates • Is aware of relevant codes of conduct relevant to the supervisee's profession and work environment • Understands all aspects of informed consent, including professional boundaries, privacy principles, duty of care, confidentiality and consent • Adheres to relevant recording and reporting mechanisms • Understands the bounds of the professional relationship, gender, power, inequality awareness that exists in the supervisor/supervisee relationship • Is clear on requirements around registration where the supervisee has such requirements • Clear evaluation framework for supervision • Has clear mechanism for resolving conflicts that may arise during the course of the supervisory relationship • Can make appropriate assessments in relation to supervisee's ethical conduct • Has a clear evidence in informed decision-making process • Incorporates policy processes							

(Continued)

Table 8.1 (*Continued*)   Supervision Capability Framework

#	Criteria	Evidence of Competency Skill Level	1	2	3	4	5	6	7
3	Training (E)	• The supervisor has attended credible and quality training on supervision that incorporates the supervisory alliance, ethical and industrial contexts of supervision, supervisor capability, the context of supervision, feedback, evaluation, etc. • Supervisor engages in own supervision • Maintains professional development points in supervision and leadership • Supervisor engages in continual development to enhance supervisory practice							
4	Evaluation (P, S)	• Supervisor has an evaluative framework to evaluate the effectiveness of supervision that aligns to the annual review process • Any evaluative framework may include • Satisfaction level of the supervisee (S) • Effectiveness of the supervisory process (A) (P) • Outcomes from supervision (A) • Enhanced practice, increase in knowledge and skills (E)							
5	Practice context (P)	• Supervisor understands relevant theoretical perspectives and practices supervisee uses • Demonstrates the use of a supervisory professional practice framework • Demonstrates principles around culture and diversity • Practices cultural and diversity practice • Engages in ongoing development to meet the needs of the practice context • Is able to engage the appropriate language framework for the practice context • Understands how to provide supervision in the organisational setting							

(*Continued*)

Table 8.1 (*Continued*) Supervision Capability Framework

#	Criteria	*Evidence of Competency Skill Level*	1	2	3	4	5	6	7
6	Research (E)	• Ability to seek out and analyse information that assists the supervisee in their practice context • Assists to generate hypotheses-based problem solving, critiquing and evaluation • Use of qualitative and quantitative methodology, analysis of relevant data and ability to draw on accurate inferences to further self and the supervisee • Able to critically analyse the effectiveness of the supervisee's approach, any interventions, models and theories as they relate to the practice context • Can seek information and use appropriately in supervision							
7	Interpersonal (P, S)	• Is able to convey supportive messages, appraise the supervisee's work, interpret information accurately and provide relevant feedback that is conducive to enhancing practice • Able to interact on a professional level that promotes a positive supervisory relationship • Able to communicate with ease, understand own and others language framework, appropriate use of words, phrases and statements • Understands how to open and close relationships appropriately • Understands how supervisory relationships fluctuate and provides flexibility for the supervisee in these situations • Owns own accountability as a supervisor • Leads by example, has depth and breadth in self-awareness • Clearly demonstrates a professional identity • Has clear and effective skills in communication and professional relationships							

(Continued)

Table 8.1 (*Continued*) Supervision Capability Framework

#	Criteria	Evidence of Competency *Skill Level*	1	2	3	4	5	6	7
8	Skills (P, A, S, E)	• Can conceptualise and contextualise issues • Has a range of interpersonal skills • Understands the art of attunement • Resolving conflicts • Mediation and negotiation skills • Engages a supervisory model • Can provide and embrace feedback • Engages depth and breadth within the reflective process • Analysis, evaluation and critiquing skills • Effectively engages the supervisee • Art of questioning • Knows developmental and transfer of learning theories							
9	Organisational (A)	• Supervisor clearly links supervisory discussion with the requirements of the supervisee's role and Position Description • Ensures supervision meets the requirements as prescribed by the organisation • Supervisor is able to balance the needs of the supervisee and organisation • Embeds the values and mission of the organisation • Supervisor meets all reporting requirements • Ensures supervision links to any relevant organisational process such as the annual review process • Demonstrates supervision is highly valued as a professional activity							

The Supervision Capability Framework incorporates nine criterion areas:

1. The supervisor's knowledge of the discipline or area of the supervisee's work and role;
2. Understanding the ethical and industrial contexts of supervision;
3. The supervisor has engaged in quality training about supervision and the supervisory role;
4. There is clear evidence the supervisor knows how to evaluate the effectiveness of aspects of supervision;
5. There is an understanding of what practices the supervisee engages in their role and how the supervisor continues to develop the supervisee;
6. How the supervisor engages in research and reading to continue to develop in the role;
7. Interpersonal skills the supervisor has;
8. An understanding of the organisational context that supervision is provided and
9. How supervision fits within the organisational system.

Each of the criteria has also been mapped to the PASE supervision model to ensure that an integrated and holistic approach is taken incorporating all four quadrants. Once the supervisor has undertaken an evaluation on their own or with the supervisee, information can be used to enhance supervision and the supervisor's capability.

The next evaluation tool outlined in Table 8.2 is based on the four quadrants of the PASE model and is called the PASE Supervision Evaluation Framework. Supervision is evaluated using the P, A, S and E quadrants and is based

Table 8.2 PASE™ Supervision Evaluation Framework

PASE Supervision Evaluation Framework (PASE Model)							
This evaluation is undertaken on an annual basis. Each of the four quadrants of the model is used to evaluate the following criterion. The evaluation is focused on 5-1. 5 Always, 4 – Frequently, 3 –Sometimes, 2 – Rarely, 1 – Never, NA – Not applicable. The evaluation is kept on file and compared over time with the previous evaluation.							
Supervisee Name/Role:	**Date:**	**Previous Evaluation Date:**					
Professional Supervisor Name:	**Date:**						
1. (P) Professional/Practice		*5*	*4*	*3*	*2*	*1*	*NA*
1. Relevant theories are used in supervision that relate to the professional/practice area of the supervisee.							

(Continued)

Table 8.2 (*Continued*)   PASE™ Supervision Evaluation Framework

	5	4	3	2	1	NA
2. An ethical decision-making framework and process is used in the discussion.						
3. The supervisor engages relevant language that demonstrates understanding and knowledge of the practice/professional area of the supervisee.						
4. Reflective frameworks are used effectively in the supervisory discussion.						
5. Supervisor demonstrates key supervisory skills, i.e., interpersonal skills, listening, reality testing, reframing, paraphrasing, mediation, etc.						
6. Supervisor assists the supervisee to use their professional practice framework in supervision to demonstrate capability and practice in the role.						
7. Engages supervisory leadership skills, i.e., analysis, assessment, evaluation, guidance, direction, deconstruction, critiquing, synthesis of information, etc.						
8. Challenges and barriers are managed professionally and ethically.						
9. Supervisory discussion clearly links to the PASE supervision model.						
10. Understands the professional needs of the supervisee.						
Comments:	**Total:** /50					
2. (A) Administrative/Organisational	*5*	*4*	*3*	*2*	*1*	*NA*
11. Supervision is linked to the organisational policy framework.						
12. Supervision is aligned to the organisational annual review process.						
13. Relevant documents are used in supervision, i.e., agreement, agenda, evaluation, minutes, etc.						
14. Discussions are minuted accurately as a formal record of the meeting.						

(*Continued*)

Table 8.2 (*Continued*)   PASE™ Supervision Evaluation Framework

	5	4	3	2	1	NA
15. Discussion moves effectively between the four quadrants in the PASE model.						
16. Both parties can effectively set an agenda.						
17. The supervisor uses the professional practice framework to ensure organisational needs are met in the role and the supervisee is performing in the role as required.						
18. Both parties understand the context of supervision, i.e., purpose, benefits, responsibility, expectations, roles.						
19. Both parties communicate clearly, conversations are relevant to the topics in supervision.						
20. Supervision is set up to maximise productive outcomes, i.e., location, agenda, understands the supervision policy, etc.						
21. Effectively evaluates the focus of the supervision discussion through the supervision model.						
Comments:	**Total: /55**					
3. (S) Support/Person	5	4	3	2	1	NA
22. Supervision discussions are positive, developmental, supportive and effective.						
23. Evidence of rapport built between both parties.						
24. The supervisor seeks support to move between the model quadrants and focus of the discussion.						
25. Validates and encourages the supervisee.						
26. Successfully engages the supervisee when debriefing.						
27. The supervisee is motivated to engage and participate. Supervision discussions can refuel and validate the supervisee.						
28. Supervision focuses on the needs of the supervisee.						

(Continued)

Table 8.2 (*Continued*)   PASE™ Supervision Evaluation Framework

	5	4	3	2	1	NA
29. Demonstration of appropriate use of professional boundaries.						
30. Supervisor is a positive role model, and is present and mindful in discussions.						
31. Supports the supervisee with appropriate style as indicated in the model.						
32. Encourages feedback in the discussion.						
Comments:	**Total:** /55					
4. (E) Educative/Professional Development	5	4	3	2	1	NA
33. Professional goals and ongoing development are identified and explored.						
34. Proactively engages the supervisee in developmental discussions.						
35. Makes a clear link between previous, current and future discussions.						
36. The supervisor looks for opportunities to develop the supervisee.						
37. Supervisor makes relevant suggestions for training, reading and research.						
38. Ongoing alignment to relevant skills, knowledge and competencies of the supervisee's position description.						
39. Maps supervision discussion to any professional development plan in place.						
Comments:	**Total:** /35					
Total Evaluation: /195						

(*Continued*)

Table 8.2 (*Continued*)   PASE™ Supervision Evaluation Framework

Under 50

The supervisor is aware that further support, coaching and development are required to effectively engage the supervisee in supervision. There is evidence of the need for further training and support in the use of technical supervisory skills and effective questioning for key outcomes. There is further need to understand the role of assessing and using reflection to ensure the supervisee is using supervision as it is intended. There is further work required by the supervisee to understand the purpose and role that supervision has in the organisation.

51–100

There is evidence of the supervisor having foundational skills in supervision. The supervisor demonstrates an understanding of some of the skills and knowledge required to focus the discussion and achieve key outcomes. Further support and development will be useful to continue growth and development as a supervisor. The supervisee understands the basic principles of supervision and how to get the best from discussions; however, further development and discussion need to occur to progress the supervisee's understanding of what is required in supervision.

101–150

The supervisor has a clear understanding of what supervision is however needs to increase their awareness of how to engage relevant tools and resources to ensure it remains effective over time. The supervisor regularly demonstrates presence and purpose in the supervisory discussions. There is evidence of confidence in the use of supervision tools and resources. The supervisor demonstrates they can focus the discussion, use key technical skills including interpersonal and mediation skills, assessment and engagement. The supervisor demonstrates confidence and motivates the supervisee. The supervisee is using and engaging supervision for its intended purpose. They attend supervision prepared, understand the key tools and frameworks used in supervision to enhance their practice and value supervision for its purpose.

151–195

Supervisory skills, techniques, knowledge and competencies are evident at an advanced level. The supervisor shows the art of attunement, has key skills, knowledge and attributes to provide effective supervision and is highly aware of the purpose and intent of supervision. They confidently demonstrate how to continually focus the discussion, evaluate the focus regularly and effective use of the PASE model. The supervisor is present and engages key technical skills including interpersonal, mediation skills and effective questioning. The supervisor can make informed assessments throughout the supervisory discussion to ascertain the effectiveness of the discussion, how to appropriately encourage the supervisee to reflect and ensure the supervisee meets organisational requirements in the role. The supervisee is fully engaged in the process and discussions. They come to supervision prepared on a regular basis, seek to gain knowledge and wisdom from the supervisor and know how to maintain a high level of professional relationship in the supervisory environment. They are able to provide and seek feedback, know how to engage with the purpose and intent of supervision and actively evaluate how supervision is effective.

on a scoring process. Each quadrant incorporates different questions from each of the four quadrants, and responses are recorded on a Likert scale 0–5. 5 – always; 0 – never.

Each section has a total score that is added up at the end of the questions. In the P (Practice/Professional) quadrant, there are ten questions with a total score of up to 50. The A (Administrative/Line Management) quadrant also has eleven questions with a score of up to 55. The S (Support/Person) quadrant includes eleven questions with a total score of 55, and the E (Educative/ Professional Development) quadrant has seven questions with a total score of 35. The total evaluation score adds up to 195. There is a comment section for both the supervisor and supervisee to add to at the end of each section.

1. Where the evaluation has a score of under 50, it demonstrates the supervisor requires further training and professional development in the role. They also require formal training to better understand the role of being a professional supervisor. The supervisee requires further support and information about what supervision is, how to engage in the process more effectively and to understand the role that supervision has in the organisation.
2. Where the evaluation is scored 51–100, the supervisor has a clear understanding of what supervision is; however, there is further work required to know how to use various tools and resources to ensure it remains effective. The supervisor is present in discussions, though more confidence is required in order for the supervisor to develop the supervisee. The supervisee is aware of what the purpose and intent of supervision is, and they attend the meetings prepared.
3. If the score is 151–195, the supervisor is demonstrating the key competencies and capabilities required at an advanced level. The supervision shows how they attune information, assess supervision in conversations to ensure it is effective, and are conscious and aware of supervision all the time. They confidently use the supervision model and engage relevant technical skills to ensure the supervisee is supported and developed. The supervisee is highly engaged and uses supervision effectively.

In the P (Professional/Practice) quadrant, the framework includes questions around the relevant approaches and theories used in the supervision conversation, the supervisor's use of an ethical decision-making framework to get the supervisee to reflect, the use of relevant language in supervision discussions and how supervision discussions are linked to the PASE model. In the A (Administrative/Line Management) quadrant, questions focus on how supervision is documented, how the agenda is set and what outcomes need to be achieved from supervision. Questions in the S (Support/Person) quadrant include how supervision is focused on the supervisee, what the supervisor does to encourage and validate the supervisee and how the supervisor is a positive role model. In the E (Educative/Professional Development) quadrant, questions explore goals identified in supervision and the linkage between historical, current and future questions.

This tool is useful for both parties to explore different aspects of supervision and enhances the supervisory alliance by having an open discussion. Once the evaluation is completed, information can be incorporated into supervision discussions.

The final evaluation framework to explore in this chapter is the Supervisee Practice Review Framework (S-PRF), as outlined in Table 8.3. This framework is based on the four areas of supervisee capability: 1. Skills, 2. Tasks, 3. Attributes and 4. Knowledge. The framework has been developed to align to the PASE supervision model and includes prompts in each section. This ensures that a holistic approach is taken in the review process. This framework is not so much about evaluating the effectiveness of

Table 8.3   Supervisee Practice Review Framework

Review Area 1: Skills (P) *(frameworks, approaches, interventions, case management practices, professional practice framework, ethics, ethical decisions, reflection, professional identity, language, client cases, reporting, evaluation, client outcomes, brings examples of successful client outcomes, can attune skills with practice)*

A skill is the ability and capacity acquired through systematic and sustained effort demonstrated on a regular basis (continually).	
Q1. Where do you draw your skills from to effectively undertake your role?	
Q2. How do your current skills connect to your practice?	
Q3. What skills do you currently use in your role and what you need to enhance the overall capability in the role?	
Q4. How do you approach your work from different perspectives?	
Q5. How do you see your ethics and practice demonstrating the organisation's values?	
Q6. When there are times where you experience tensions between the organisation's values and your own practice, how do you reconcile these?	

Table 8.3 (*Continued*) **Supervisee Practice Review Framework**

Review Area 2: Tasks (A) (*quality assurance, compliance, policy, procedures, position description, planning, resourcing, leave planning, workflow and workload management, client satisfaction, service agreements, government and legislative requirements, organisational requirements, organisational objectives*)	
A task is an identified activity that requires practical completion within a given period of time. The task may be a single activity or series of components to make up a larger piece of work or project.	
Q1. How do the tasks in your role deliver the vision and mission of the organisation?	
Q2. How do you identify your successes and challenges in undertaking the tasks in the role? Is there anything you find difficult?	
Q3. What is your approach in undertaking the tasks in the role?	
Q4. Where there are times that you do not feel connected to the tasks in your role, what may need to change?	
Q5. How do you perform the tasks in your role to reflect the organisation's values? What do you think needs to change in order to achieve the organisation's values to connect you to the tasks in your role?	
Q6. How do the tasks in your role connect to your personal and professional beliefs and values?	
Q7. How do you support others to connect to the tasks in their role and the organisation's values?	

(Continued)

Table 8.3 (*Continued*)   Supervisee Practice Review Framework

Review Area 3: Attributes (S) (*neuro self-care, personal vs. professional, team functioning and dynamics, debriefing, work and life balancing, stress, fatigue and burnout, job and role satisfaction, workplace relationships, personal responsibility and professional accountability, bounceability, personal resourcing, health and well-being, encouragement, validation, hope, beliefs and values, refuelling, appreciation*)	
Attributes are the qualities and characteristics that are owned and valued by an individual to demonstrate professional identity.	
Q1. How do your attributes/qualities, beliefs and values align to the organisation's mission and vision?	
Q2. How does this impact and influence you when they don't? What would others notice? What do you notice? How do you reconcile this in order to be effective in your role?	
Q3. As a person and professional what do you bring to the workplace that ensures you feel successful in your role?	
Q4. How is your professional identity reflective of you as a person? Do you understand what your professional identity is?	
Q5. How do you engage in self-care whilst at work and outside of your workplace to remain effective in your role?	
Q6. How do you encourage and support your colleagues and your team members in living out the organisation's vision, mission and values to maintain positive workplace relationships? How do you establish and maintain relationships for the organisation's common purpose?	

(Continued)

Table 8.3 (*Continued*)   Supervisee Practice Review Framework

Review Area 4: Knowledge (E) (*professional excellence, professional development, training needs, qualifications, competencies/capability, transfer of knowledge and information into the role, research, evidence base, career planning, learning and development plan, adult learning*).	
Knowledge is the collection of information; understandings; insights and consciousness in our mind library that is gathered over time through experience, education, training and relational interactions.	
Q1. How do you use your knowledge to consciously demonstrate your skills in performing the tasks in your role? How do you demonstrate the breadth of knowledge in your role to others?	
Q2. What knowledge do you need to increase to remain effective in your role?	
Q3. How have you been encouraged to grow and develop both in your role and as part of the organisation?	
Q4. What opportunities have you taken to increase your skills and further your knowledge base?	
Q5. How can the organization provide you with opportunities to grow your skills and further your knowledge base?	
Q6. How do you regularly demonstrate your breadth of knowledge in your role?	
Q7. What is your reflective process to understand and demonstrate the knowledge you have gained from life experience that you have transferred into your role?	
Q8. How do you share your knowledge across your team and the organisation?	

(*Continued*)

Table 8.3 (*Continued*)   Supervisee Practice Review Framework

Review Plan: Supervisee Practice Review Framework			
(*This document outlines the key elements of the framework and supports the review discussion and what the supervisee would like to prioritise and take back into supervision discussions during the next twelve months*) **Supervisor Name:** **Supervisee Name:** **Review Date:**			
Review Area 1: Skills (P)	**Review**		
	Priority 1–10	**Perspective P, A, S, E**	**Development Detail What is the focus from now to the next review?**
A skill is the ability and capacity acquired through systematic and sustained effort demonstrated on a regular basis (continually).			
Q1. Where do you draw your skills from to effectively undertake your role?			
Q2. How do your current skills connect to your practice?			
Q3. What skills do you currently use in your role and what you need to enhance the overall capability in the role?			
Q4. How do you approach your work from different perspectives?			
Q5. How do you see your ethics and practice demonstrating the organisation's values?			
Q6. When there are times where you experience tensions between the organisation's values and your own practice, how do you reconcile these?			

(Continued)

Table 8.3 (*Continued*)   Supervisee Practice Review Framework

Review Area 2: Tasks (A)	Review		
	Priority 1–10	**Perspective P, A, S, E**	**Development Detail What is the focus from now to the next review?**
A task is an identified activity that requires practical completion within a given period of time. The task may be a single activity or series of components to make up a larger piece of work or project			
Q1. How do the tasks in your role deliver the vision and mission of the organisation?			
Q2. How do you identify your successes and challenges in understanding the tasks in the role? Is there anything you find difficult?			
Q3. What is your approach in undertaking the tasks in the role?			
Q4. Where there are times you do not feel connected to the tasks in your role, what may need to change?			
Q5. How do you perform the tasks in your role to reflect the organisation's values? What do you think needs to change in order to achieve the organisation's values to connect you to the tasks in your role?			
Q6. How do the tasks in your role connect to your personal and professional beliefs and values?			
Q7. How do you support others to connect to the tasks in their role and the organisation's values?			

(*Continued*)

Table 8.3 (*Continued*)   Supervisee Practice Review Framework

Capability Area 3: Attributes (S)	Review		
	Priority 1–10	Perspective P, A, S, E	Development Detail What is the focus from now to the next review?
Attributes are the qualities and characteristics that are owned and valued by an individual to demonstrate professional identity			
Q1. How do your attributes/ qualities, beliefs and values align to the organisation's mission and vision?			
Q2. How does this impact and influence you when they don't? What would others notice? What do you notice? How do you reconcile this in order to be effective in your role?			
Q3. As a person and professional what do you bring to the workplace that ensures you feel successful in your role?			
Q4. How is your professional identity reflective of you as a person? Do you understand what your professional identity is?			
Q5. How do you engage in self-care whilst at work and outside of your workplace to remain effective in your role?			
Q6. How do you encourage and support your colleagues and your team members in living out the organisation's vision, mission and values to maintain positive workplace relationships? How do you establish and maintain relationships for the organisation's common purpose?			

(*Continued*)

Table 8.3 (*Continued*)   Supervisee Practice Review Framework

Capability Area 4: Knowledge (E)	Review		
	Priority 1–10	Perspective P, A, S, E	Development Detail What is the focus from now to the next review?
Knowledge is the collection of information; understandings; insights and consciousness in our mind library that is gathered over time through experience, education, training and relational interactions			
Q1. How do you use your knowledge to consciously demonstrate your skills in performing the tasks in the role? How do you demonstrate the breadth of knowledge in your role to others?			
Q2. What knowledge do you need to increase to remain effective in your role?			
Q3. How have you been encouraged to grow and develop both in your role and as part of the organisation?			
Q4. What opportunities have you taken to increase your skills and further your knowledge base?			
Q5. How can the organization provide you with opportunities to grow your skills and further your knowledge base?			
Q6. How do you regularly demonstrate your breadth of knowledge in your role?			
Q7. What is your reflective process to understand and demonstrate the knowledge you have gained from life experience that you have transferred into your role?			
Q8. How do you share your knowledge across your team and the organisation?			

(*Continued*)

Table 8.3 (*Continued*)   Supervisee Practice Review Framework

Supervisee Name:
Supervisee Comments:
Line Manager/Supervisor Name:
Line Manager/Supervisor Comments:

supervision, but is more an evaluation for the supervisee to review aspects of their role and inform their annual review process. It is completed by the supervisee during probation and responses made by the supervisee are then incorporated into supervision discussions. If the supervisee is not in the process of probation, the review questions can be completed at any time and then discussed in supervision.

The framework has a developmental plan included for the supervisee to identify what areas they would like to enhance or develop over the next twelve months from their responses. The supervisee then chooses what perspective in the PASE model that they would like to focus their goals on.

Review area 1. Skills, focuses the supervisee to think about where they draw their skills from to perform in their role. The questions explore what skills the supervisee uses in their role, how they approach their role from different perspectives and how they manage tensions between their own practice and the organisation's values.

Review area 2. Tasks, focuses on how the supervisee undertakes the tasks in their role. Questions focus on how the supervisee identifies successes and challenges in the role, what happens when they are not connected to the tasks in the role and how the supervisee supports others in the team to connect to their tasks as well.

Review area 3. Attributes, asks the supervisee to consider how they align their own beliefs and values to the organisations, and how do they manage when they don't. Other questions focus on how they live out the organisations vision and values, what their professional identity is and how they establish and maintain positive relationships in the workplace.

Review area 4. Knowledge, asks questions around how the supervisee uses their knowledge to demonstrate skills in the role, how they have been encouraged by the organisation to grow and develop and what opportunities the supervisee has taken to increase skills and knowledge. The supervisee is also asked how they share their knowledge with colleagues and how they encourage others to develop as a professional.

Summary

We have discussed the importance of evaluating different aspects of supervision to ensure it remains effective. In this chapter, there are tools for both the supervisor and supervisee to use in the evaluation process. Consider the following reflective questions as a summary to this chapter about evaluating supervision.

What have been the key things you have gained from reading this chapter on the importance of evaluating supervision?
What have been your reflections about this chapter?
List three things that you will take from this chapter to incorporate into your supervisory role.
What do you think will be useful to talk to your supervisee/s about regarding this chapter?

Chapter 9

Supervising Student Placements

Key focus for this chapter

- The different faces of student placements
- The role of the field educator on placement
- Placement stages
- Understanding the integrated learning environment
- Setting expectations in the learning environment
- Structuring the placement for success
- Transitioning from student to professional
- Different placement timelines
- Providing effective supervision for students

Introduction

Deciding to have a student on field placement takes energy, resources and time. It is also possibly one of the most rewarding and positive experiences that a supervisor can have in their career. Being able to mentor and guide a student in a professional practice setting during their field placement is fulfilling. It provides professional satisfaction and the opportunity for supervisors to give back to their profession and influence good practice outcomes. When providing supervision to students on field placement, it is crucial to integrate their learning. When supervision and support is set up well, the placement will be very successful. This chapter explores different aspects of placements, including the role of the field placement educator, placement stages, how to select the right students and how to ensure supervision is effective.

There are various time frames where students may be on placement for two weeks at a time, and others that are on placement for sixteen weeks. No matter the duration of placement, it needs to be a purposeful and meaningful learning experience for the student and a worthwhile experience for the supervisor or field educator. Having students on field placement also motivates supervisors to refresh their professional identity and keep up to date with the latest theories and best practice approaches.

When deciding to have a student on field placement, it is important to understand the context and principles in which practicum takes place. This will assist you and your agency, organisation or business to set up a field placement framework and process that can be easily implemented each and every time you have a student. If you do this, it will save you a lot of time and energy throughout the placement timeline. It also assists you to clearly understand the requirements of the university, any professional body and your own expectations as the supervisor and field educator.

Setting up a quality placement provides students with an integrated learning experience where they have unique opportunities to learn new skills and enhance existing ones in a facilitated learning environment. In this type of placement environment, students can test out what they are learning at university and how they apply these in the organisational context. Being a student on placement is the only time during their career that they can reflect and enjoy the opportunity to engage in an action-learning environment knowing they are in a student role. At no other time in their career will the student have this type of learning experience again. The student also learns the importance of developing a professional identity, to understand the process of reflection, and how to maintain professional excellence throughout their career. The placement experience is also a collaborative and complex partnership between various parties, including the student, placement organisation, professional body, educator and the university.

The principles of the placement experience are far reaching for the field educator in understanding different theories and practices the student needs to use on placement, knowing the different phases of the placement process and understanding how students learn. It also involves the development of a learning agreement that includes reflective goals and objectives to maximise learning.

As the placement sits within an experiential learning context, supervising students is a critical component to ensure linkages are made between the learning processes and what occurs in the placement environment. Having an experienced supervisor who understands the critical nature of the supervisory process and engages an effective supervision model and framework is crucial for student learning.

Faces of Placement

There are various stakeholders involved in the field placement process. Visual 9.1 provides an overview of the different faces of the placement context. Students have to juggle various relationships because of the

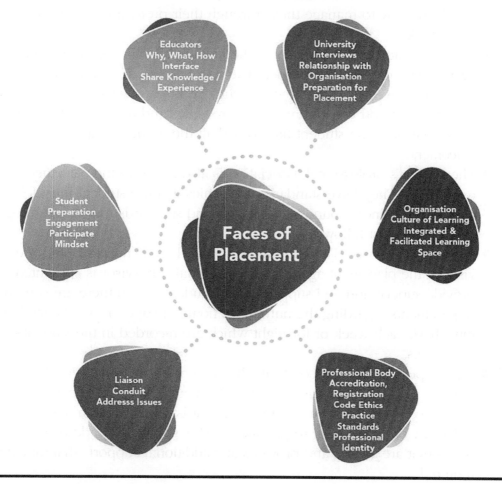

Visual 9.1   Different faces of placement.

different requirements placed on them throughout the placement experience. In understanding all the faces of placement:

- The university provides a lead role as the key decision maker. They act as the interface between the university and the placement agency and engage processes to prepare the student for their learning experience. They check in at regular intervals to support or resolve any issues that arise and celebrate the student's successes along the way.
- The placement agency provides a positive culture of learning through an Integrated Learning Framework (ILF). The agency or organisation offers different learning experiences and provides the student with the time and space to reflect at a deeper level to maximise their learning. Through this process, the student comes to understand their personal beliefs and values that intersect in the professional environment. They also learn how to manage these through their professional identity framework.
- The field placement supervisor is the main contact in the placement agency who oversees the student learning process. They are the interface between the placement agency and the university. The field educator signs off on administrative processes and usually makes the final decision if the student has passed all the requirements of the field placement.
- The student's professional association is also a face in the placement experience. They have standards and ethics that the student must follow and set guidelines around accreditation and standards that the learning institutions must follow.
- External supervisor. There are times where there is no available supervisor in the placement agency, so an external supervisor is appointed to provide supervision and support to the student. Often there are certain requirements regarding the number of hours of supervision, the student must have each week or fortnight which are recorded in the student's timesheets.
- Liaison person. This person visits the student throughout their placement to assess how things are going. They meet with the supervisor or field educator to ensure that the student is progressing in line with university or educational requirements. This person also addresses any issues that are arising and provides any additional supports that may be required.

The role of the field placement supervisor in any organisation is crucial to the field placement being successful. If you have had many students on placement or are considering having one or two, consider the following questions to guide your thinking.

What would be your interest in having a student on placement? How many students have you provided a field placement to and why?

_____

_____

_____

_____

_____

What do you see as the role of the field educator or placement supervisor?

_____

_____

_____

_____

_____

What would you find the most challenging about having a student on placement?

_____

_____

_____

_____

_____

What do you think are the rewards in having a student?

_____

_____

_____

_____

_____

The role of the field placement supervisor is one of the most important roles within the field education process. Supervisors are instrumental not only in the success of the placement process but also in providing the student with key learning opportunities to learn specific skills and knowledge and qualities. They are a role model demonstrating ethical practice, showing students how to integrate theory to practice and provide support during the different stages of the placement process.

The supervisor's role is to

- Develop an outline of the learning opportunities the student can expect whilst on placement;
- Assist the student to develop their goals and complete all the required documentation;
- Support the student to integrate and use the learning documents as part of their daily work;
- Provide effective professional supervision;
- Assist the student to develop reflective objectives in the learning plan to maximise outcomes during the field placement;
- Understand a range of approaches to support the student to integrate learning from their course;
- Understand the role of practice vs. task and process in the learning process;
- Provide an integrated learning environment in which the student can articulate and measure their learning success;
- Ensure the student provides information and course materials that allow the field supervisor to support the student to make the linkage between the learning environment and the placement;
- Assess and evaluate the student's progress throughout the placement;
- Resolve any challenges that may arise during the placement;
- Appropriately induct the student into the organisation agency;
- Assist the student to develop a number of key frameworks that may include a critical reflection framework, ethical decision-making framework, supervision framework and a professional practice framework;
- Oversee any reporting processes;
- Attend any supervisor workshops;
- Understand the principles of adult learning and how the student takes information and learning from the placement back into their course and
- Assess the students' learning achievements.

In thinking about all these things, consider what you would see as the role of the field placement supervisor in Visual 9.2?

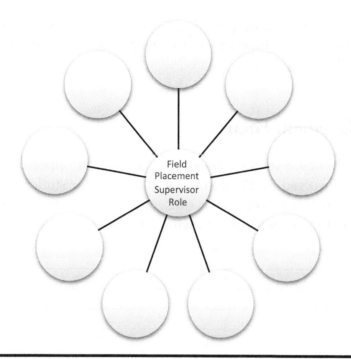

Visual 9.2   Field supervisor role.

Initial questions to consider

Now that we have explored the role of the field placement supervisor, we can now consider what things are important when having a student on placement. These questions can assist the field supervisor think about what the induction process will look like, what the student will be doing during their time on placement, who will provide support and where the student will be located.

1. What induction process will the student go through? How will the student be orientated into the organisation?
2. What will the student be doing, will the placement be project focused, clinical, professional, with clients, not with clients, etc.?
3. Who will supervise the student during the placement?
4. What expectations does the university or educational environment have for the organisation?
5. How would you like the student demonstrate their skills and knowledge during the placement?
6. What support processes need to be put in place to maintain the student's self-care?

7. How will supervision be provided? How will you ensure they know how to use a supervision model to ensure it remains effective?
8. Where will the student be located?

Student Placement Focus

What do you think are relevant activities and learning opportunities for students to be involved in? Do you see a difference for students who may be undertaking their first placement or subsequent placements? Do you see any differences for students who are studying different qualifications?

_____

_____

_____

_____

_____

During placement, students can be involved in a whole range of activities that support the work of the organisation, promotes learning, integrates practice skills and engages reflection. Mapping placement activities to the students learning process also maximises the transfer of knowledge and skills. The type and complexity of the activities on placement can also be mapped to the different stages of the placement. This way, the student feels supported as they embark on new activities and feel confident in the process. When students are fully engaged in the facilitated learning environment, they are motivated to learn and feel supported. Table 9.1 provides an overview of the types of activities that students might be involved in. Reflect on the focus of the placement and then document what types of activities the student could be involved in.

Selecting Students

With the demands placed on universities and other educational institutions to secure student placements each year, there are many challenges for organisations in having students regularly. Some students require additional support due to different health issues. Finding the right organisation for particular students can be difficult, particularly if the environment is not conducive to having a student with particular challenges. It is often easier to have a small

Table 9.1 Placement Focus

Focus	Activities
Working with clients	
Client observations Patient/client case load	
Non-client work	
Organisational practice/administration	
Projects – evaluation, program development, implementation, policy, research	
Report writing	
Development of grants and funding submissions	
Sector/peak/organisational meetings	
Professional association activities/events	
Peer discussions	
Program reviews	
Reading	
Journaling/writing	
Marketing/promotional work	

group of students on placement rather than just having one, so they work on projects together. Finding a student that is a good match for your organisation can be easier using the following questions and thinking about what questions are important to ask students during the pre-placement process.

1. What attributes are important to look for as a good match with the organisation?
2. What requirements does the university, educational institution or professional body have?
3. Is it easier to take more than one student so they can work together during placement?
4. How do you assess the students' readiness for the placement context?
5. What approach does your organisation take in preparing a student for placement?
6. Do you ask for the student's resume?

7. Do you take a first or final placement student?
8. Does your organisation have the ability to take a student with any challenges?
9. What supports does the university or educational agency provide during the placement?

The following questions provide a guide for the organisation to ask students during their interview prior to being chosen for placement?

1. What are you looking forward to during the placement?
2. What types of things are you interested in doing on placement?
3. What might be the challenges you see arising during the placement?
4. Is there anything particular the organisation needs to know to support you on placement?
5. What are your learning goals for the placement?
6. How do you think you learn best?
7. What has been your success during your course to date?
8. What previous work experiences have you had?
9. How many days a week will you be on placement?
10. Start dates, length of placement, expected finish date?

Placement Stages

The student goes through different stages where they feel at times that things are going well. Equally, there are times when they feel overwhelmed due to the amount of juggling that needs to occur. Understanding the stages of the placement process will support the student and alleviate any fears or concerns they may have during the placement. The following provides an overview of how a placement can be divided into different stages. This can be changed depending on how many weeks or months you have the student for. When the field placement is for a much shorter period of time, each of the stages can be reduced. This framework is very useful to show students at the beginning of their placement, so they understand the activities and tasks they will be undertaking and when they move from one stage to another.

Weeks 1–5 is the Orientation Stage
Weeks 6–10 is referred to as the Engagement Stage
Weeks 11+ is the Consolidation and Termination Stage

In each of the stages, students undertake and complete particular tasks and activities that are aligned to their learning plan. All requirements need to be completed prior to the student finalising their placement in the organisation.

Stage One – Weeks 1–5

The first stage in the placement process is referred to as the '*Orientation Stage*'.

This stage typically occurs between Weeks 1 and 5. During this time, the field supervisor and university or educational institution leads the process. The student is orientated into the agency, gets to know the team they will be working in and they tour the work environment. The student usually completes the necessary paperwork that is required by the university or educational institution and the agency/department, including an ID badge or other identification, email and computer access, etc.

During Weeks 1–5, the student usually shadows the field supervisor or other staff to understand the placement context and what the organisation does. The student commences supervision and completes their intake questions. During the **Orientation Stage**, the student develops their Learning Plan/Agreement. The Learning Plan is usually mapped against the student's professional association's Practice Standards and other relevant documents that the university or educational institution may require for any reporting processes. We discuss later how to develop a Learning Plan and the importance of developing reflective goals rather than task and process goals. There will be various disciplines where students are only required to develop task goals, so it is important to check this out when the student commences. It is also vital that the students review their *Placement Manual* and clearly understand any assessment requirements they may have. The field placement manual usually outlines information about what is required on placement. If a student can spend some time during the week to work on documentation, this assists students to feel supported and reduces stressors that may arise during this phase.

Stage Two – Weeks 6–10

Stage two, referred to as '***The Engagement Phase***', is where the student begins to settle into the organisation, feels part of the team, understands their role and has been successfully inducted. This stage is led by the supervisor and student with support from the university or educational institution. The students will now know what they are doing on placement and may be working directly with clients. They will have shadowed others in the organisation and feel more confident about what their focus is. Supervision has been commenced; the student has completed their supervision agreement, plans the agenda for supervision meetings and is transferring learning from supervision into their role on placement. The student is now working to the Learning Plan through a critical reflective framework and are writing about their experiences on placement. The student will be thinking about and starting to develop a mid-placement report of their achievements, challenges and how they are meeting placement requirements. Many universities or educational institutions require a mid and final placement report to assess the student's capability to pass their course. The student will have (where required) attended their first contact visit from the university any issues will have been identified by this stage. It is also ideal if it is a first placement, that students are able to articulate how they will develop a reflective framework, ethical decision-making framework and professional practice framework.

Final Stage – Weeks 11+

The final stage of the placement is referred to as the '***Consolidation and Termination Phase***' and usually occurs from Week 11 until the student finishes their placement. By this stage, the student is leading their learning process and the field supervisor provides support. Students understand the importance and role of supervision, are progressing their Learning Plan and are beginning to consider their professional identity as an emerging professional. The student is showing confidence contributing to or leading discussions. The student is proactive in their own learning process through the integration of the Learning Plan into the placement environment. The student is preparing to finish the placement and is having discussions in supervision about how to exit client cases and end relationships both in side and outside of the organisation. Final year students have now fully developed their professional practice framework, and for first placement students, they are still in the developmental stage with additional support from the supervisor. The final placement report is finalised and students can articulate how their learning has progressed, what they have achieved and what needs to be finished. Visual 9.3 provides an overview of the phases of the placement process.

Orientation Phase Weeks 1 - 5	Engagement Phase Weeks 6 - 10	Consolidation & Termination Phase Weeks 11 – 16+
ORGANISATIONAL EDUCATOR LED	**EDUCATOR /STUDENT LED**	**STUDENT LED EDUCATOR SUPPORT**
Placement orientation in context & environment	Participates in workplace activities, meetings, fully orientated to the work team	Professional identity developing or established - presenting as a professional
Orientation to work team and wider organisational teams Completion of Admin processes (system & email sign on, ID Badge, relevant documents)	Networks within the team, placement environment and with relevant external stakeholders	Autonomous in role
Observation of Educator in the placement context, develop initial understanding of the role & practice within the placement context	Participate in the practice context, commences client interactions/case lost	Student led discussion, professional & clinical skills developing and evident
		Observations conducted by others/assessing practice
UNIVERSITY EDUCATOR LED	**UNIVERSITY SUPPORT EDUCATOR/ STUDENT LED**	**UNIVERSITY SUPPORT STUDENT LED/ EDUCATOR LED**
Orientation to placement environment Development of Learning Agreement	Supervision framework set up.Learning Agreement completed	Preparing for termination of placement
Set up supervision process/timelines, introduction to supervisor, develop agreement, review policy, supervision documents, explore role of student status and role within the placement, understand SV model in context	Developing Professional Practice Framework	Professional Identity established or developed
	Developing Ethical Decision Making Framework	Student able to articulate what professional practice is within placement environment
Review Placement Education Manual and university requirements	Developing Reflective Practice Framework	Professional Practice Framework developed
Link Learning Agreements to relevant professional body documents	First Liaison contact Any issues identified and resolved	

www.amovita.com.au
1800 YES AMOVITA (1800 937 266)

© Amotovita Consulting and R Majcen

Amovita
CONSULTING

Visual 9.3   Placement phases.

Table 9.2   Placement Activities

Stage 1 Weeks 1–5 Orientation	Stage 2 Weeks 6–10 Engagement	Stage 3 Weeks 11+ Consolidation and Termination
Orientate the student on placement Overview organisational policies Structure Clarify expectations Set up supervision Understand university requirements Develop learning plan Map to student graduate attributes Develop integrated learning plan Observe others work Set up university visit where there is a liaison person in place	Finalise mid-placement report Develop professional practice framework Client case load commences Using the PASE™ supervision model for effective supervision Completed written documents such as client case notes and reports Develop self-care and well-being plan Timeline for university or educational institution assessments Spend time in reflection for practice First liaison visit	Develop final placement report Develop ethical decision-making framework Review resume, interview skills Prepare for closing the placement Finalise work activities Close client cases Supervision focus transition from student to professional

Now we have explored the three stages of the placement process; it is important to consider what key activities and learning the student will cover in each of the stages. Table 9.2 provides a brief overview of the types of activities the student may be involved in during each of the placement phases. What things would you envisage are required as part of each phase?

Visual 9.4 provides an overview from Sweitzer and King's (2004) placement process as students are often challenged by the placement context.

1. **Anticipation ('What if …?' Stage)**

   This phase of the placement is usually mixed with excitement and anxiety as students look forward to putting into practice what they have learned but may also be concerned with being successful on placement. The student may feel anxious about the role that they will be expected to do as they try to settle into the placement.

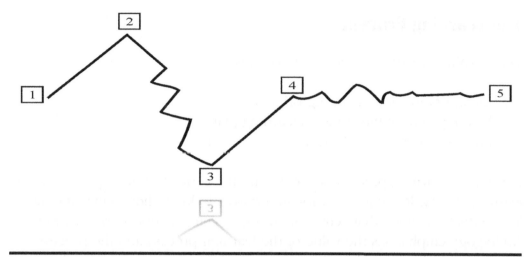

Visual 9.4   Stages of placement: (1) Anticipation, (2) Disillusionment, (3) Confrontation, (4) Competence, and (5) Culmination (Sweitzer & King, 2004).

2. **Disillusionment ('What's wrong?' Stage)**

   By this stage, students often feel the placement is not what they thought it would be. There is a difference between what they expected and what is taking place. There may be times where the student lacks confidence to try new things and the field educator also has expectations that the student is not meeting.

3. **Confrontation ('The only way around is through...')**

   This is the time where students often feel the only way to get through the disillusionment stage is to spend time reflecting, speak with their supervisor push through. It is a time where they may be lots of assessments due, work tasks that need completing and the organisation requires the student to demonstrate skills and knowledge required of them.

4. **Competence**

   The student pushes through to feel more confident, and this phase can bring a sense of achievement as things start to be finished and the end is in sight. The student is recognised for what they have completed and feels part of the team.

5. **Culmination**

   As the placement ends, students may feel a sense of urgency to consider their employment opportunities. Relationships are concluding and clients are exiting. Field educators can play an important role at this time by ensuring they have achieved all they needed to during the placement timeline.

The Learning Process

The learning process includes three key principles:

1. Incorporating adult learning principles.
2. Development of the students learning plan.
3. Engaging a facilitated learning environment.

Engaging a learning process occurs within the context of andragogy or adult learning theory. It is important for supervisors to know how adult students learn effectively and what activities during placement support the learning. Andragogy emphasises the value of the learning process and the process required to facilitate the learning process at different points of time during the placement. The study of adult learning originated from Europe in the 1950's from the work of Knowles (1990). He identified six adult learning principles for adult learners:

1. Adults are more motivated and self-directed internally than externally, so motivation is an intrinsic process;
2. Adults need to bring life experiences and knowledge to their learning experience to learn effectively;
3. Adults are goal orientated;
4. Adults need experience relevance in the learning process;
5. Adults are practical learners and
6. Adult learners like to be respected in the learning process.

1. **Adults are motivated and self-directed internally**

   Have you ever noticed adults switch off when information and learning is imposed upon them? Adults learn best when they feel fully engaged in the learning process, want to learn and are in the right mindset to receive the information. When a student engages in a facilitated learning environment, they step into a learning space where they want to take on information and therefore take responsibility for their own learning. To maximise the learning process, it is important to
   - Provide structure, boundaries and flexibility in the learning environment.
   - Pace the student's learning through a developmental framework to maximise their curiosity.
   - Ensure the student feels responsibility for their own learning without feeling overly responsible.
   - Ensure the student remains in the learning space as a student.
   - Encourage reflection throughout the placement.
   - Provide regular and developmental feedback.
   - Understand how to provide developmental feedback.
   - Ensure the student develops reflective goals in their learning plan rather than being task and process orientated.
   - Understand the student's personality and learning style.
   - Provide students with an understanding of how the learning process takes place.

2. **Adults bring life experiences and knowledge to their learning experience**

   Students often come to field placement having had extensive work and life experience. Some students continue working whilst studying; therefore, it is important to acknowledge the experience the student brings and integrate this into the learning experience. Get to know the student and understand what they like to do outside of their course/study as you never know when a hobby or talent will be useful in the placement context, i.e., playing the guitar, singing, etc.

   Understanding this adult learning principle also assists to understand how personal values and beliefs influence the placement context. Students come with beliefs and values from other study, childhood and family of origin. This can create a pattern of thinking in how the student engages with clients, other team members and the organisation.

It is important that the student engages a professional practice framework within the professional context and understands what biases and beliefs can impact on the work they do.

3. **Adults are goal orientated (developing an attention plan)**

   Engaging the student in critical reflection and appreciative inquiry in the learning process assists them to set appropriate goals to achieve on placement. Setting goals is more effective when we ask the student to forecast their success in achieving the goal and work from that retrospectively. For example, setting goals is more effective through the following: 'it is now (date, month) and I have/am…', rather than 'I am going to…'. Setting goals in the learning plan needs to be reflective so that the student can be curious about their learning. When a student develops goals that are predominantly task and process, it becomes a tick and flick exercise rather than a rich learning experience. When goals are developed from a reflective perspective, the student is more likely to achieve their goals and it is an enjoyable learning experience.

   Reflective Goals

   Task and process goal

   I want to learn how to communicate more effectively on placement.

   Reflective goal

   To understand the role of communication within the organisation and demonstrate the key skills of communication with clients.

   Task and process goal

   Participate in meetings and look at how team members work together.

   Reflective goal

   Explore and understand the framework in which relationships develop and how they align to professional identity.

   Task and process goal

   Read a number of organisation policies.

   Reflective goal

   Understand the context policy that plays a role in incorporating the wider social policy environment.

4. **Adults are relevancy based in the learning process**

   As adult learners, students need to know the relevance of the learning in the field placement context. To assist students to see the value of the learning experience, it is important to engage a reflective framework as part of the placement. Having a reflective framework means that the supervisor asks relevant questions that invite curiosity, therefore better connection to the learning experience. More organisations set goals with students and advise what they would like the student to incorporate into the learning experience. Given many university programs are now often two-year intensive programs, it can be more challenging for students to receive a comprehensive array of skills required for their professional role when they finish placement. Providing students with a project or client case load can test out skills learned and provide the opportunity to reflect on these in supervision. Ensuring key documents such as the Learning Plan and Practice Standards, education manual and associated documents provide context in which the placement and learning experience are relevant.

5. **Adults are practical**

   Students enjoy direct client work that supports the practical application of theory to the practice environment. Despite many students working as a professional, having a placement experience in a different workplace ensures other real-world experiences are useful during placement. Using problem-based solving methods are good for different learning styles. Wherever possible, it is useful to provide opportunities for students to participate in learning rather than observe for much of the placement. Any opportunity to 'get their hands dirty' is usually at the forefront of most students minds on placement.

6. **Adult learners like to be respected**

   As adult learners, students on field placement like to be respected by
   – The field educator taking regular interest in what they are doing.
   – Setting consistent and regular times for professional supervision.
   – Acknowledging their contributions on placement.
   – Encouraging and validating them and their work.
   – Providing developmental feedback on a regular basis.
   – Facilitating an integrated learning experience through the learning plan.
   – Understanding how to support a student even when they say they are doing well and may be overwhelmed.

Facilitated Learning Environment/Process

A facilitated learning environment occurs when the field educator aligns the placement experience with the learning plan and maps activities to maximise learning outcomes. The field educator takes on the role of a facilitator, coach and mentor. They organise the environment to maximise the student's learning and provide the necessary resources to ensure this occurs. The student is provided with a solution-focused framework to ask questions, resolve issues and focus on the developmental process as it unfolds. The field educator who has a leading role in the process however allows the student to explore, critique and reflect regularly to ensure best learning outcomes. This can be challenging given that some students in a clinical setting have a patient load, so ethics and adequate clinical supervision are crucial.

There are many advantages of setting up a facilitated learning environment, which include

- The student takes control of their own learning process.
- The student is an active and motivated learner as they assist in the placement process and program of activities.
- It provides a range of learning opportunities.
- It provides a critical reflection framework for the student to engage in reflective practice.
- The student is encouraged to ask questions, rather than the educator providing all of the information.

Learning Plans

The student's *Learning Plan* is one of the key pillars of any field placement. Students often find it difficult to develop their Learning Plan during the first stage of the placement as they are finding their way around organisation, settling into the team and understanding the expectations of the organisation and educational institution.

Incorporating adult learning principles and reflective goals into the Learning Plan enhances the learning experience. The student's learning plan is usually developed in the first stage of the placement and is the guiding document to highlight the student's success and completion of professional activities. The learning plan forms part of the supervision agenda at each meeting, and the student demonstrates continued learning through this reflective process. The learning plan is also developed in line with appropriate Code of Ethics, information from the student's field placement education manual and any relevant practice standards. It is important that the learning plan is not developed using task-centred goals as the student will engage with them more from a cognitive process where it is more about completion of the task. When the student's learning goals are developed using reflective language, the learning is embedded from a professional practice perspective. Table 9.3 provides an example of a learning plan that incorporates task-oriented goals, and Table 9.4 provides an example of a learning plan that includes reflective goals.

Some universities and educational institutions incorporate student graduate attributes that need to be evidenced by the student by the time of graduation. It is important to incorporate these attributes into any learning plan to ensure the student is focused on them – particularly if it is the student's final placement before they graduate. Table 9.5 provides an example of student

Table 9.3   Example Learning Plan – Task and Process Goals

Learning Objective (Task and Process)	*How Will I Achieve This Objective?*	*Evidence of Achievement How I Will Evidence My Understanding and Demonstrated Skills and Knowledge*
1. I want to ensure that I communicate effectively throughout placement		
2. Make ethical decisions		
3. Understand the purpose and services provided by the organisation		
4. Get to know other professionals to do networking and build professional relationships		
5. Outline the values and beliefs that intersect between the personal and professional		
6. Develop a professional identity for my career		
7. Assume responsibility for a range of administrative procedures within the organisation		
8. Attend supervision with an agenda developed for each meeting		

Table 9.4 Example Learning Plan – Reflective Goals

Learning Objectives (Reflective Goals)	How Will I Achieve This Objective?	Evidence of Achievement How I Will Evidence My Understanding and Demonstrated Skills and Knowledge
1. Develop an understanding of how collaborative and respectful relationships are developed and exited in the organisation		
2. Explore and understand what an ethical decision-making framework is and evidence throughout the placement		
3. Understand the role the organisation has in the community and articulate its purpose and mission to others		
4. Understand how to develop a professional identity and evidence throughout the placement		
5. Explore a range of beliefs and values that intersect between the personal and professional context and how they influence practice in the organisation		
6. Explore the reflective process and its relationship to the organisation's role and practice as a professional		
7. Demonstrate an understanding of the importance of administrative tasks and how they relate to practice		
8. Understand and articulate the important role that supervision plays as it underpins the placement context		

Table 9.5 Example Student Graduate Attributes

Student Graduate Attributes	Learning Outcomes
1. The student demonstrates a clear professional identity	• Demonstrates an understanding of the role and value of being a professional in the student's chosen profession • Acts in accordance with professional knowledge, values and ethics within their profession • Can articulate key elements of a professional identity framework • Evidences a professional identity during the field placement
2. Professional values and ethics	• Demonstrates and articulates a clear ethical framework • The ability to conceptualise, contextualise, assess and synthesise ethical issues • Demonstrates ethical practice through professional behaviour and conduct and positive relationships • The ability to critically analyse information, bring together to synthesise in order to make sound judgements and professional decisions • Understands how own beliefs and values intersect between personal and professional contexts • Demonstrates principles around informed consent (duty of care, privacy, confidentiality, industrial issues, etc.)
3. Reflective practice	• Understands the process of reflection and how it relates to practice • Demonstrates use of reflection to achieve key goals during placement • Can articulate what reflective practice is and how it is engaged during the placement
4. Research and project management	• The ability to undertake research to inform and influence organisational practice and policy • The ability to undertake evidence-informed practice in working with clients and consumers • The ability to plan and execute project work and/or a piece of research with semi-independence • Demonstrated ability to apply knowledge and skills to undertake research congruent with practice values and ethics in the organisation

(Continued)

Table 9.5 (*Continued*) Example Student Graduate Attributes

Student Graduate Attributes		Learning Outcomes
5.	Communication and interpersonal skills	• Demonstrates key communication skills around communicating with influence, advocacy, mediation, negotiation, conflict resolution, technical communication skills • Ability to write high-level documents, use of appropriate language and can document clear messaging for the intended audience • The ability to relate interpersonally with internal and external stakeholders
6.	Diversity and cultural respect	• Knowledge and understanding of the principles of diversity and cultural backgrounds integrating into the work environment with respect • An appreciation of the historical and contemporary interface between different cultures • Knowledge of the cultural context of practice and the ability to apply that to practice
7.	Supervision and professional development	• Positively and proactively participates and engages in professional and line management supervision • Understands the value and use of supervision to achieve highly skilled professional practice, role accountability and professional development • The ability to articulate the integration of knowledge and practice during placement • Effective use of supervision model and relevant documentation to evidence professional success during placement

graduate attributes that students may be required to evidence to their professional association by the conclusion of the field placement.

Transitioning from Student to Professional

Preparing students to transition from student to professional during the final stage of their placement is crucial. Ensuring that students are ready to complete placement and move into their profession is a transition process in itself. Having a professional identity is key for students in understanding and articulating what it means to be a professional, and how to articulate this if looking for a professional job after placement is finished.

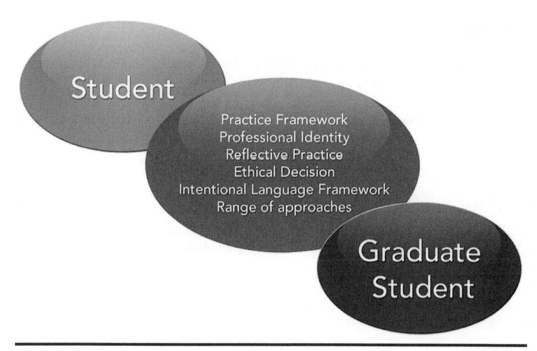

Visual 9.5   Transition from student to professional.

The process of transitioning from student professional is about the student having developed their professional excellence framework, professional identity framework, reflective practice, ethical decision-making framework, a range of practice approaches and a professional language framework. All of these components demonstrate if the student is ready to progress into a new professional role. Having a discussion in supervision about this transition process will support the student to feel comfortable and move through the process successfully. Without supporting the student to understand this transition process, some students can become 'stuck' between being a student and preparing to be a professional. Visual 9.5 overviews the key frameworks the student completes in the transition process.

Summary

This chapter has explored the importance of setting up a successful student placement where students are provided with effective supervision.

What have been the key things you have gained from reading this chapter?
What have been your reflections about this chapter about the importance of setting up a successful placement?
List three things that you will take from this chapter to incorporate into your supervisory role.
What do you think will be useful to talk to your supervisee/s about regarding this chapter?
What steps are important to ensure supervisees have a successful placement?

Chapter 10

Providing Supervision in a Cultural Context

Key focus for this chapter

- Caring communication in cultural supervision
- Understand what types of yarning are important in cultural supervision
- What can be discussed in Yarn Up Time and what may not be discussed
- Supervision and the third space
- Cultural priorities and protocols and their impact in a professional role
- The concept of cultural infusion
- Cultural respect in Yarn Up Time
- Understand community responsibilities in the mainstream environment
- Sharing knowledge in Yarn Up Time
- Discuss how culture relates to confidentiality
- Exploring the CASE™ supervision model of Yarn Up Time

Introduction

Please note: This chapter overviews a supervision model and process for providing culturally appropriate supervision for various cultural backgrounds, including Aboriginal staff across Australia. This chapter does not, however, provide information or commentary about supervision for all or many cultures, and this needs to be taken into consideration when using information from this chapter and adapted for other cultures. This chapter also mentions the work of a deceased Aboriginal Elder and permissions have been provided by Uncle Bob's wife, Barbara, to use in this book. This chapter may apply to Torres Strait Islander people; however, there are cultural differences to be observed. As the supervision model outlined in this chapter has been developed for Aboriginal people, only reference has been made in that context.

Whilst it is commonplace to provide professional supervision in a mainstream context through line management and operational supervision, too often cultural considerations are not included in the context of supervision. This chapter is crucial to consider how to provide cultural supervision for any cultural background. Given the author's work and professional experience, this chapter has been written with a focus on cultural supervision with Aboriginal staff. It is not intended to cover all cultures but provides some general information that can assist supervisors to reflect on how they provide supervision in a cultural context. This chapter includes the Yarn Up Time CASE (Cultural Practice/Professional, Administrative/Line Management, Support/Person, Educative/Professional Development) supervision model that is used in cultural supervision with Aboriginal staff across Australia.

Kanyini and Oneness

Providing supervision to staff from any cultural background needs to take place using the principles of Kanyini as overviewed in Aboriginal culture. In parts of Australia, Kanyini is an Indigenous word for the 'oneness' of Aboriginal people, as they are connected through caring and responsibility. Often spoken about by Uncle Bob Randall from the Northern Territory in Australia, Kanyini is having connection through Tjuukurpa (spirituality), Ngura (belonging to home and land), Walytja (family and kinship) and Kurunpa (spirit of the soul). It is about being nurtured through caring and practicing responsibility for all things. Kanyini is all about eternal relationships with the earth and with each other. The strength of Aboriginal people through their Kanyini is evident when working with them through supervision, or in a cultural context, Yarn Up Time. Supervision cannot be

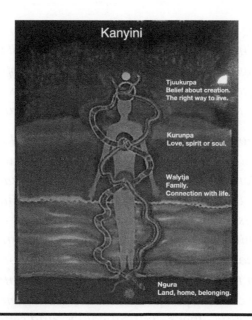

Visual 10.1   Kanyini elements.

provided in a cultural context without infusing the principles of connectedness (Visual 10.1).

> ***'Kanyini' – Connection and belonging to home, land, family and animals. It is about our beliefs, values and spirituality (Uncle Bob Randall).***

> ***The land owns us, not the other way around***
> ***The land has grown us all up***
> ***The land is older than us***
> ***(Uncle Bob Randall 2009)***

There are many definitions for the word, culture. You may have heard of terms such as cultural awareness, cultural sensitivity and cultural competence. So, what do they all mean? Loosely defined, words that represent these terms are

Culture: *General customs, social interactions, behaviours, ideas and values shared by a group of people in society. These may be shared by a particular member of a group or the group as a whole. It may include ways of communicating, expressing and interpreting.*

Cultural Sensitivity: *Being open and inclusive of all people from any culture. Having a commitment to ensuring that all individuals are engaged, received and approached with openness and non-judgement. That an individual's culture is received with respect and no biases are placed on the person from that culture.*

Cultural Competence: *Demonstrating the skills, knowledge and understanding about various cultural perspectives and contexts. There is an understanding of cultural nuances, languages and protocols that are practiced consistently and continually. Being conscious of engaging cultural respect, trust and integrity when working with people from different cultural backgrounds. Demonstrating the ability to expand knowledge and skills from the cultural perspective of others, and less from one's own cultural perspective. Having an open heart and mind, accepting other's cultural values, and setting aside one's own beliefs to support others.*

Cultural Awareness: *Being aware of the difference between cultures and demonstrating that understanding to others. Engaging relevant and appropriate language, words, terms and phrases with those from other cultural backgrounds. Being interested in learning, training and ongoing professional development to gain more information and understanding about other cultural protocols and responsibilities.*

Cultural Infusion: *Cultural information, understandings, protocols, priorities and responsibilities are incorporated and embraced across all aspects of the organisation. All staff from any culture have a sense that the organisation makes them feel valued and appreciated in their cultural beliefs. The organisation demonstrates integration of mainstream and cultural aspects that culturally infuses everyone into the one team and the third space. The organisation recognises and incorporates a strength-based, deep-listening approach to its operations and practices. It harmonises the organisation so all staff feel part of a collaborative approach towards cultural integrity. Infusion extracts the best from all cultural perspectives, and takes these elements, infuses them together and produces an environment that is highly effective both operationally and as a team.*

Infusion: *Taking a number of elements or components that work well together, complement each other and embed to become one whole element. Bringing different elements together in a slow and meaningful process that can take on a new meaning with purpose, intention and integrity.*

Principles of Cultural Supervision

Cultural supervision needs to clearly demonstrate particular principles, and it is important to include these principles in the organisation's policy framework, so all staff can support and understand them.

- Engagement in supervision is purely relational;
- To ensure performance in the role, a trusting relationship comes first;
- The relationship is built on belonging and connection;
- Celebrate cultural identity;
- The organisation needs to infuse all cultural backgrounds through the policy, governance and professional practice frameworks;
- Seek shared agreements about outcomes from the role;
- Cultural integrity needs to be clearly evident across the organisation;
- Understand the struggles of Aboriginal people as one people;
- Provide an environment where cultural obligations and protocols are supported and valued by everyone in an organisation;
- Involve staff in the development of all cultural frameworks, practices, processes, program development, delivery, policies and procedures in the mainstream environment;
- All self-care and well-being strategies, employee assistance program services and supervision need to observe cultural protocols and obligations and
- Ensure that non-Aboriginal staff understand the principles of Kanyini and observe these practices.

Supervision in a Cultural Context

Providing professional supervision in a cultural context incorporates cultural awareness and an understanding of the struggles that many people had, and continue to endure, due to intergenerational experiences.

Supervision incorporates trust, respect and an understanding of the culture and life experience of the supervisee. For many professionals, the relationship is integral in having authentic conversations in supervision. When providing supervision in a cultural context, it is important to consider the professional relationship first and business second. The success of supervision is often dependent on the connection developed in the supervisory relationship, and the skills of the supervisor to build rapport and respect the cultural background of the supervisee. The essence of one's cultural background is crucial in the workplace given that we spend so much time there (Table 10.1).

If you have ever attended training on cultural awareness or cultural competency, you may have experienced some valuable insights into the transgenerational experiences of different cultures and how from the time of colonisation as a people, they have continued to experience ongoing challenges. Because of the story and the transgenerational experiences, some cultures continue to feel these impacts. For many people, transgenerational experiences have stripped away their beliefs and values, sense of culture, connection to land and spirituality. For Aboriginal people to be connected and feel the 'Kanyini', they need to be connected to all four elements of Kanyini to experience oneness (Harris & O'Donoghue, 2019).

Think of your own family background, culture and ancestry.

Table 10.1   The Context of Cultural Supervision

What do you believe is meant by the term cultural supervision?	
What things contribute to supervision being useful and effective for any person's cultural background?	
What is the benefit of providing supervision in a cultural context?	
What do you think the supervisor needs to be aware of?	
How can the supervisee ask you for what they need?	

What do you know about your family ancestors over the last few hundred years?

_____

_____

_____

_____

_____

What cultural protocols does your family observe?

_____

_____

_____

_____

_____

How long have these values or protocols been in place?

_____

_____

_____

_____

_____

From a cultural context, it is crucial to explore the supervisee's cultural responsibilities, obligations and protocols and incorporate this into the supervisory context. This gives the supervisee a clear message that you respect their cultural needs. As a supervisor, the other important thing to remember from a cultural context is the process of invitation. This means that the supervisor engages with the supervisee through the process of being invited to undertake supervision each time. For example, when I am supervising staff from different cultural backgrounds, I show respect through my language by asking questions about how comfortable they are meeting in the workplace, how they would like the conversation to be, what is important for them in the supervision discussion and are there any cultural needs they have. It shows that I am interested in how the supervision environment can assist them to feel comfortable and meet their needs. The process of invitation is highly brain friendly as it shows that the supervisee is put first in supervision. In Visual 10.2, the four elements of Kanyini and the connection to culture overview beliefs and values, spirituality, land and family. In mainstream supervision, family is not considered as part of the

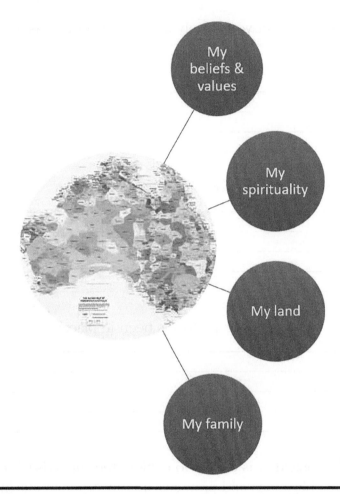

Visual 10.2   Components of Kanyini.

supervision discussion; however with many cultures, this comes foremost for people into their work, where family and work cannot be separated. The CASE supervision model outlined in this chapter can assist with this and maintain professional boundaries at the same time (Harris, 2018).

The Supervision Process

Most organisations provide supervision in a mainstream process by incorporating various supervision documents, written minutes and informal evaluation processes. Whilst supervision fits within an ethical and industrial environment, in many instances, mainstream supervision does not fit or align to cultural supervision. For cultural supervision to be accepted and useful for cultural backgrounds, it is crucial to use the process of cultural infusion. This means that all supervision processes and documents include cultural language, context and information. This can positively change the supervision, as the supervisee feels important and valued instead of supervision being a tick and flick process.

When providing supervision to staff with different cultural backgrounds, try not to overuse documents. Whilst this is normal practice in a mainstream context, in a cultural environment, presenting too many documents in supervision can provide a different message. When I provide supervision to staff with different cultural backgrounds, I ask questions in the first or second meeting that includes some of the intake questions from Chapter 2. I do not use all the documents in the conversation; instead, I complete the documents after the meeting. I also do the minutes differently. In a cultural context, I have a minute book with a copy of the CASE supervision model and handwrite minutes, so it is not overly formal. The relationship is one of the most important aspects in supervision. As long as I ensure that the documentation is accurately completed and meets industrial requirements, being flexible is the key to providing effective cultural supervision. Visual 10.3 shows what the supervision minute template looks like.

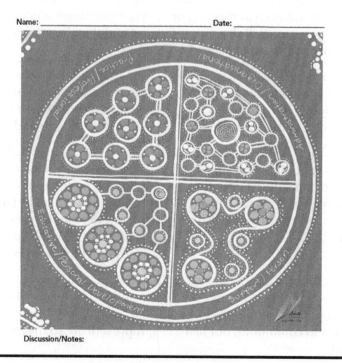

Visual 10.3 CASE™ supervision minute template.

Supervisees may have to manage various complex situations given the duality of their roles in both the organisation and their community. Staff often manage situations where they are required to communicate particular things in their family and community that an organisation may see that is confidential – i.e., information about particular individual or family members. This needs to be managed carefully and with integrity in the organisational environment.

The supervision process is useful as it assists the supervisor to reflect on what to consider in supervision discussions. It also assists in setting the agenda, documenting conversations, knowing where to meet and understanding what outcomes are expected. Table 10.2 reminds supervisors of what is important when setting up the supervisory process from a cultural perspective.

Table 10.2   Facets of Cultural Supervision

Particular stories, focus of discussions, articles, etc. can be a difficult reminder of past cultural struggles, so it is important to keep discussions positive	Ask the supervisee what is important for them and their culture in supervision
Asking permission, seek permission to be invited into any space such as meeting or professional supervision will show a supportive stance as the supervisor	Explain what you mean, ensure that your intentions are known, listen a lot and then listen some more
You may want to know the other person's story; however, they may not be able to talk about particular things, i.e., health, family, etc. so respect that and don't let it be a barrier in supervision	Due to cultural aspects, some supervisees may be hesitant to talk about aspects of their role, their culture, protocols and obligations and not be able to tell you that
The supervisory space is about building the relationship and cultural integrity first, then focus on aspects of the role, responsibilities and organisational requirements	Time may be seen as something different in different cultures, so having ample time to talk is crucial, try not to rush the person in the conversation. Use your language skills to let the person know about the time.
In some cultures, working with one person represent their people as a whole culture and community, not just the individual	In some cultures, celebration is about all people, they celebrate all, they represent all, so things affect all

(Continued)

Table 10.2 (*Continued*)   **Facets of Cultural Supervision**

Culture carries and holds all members of the community in a connected space and time	Supervisees generally see any issues and concerns in their role or work is not just about them, but all their community
Culture is often founded and respected by storytelling and being with each other, not about mainstream processes and frameworks	Supervision needs to be focused and held in a storytelling and yarning space so that both people are connected
For storytelling to occur, it needs to be held in a relaxing environment, not a formal clinical space or process environment	Yarning (conversation, supervision discussion, storytelling) is not about time, it is about the relationship
Yarning and storytelling are important to ensure key outcomes in the role are achieved	There needs to be meaning and rhythm in the conversation, not just about the task and process
Ask what language is useful and be invited to use it in the supervision discussion	If you understand cultural infusion, outcomes in the role can be more readily met
Supervisees need to feel culturally respected and safe to feel a connectedness of belonging in supervision	Supervision can be more effective if meetings take place in the third space (i.e., by invitation so the supervisee feels it is their space and the supervisor is coming to that place with them rather than vice versa)

Can I come into your world so we can yarn?
rather than me asking you to come into mine
Tracey H

I need to understand both systems
We need to walk in a culturally infused system
Can we talk in your world?
Let's think like you and I are connected in the one cultural space
Resect is to speak in your culture
I will listen to your world
May I ask you through invitation
I will ask you about how you like to work
I will be mindful of how we work together to achieve
(Adapted from Uncle Bob Randall)

**We are first answerable to our communities, then to
the organisations in which we work, that is when I feel my culture
is respected**
Lucy P

Connecting to the Third Space

From a cultural perspective, supervisees interact with their work environment through connection to their cultural landscape, family networks and values. Supervision is a connective experience whereby both parties come together in a space to share information that is intentional, meaningful and purposeful.

Providing culturally respectful supervision means setting up the third space. The third space concept is about the supervisor being invited into the supervisory space that connects both people together. This does not mean that the supervisor formally asks the supervisee if they can attend supervision, it is more about the supervisor being respectful in their language and leadership skills. In mainstream organisations, cultural aspects are often not considered and supervisees can feel as though they are going into the supervisor's space driven by the supervisor, *'My Space'*. This does not meet the supervisee's needs as it does not include cultural aspects in the context of the supervisee's role, cultural approaches or consider the principles of Kanyini (Bhabha, 1994). If the supervision is set up in *'Your Space'*, this is referred to as the supervisee's space. Whilst supervision is predominantly about the supervisee and meeting the requirements of the role, having supervision in Your Space is not conducive to high-performance outcomes. When supervision is set up using the third space concept, both parties come together in a united and connected time and place. It is a mutually respectful space where both the supervisor and supervisee interact from their own culture as individuals, and with each other's culture. Even with the power difference given the supervisor is in a higher-level role in the organisational structure, the third space assists to neutralise the power differential. Using language such as the third space reminds the supervisor to minimise the power aspect in the conversation and engage the supervisee in a way where they feel supported and valued in their role (Falender & Shafranske, 2017).

Connecting through the third space encourages the supervisee to think about where they would like to meet and opens up the supervisory conversation so that both parties feel comfortable. It allows the supervisee to consider how information is shared in a collaborative space and ensures the supervisor remains conscious and intentional in the language used during the supervisory discussion. It also ensures that the supervisor is aware of what is culturally appropriate to discuss, and what areas may not be appropriate for the supervisee given their cultural background.

We generally feel connected to something. It may be the bush, the sea, other people or a place that is special. Something that makes us feel as though we can be open, ourselves and have a connection to it. From a cultural context and thinking about your own background, reflect on the following questions on where you feel connected the most.

- Do you feel more at home near water, in the bush, at one with the clouds or the sky?
- Where do you feel more at peace?
- How do you feel when you are near fresh or saltwater?
- What does it feel like when you are in the bush or out of the city?
- Where do you feel a sense of belonging?
- Do you feel at one with the tides, like to be with the moon and the stars?
- What energy do any of these given you?

If you think back to your childhood, what was your identity as a child growing up? What was your first memory of?
Saltwater

Freshwater

Land

Sky/Moon/Sun

Saltwater

Saltwater provides us with the fruits of the ocean. It has power, energy and is majestic under different weather conditions. It is full of energy, can be calm one moment and when the winds arise, it becomes a forceful energy. Saltwater comes and goes with the tides. It interacts and connects to the sun and moon. Saltwater has healing properties and a sour taste.

Freshwater

Freshwater is calm, but if you listen you can hear its voice and how it talks. It is steadfast in how it allows the water to travel downstream and out into the saltwater. It changes temperature with the changes of season. It can dry up in drought and be plentiful when the rains come. Freshwater is the place where many birds and animals come to bathe, drink, gather and communicate together. It has a rhythmic power that brings a sense of peace and calm.

The Land

The land and bush provide food and nourishment. It can be harsh and hold such beauty. The sun and moon change their colours and look depending on the seasons. It provides a space of peace and quiet and is a resting and living space for birds and other animals. Whilst it changes, there is a predictability with the seasons. It withstands Mother Nature's elements and despite being ravaged by fire, floods and other elements, it continues to respond strongly.

Sky/Moon/Sun

The sky is a place of dreaming. It allows us to vision and imagine. The sky is about Mother Nature and is the link to mother earth. We look up to it, we speak to it and it provides us with answers allowing us to reflect. It also provides the much needed nourishment to the land through the rain that comes from the sky. This water then runs into the freshwater and in turn the freshwater runs into the saltwater. Visual 10.4 provides an overview of the relationship between each of these elements.

Cultural Infusion Practice

In the majority of organisations and businesses, staff conduct their role in a professional capacity adhering to organisational policies, procedures, legislation, practice standards, codes of ethics and the organisational structure. They are also directed in their work by their position description, and performance is usually evaluated on an annual basis through a

Visual 10.4   Sky, land, fresh and saltwater.

formal review process. The organisational business system dictates how the employee works and how they operate in their role, keeping in mind what the organisation needs first.

From a cultural perspective, employees often undertake their role first through cultural beliefs, values and protocols and then the needs of the organisation and the business system second. I see the tensions in many organisations where cultural awareness is evident; however, cultural infusion practices have not been put into place. By this I mean that the organisational structure, policy framework and practices have not fully implemented cultural aspects across all parts of the organisation. There may be policies that relate to particular cultural aspects; however, it is often tokenistic in its intent and practice. Cultural infusion demonstrates that the organisation considers cultural practices and processes in everything it does. For supervisees to engage fully in the supervision space, cultural infusion is critical. When cultural infusion is absent or has limited presence, it sends confusing messages to staff. It can be interpreted that the organisation is culturally aware and mentions cultural practice in various policies; however, the organisational is predominantly operated through a mainstream lens. Cultural infusion sends the message that staff from all cultures are valued and that all aspects of the organisation align with cultural protocols and practices. Through the following questions, consider how your organisation or business considers cultural infusion (Harris & O'Donoghue, 2019).

How does your organisation demonstrate cultural infusion practices?

_____

_____

_____

_____

How has your organisation implemented cultural infusion practices and over what time?

_____

_____

_____

_____

What do you think your organisation can do to further demonstrate cultural infusion practices?

_____

_____

_____

_____

As a supervisor how do you demonstrate cultural infusion practices?

_____

_____

_____

_____

What else could you do as a supervisor to demonstrate this to your supervisees?

_____

_____

_____

_____

> ***Review the organisation through a cultural infusion lens as this will assist to find the gaps and promote a more inclusive workplace.***

Cultural infusion is about evidencing an integrative way of thinking and being in an organisation. It is about moving all aspects of the organisation into third space thinking. It is where culture is infused into the very fabric of the organisation, including

- Organisational documents and how they incorporate cultural language
- Policies and procedures include cultural protocols
- Meetings both formal and informal are held in the third space
- Language, words, terms and phrases incorporate cultural language
- Meeting places are culturally infused
- The physical environment is about culture
- Decision-making processes are evidence informed through culture
- Leadership approaches are culturally dynamic and led by third space mindset
- The organisational structure enhances cultural integrity
- The values are infused by cultural language
- The Board of Management engages in culturally appropriate supervision and training
- Discussions and conversations are all held using cultural values
- The organisation's employee assistance program service demonstrates cultural infusion practices
- Supervision is all about culture and relationships
- Publications (i.e., Annual Report)
- Mainstream practices are moved to be culturally infused
- Social media platforms demonstrate cultural infusion

When organisations incorporate culturally infused practices, it is easier to ensure the organisation operates within high-performance principles. It assists leaders and supervisors to have difficult discussions when issues arise, as staff clearly know the intent and purpose of the open conversation. I am often asked to work with businesses and organisations to assist them to manage performance and industrial processes with staff who are not performing in the role as required. Usually, an assessment has been made by the organisation that the employee is not achieving the requirements of the role or there are conduct issues. What I often find is that the organisation has not put into place cultural infusion practices and does not understand cultural aspects, and therefore does not get the best from the employee. On many occasions, the issues have not been around performance, but more that the employee does not understand organisational requirements, nor does the organisation understand how to incorporate the third space concept, cultural infusion or an effective language framework to resolve issues.

The end result is that the employee may be terminated or disciplined in a way that affects them in the longer term. When performance processes occur in the third space, the organisation uses particular language to show that the conversation is more positive and developmental in its intent.

Steps towards Cultural Infusion

The following features foster the process of cultural infusion and continue to enhance it (Visual 10.5).

Visual 10.5   Cultural infusion framework.

1. Train staff, supervisors and leaders to understand how to provide cultural supervision. Remember, it is not a mainstream process but a cultural experience in yarning and storytelling;
2. Engage the process of invitation in supervision and meetings;
3. Gather information from staff in culturally specific roles to continue to build the organisation's cultural knowledge base;
4. Understand what is important for staff to bring to supervision that supports cultural conversation;
5. Train all staff to understand the concept of cultural infusion practices;
6. Ensure all staff understand that many cultures continue to feel the struggles from transgenerational experiences;
7. Ensure the workplace has a third space as a meeting place;
8. Review all organisational documents, frameworks, tools and resources to ensure they follow the principles of cultural infusion and
9. Develop a language framework that represents cultural infusion.

Important things for supervisors to consider

- Demonstrate an understanding of the intergenerational experiences of all cultures;
- Understand that different cultures are a living culture;
- Cultural obligations and protocols may not finish at 5 pm;
- Each cultural community is the same and different;
- Be invited to engage – use the third space concept to demonstrate respect;
- Be able to articulate values and attributes of culture around Kanyini and the oneness of culture;
- Understand how to connect in a relationship of trust, respect and understand the cultural needs of the employee;
- Use language that is culturally relevant and appropriate;
- The supervisor needs to check any pre-conceived ideas, assumptions or biases that may be hidden in their own self-talk;
- Supervisors have attended cultural awareness training and bring this into Yarn Up Time;
- Understand how to engage cultural safety practices;
- Always ask to enter Yarn Up Time in their space, not assume that you are requesting the staff member to come to Yarn Up Time;
- Understand if the staff member is connected more to land, sky, fresh or saltwater;

- Understand the concept of yarning, what might be appropriate to bring into Yarn Up Time and what staff may not be able to bring into the conversation;
- Be clear on what the staff member's cultural responsibilities, protocols and obligations are;
- Understand the importance of non-verbal communication, including the language of silence and deep listening;
- Be aware of significant days that are important to any culture;
- See what your role is to embed cultural infusion in the organisation;
- Ensure any external supervisors understand the skills and knowledge required to provide Yarn Up Time supervision in the intent in which it is provided;
- Ensure any external supervisors have attended cultural awareness training;
- All supervisors have had appropriate Yarn Up Time training prior to providing supervision;
- Be clear on how administration processes will be undertaken in Yarn Up Time, given it is not a mainstream process;
- Know which community your staff are from, learn about their history and background;
- Have cultural supervision using a Yarning Mat and
- Work with community to demonstrate the spirit of collaboration (Visual 10.6).

When you think of professional supervision in both a mainstream and a cultural context, what do you see as the differences in the following areas given what has been discussed in this chapter?

1. Documentation (i.e., taking and recording minutes, schedules, etc.).

_____

_____

_____

_____

2. Supervision process.

_____

_____

_____

_____

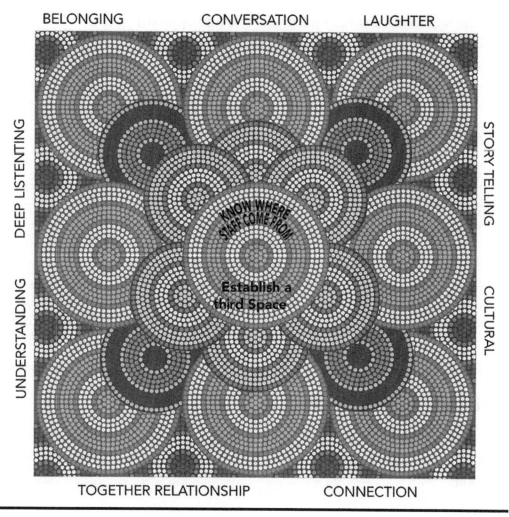

BELONGING   CONVERSATION   LAUGHTER

DEEP LISTENING

UNDERSTANDING

STORY TELLING

CULTURAL

KNOW WHERE
STAFF COME FROM

Establish a
third Space

TOGETHER RELATIONSHIP   CONNECTION

Visual 10.6   Yarn Up Time framework.

3. Evaluating supervision.

_____

_____

_____

_____

4. The environment where supervision takes place.

_____

_____

_____

_____

5. The supervisor's communication, style and approach.

_____

_____

_____

_____

6. The skills and knowledge of the supervisor.

_____

_____

_____

_____

7. How an agenda is developed for each meeting.

_____

_____

_____

_____

Culturally Specific Roles

Now that we have talked about cultural infusion and how organisations need to incorporate a cultural infusion framework, let's look at Julie's situation:

Case Study

Anne is a cultural practice advisor. She has been in her role for one year and is the primary contact for all staff in the organisation where they have cultural questions or need cultural advising. Anne works closely with her supervisor/ manager Dan to ensure that staff are well trained in cultural awareness and bring cultural principles to their work. Anne is a community Elder and is often required to attend to community business. On this occasion, Anne is required to attend to Sorry Business (her Aunty has passed away and there is time for reflection and ceremony). Anne has only three days leave available; however, she needs to be away from work for just over six weeks.

Dan, her supervisor is supportive of Anne's role and has allowed her to take time off in her senior role when needed, however believes that this has been taken advantage of during the time she has started in her role. Not only is Dan (non-Indigenous) not supportive of Anne having this additional time off for Sorry Business, he indicated that she would need to seek special leave from the director, and this was going to take four working days. He offered to start the paperwork for Anne, but advised that approval would need to be granted for that amount of time off prior to her attending to cultural business.

Anne did not feel confident in advising or speaking with her supervisor about her role in community and that she did not have a choice not to undertake the business she was required to do. Anne did not know how to assert herself to say that she was required to be away for that period of time and that she did not have a week to seek approval. Anne felt as though her supervisor did not understand her cultural responsibilities and did not speak to anyone in the workplace or her family about this. Anne is feeling overwhelmed, angry, disappointed and all trust has been broken with Dan.

This scenario is not uncommon in many of the workplaces I have provided consulting services to. It is typical of what occurs when there is a lot of time needed to attend ceremony in relation to Sorry Business. It is equally as challenging for workplaces to be able to provide adequate coverage whilst staff are away on cultural business. The other challenge I find is that organisational policies are often not reflective of cultural infusion practices and reflect mainstream thinking. For staff to feel valued, it is important that cultural infusion is incorporated across all aspects of the organisation. In thinking about Anne's situation, consider the following questions.

1. What are your thoughts and feelings when you read a scenario like Anne's?
2. What personal values and beliefs are challenged for you?
3. What beliefs do you think Anne's supervisor Dan holds? What management responsibilities does he have?
4. What dilemmas come up for Anne and for her supervisor Dan?
5. What would you do in this situation and why?
6. How might other staff see this situation?
7. What does the organisation need to do in these situations?
8. What might Anne need to do to follow her supervisor's instructions given the lack of leave she has?
9. What things can be implemented for this situation not to occur again?
10. How might you incorporate a third space?
11. How might the organisation have handled this more effectively?

Many organisations now have the provision for culturally specific roles and cultural leave, however what does this really mean?

Roles like Anne's may have a job title as cultural advisor, or cultural practice supervisor. These roles provide specific cultural information, support, advice and consultation to staff in the organisation. They can provide cultural awareness training and contribute specifically to policy and procedures to ensure that cultural infusion is across the organisation. These staff play an important role in their own position and across the whole organisation through supporting leaders, managers and supervisors to understand things such as

- The transgenerational experiences of many cultures
- Cultural integrity
- Inclusion of cultural language and messaging in organisational policy and frameworks
- Kanyini and other cultural protocols and language
- Deep listening, being in the quiet
- Understand how to meet in the third space
- Assist staff and leaders to understand how to work with cultural obligations and protocols and still meet organisational imperatives, outputs and outcomes
- The importance of infusing cultures

There are many staff like Anne who are employed in a mainstream role. It is equally important to engage their cultural expertise and understand the things that have been mentioned above. In both situations, staff like Anne have obligations and protocols they need to follow, and this can cause tension between other staff and impact on organisational requirements. From a cultural perspective, beliefs and values are foremost and when staff are compromised in the role they have in community, the organisation can be viewed by community as being disrespectful. It is crucial that leaders and supervisors understand the dilemmas that arise for staff and the tensions and challenges they experience when they work in mainstream organisations that do not incorporate cultural infusion practices. It is crucial to develop a plan of how cultural obligations and protocols are managed, what the organisation's role and expectations are in particular situations, how support is provided and how these things are communicated to all staff.

Cultural Priorities, Protocols and Responsibilities

When you think about various cultural priorities, protocols and responsibilities of staff, what comes to your mind?

_____

_____

_____

_____

What cultural protocols are you aware that different cultures have?

_____

_____

_____

_____

What cultural protocols and obligations does your organisation include in policy and process?

_____

_____

_____

_____

This gives us some perspective on the importance of culture for staff, and how as supervisors it is imperative to understand, remember and respect cultural perspectives. It can assist you as a supervisor to include particular words and language around cultural priorities, protocols and responsibilities in policies so that cultural infusion is achieved. Remember that supporting staff from different cultures to attend cultural events are important. This sends a message to all staff and the community that you have undertaken a cultural infusion process. Connecting to community whenever you can also demonstrates support for cultural priorities, protocols and responsibilities. When possible, work alongside Elders as this brings cultural integrity into the workplace. We have been discussing the importance of integration of cultural infusion into the fabric of the organisation through cultural integrity, but this can be challenging at times. You may feel torn between supporting staff to meet their cultural priorities; however, other staff may feel that there is a difference between how the organisation manages different situations.

So, let's consider this for a moment!

Whilst in supervision, one of your staff raises concerns that they are being treated differently to one of their colleagues from another cultural background. The employee suggests that you do not take seriously their cultural protocols and obligations in community and that you treat them with cultural disrespect. The employee reports that you make them conform to the policies in the organisation where they are not culturally appropriate or fit cultural protocols. They provide an example where you have asked them to stop referring to yourself in cultural language and to use more mainstream language.

This raises a lot of questions for consideration.

What are your initial thoughts about the scenario?

_____

_____

_____

_____

What do you see as the ethical dilemmas?

_____

_____

_____

_____

How would you manage this situation?

_____

_____

_____

_____

How would you ensure that your organisation supports staff to feel supported and holds cultural integrity in their own community and in the organisation?

_____

_____

_____

_____

What would you change in your organisation's policies to encourage cultural integrity?

_____

_____

_____

_____

Yarn Up Time Supervision

What Is Yarn Up Time?

In many cultures, the word yarning is used to have a conversation. Yarning is a place where two people come together with the intent of having a respectful and relational discussion. As Harris (2018) suggests, Yarn Up Time is about having an intentional conversation within the context of professional supervision, which incorporates the principles of yarning from a cultural perspective. Using cultural language, Yarn Up Time is the opportunity for staff to meet in the third space with their supervisor, and to engage in yarning about their role, cultural perspectives, organisational needs, family, community, connection and ongoing development in their professional role (Harris, 2018).

Amovita has designed a supervision model that has been developed specifically for Aboriginal staff in Australia. Whilst many Aboriginal staff use the PASE™ (Professional/Practice, Administrative/Line Management, Support/Person, Educative/Professional Development) model as outlined in Chapter 4, it was important to design a visual model that aligned to the yarning process. The visual supervision model titled CASE Yarn Up Time supervision model aligns to the other models, i.e., the PASE model of professional supervision as outlined in Chapter 4. As with the other models, CASE model has four quadrants that focus on the C (Cultural Practice/Professional), A (Administrative/Line Management), S (Support/Person) and E (Educative/Professional Development) aspects of the supervisee's role.

> **C: Cultural/Professional**
> **A: Administrative/Line Management**
> **S: Support/Person**
> **E: Educational/Professional Development**

There are clear differences in the way the CASE Yarn Up Time supervision model has been designed and developed when compared with other supervision models developed by Amovita. It has been titled Yarn Up Time to ensure that supervision is undertaken from a cultural perspective and considers the cultural background of the supervisee. Having the CASE Yarn Up Time supervision model highlights the difference between cultural and mainstream supervision. When providing supervision from a cultural perspective, consider how to reduce or limit documentation in supervision. I have found with some cultural backgrounds that incorporating too many documents into supervision can be taken as disrespectful and break the relational connection. Consider what to include in the supervisory process such as minutes, policy, the process and what framework to use. The CASE Yarn Up Time supervision model is useful to maintain integrity in supervision as the visual model can also act as a minute template to document discussions.

Cultural integrity in supervision

- Where possible, reduce administrative processes, templates and documents;
- Incorporate cultural infusion language into conversations;
- Agree on how to document discussions;
- Be respectful about things that cannot be discussed from a cultural perspective;
- Use language that shows deep listening;
- Learn new words, phrases and statements that are from the supervisee's cultural background;
- Where possible, seek permission to meet on country;
- Each and every meeting seek invitation to meet in the third space;
- Have supervision meetings in the process of storytelling and yarning and
- Agree on how the yarning is documented, particularly in mainstream purposes.

It is important to ask the supervisee what things may not be appropriate to talk about in Yarn Up Time. Check what the protocols are important to adhere to. These things may include:

- Not being able to talk about particular topics, i.e., mental health;
- Using the name of a person who has passed;
- Men and women's business;
- Using directive questioning;

- The supervisee not being able to talk to particular staff in the workplace, i.e., a family member;
- When topics have to be discussed in the presence of an Elder;
- Engage in the third space;
- Ensure that questions in Yarn Up Time are not overly directive but allow the supervisee the space and time to respond to any questions that support the yarning conversation;
- Try not to overly use closed questions.

Each of the quadrants are represented by different symbols that are all related and integrated. The colours have been chosen intentionally as they allow both the supervisor and supervisee to use a storytelling approach and derive their own meaning from the supervisory conversation (Harris & O'Donoghue, 2019). The agenda is developed for supervision as the meeting commences, and relates to the C, A, S or E quadrants. The symbols can assist the supervisee to relate the conversation to their cultural background and therefore feel culturally respected and valued (Visual 10.7).

Visual 10.7 CASE™ Yarn Up Time model.

The CASE Yarn Up Time Model Quadrants

Cultural/Professional

In the model, the C (Cultural/Professional) (top left) quadrant focus the supervision discussion on the professional aspects of the supervisee's role. The symbols in the C (Cultural/Professional) quadrant have been used to demonstrate how the supervisee demonstrates their professional identity through a cultural lens. As outlined in this quadrant, the symbols are connected through lines that depict the journey that everyone in the organisation takes to achieve a collective outcome. The circles represent a never-ending positive energy that radiates to others in the professional environment. The lines also display strength as they are parallel to each other in unity. This is the only way that individuals in the organisation can come together to ensure success is achieved. The C (Cultural/Professional) quadrant includes principles of Kanyini, as the supervisee connects their sense of self, culture and heritage in their role as a professional and person. This quadrant encourages supervisees to demonstrate their cultural skills as they share their heritage that empowers others to be connected to the work they do. Discussion may include how the supervisee integrates cultural knowledge and experience into practice. Topics discussed in this quadrant also include the supervisee's professional role, professional practice using cultural skills, cultural ethics, professional boundaries, cultural infusion, cultural integrity, use of language in the organisational context and how the supervisee articulates their approach to the work they do.

Administration/Line Management

The symbols in the A (Administrative/Line Management) (top right) quadrant are small circles that join with each other. The circles represent how the supervisee meets the requirements of their role in the organisational system, and how they inter-relate to each other in a web of networking and connection. It shows how each person in the organisation is important, for without each individual the team would not be effective. The use of the Blue tones is indicative of open and transparent communication, trust and integrity. They represent the space and energy for free-flowing supervision conversations to ensure the organisational requirements of the role are met. In this quadrant, there are many small circles that all connect to the one larger circle in the middle, which is the organisational system. There are different colours and symbols in the small circles to demonstrate how the system has to integrate together to achieve its desired result. All of the lines connect to each other to also represent the perfect synergy and balance that organisations need. Agenda topics in supervision include how the supervisee meets the requirements in the role, connections between community and organisation, policies and procedures, leave planning and workflow management.

Support/Person

The S (Support/Person) (bottom right) quadrant provides a focus in supervision to support the supervisee in their role. It gives the professional supervisor the opportunity to support the professional so that they can meet the requirements of the role and their community. The larger circles and smaller circles represent the different levels of support for the professional in the organisation, and how this links to the supervisee's cultural background. The use of the yellow and orange tones represents warmth and compassion, whilst the lines and dots around each of the circles represent the pathway of support between each of the elements. The lines and dots are the supervisor and supervisee sharing the journey together and remind the supervisor to engage in deep listening. The symbols characterise how important the connection is between the supervisor and supervisee. When communication does not flow properly, challenges arise between organisational needs and cultural responsibilities of the supervisee in their role. Agenda topics that may be discussed in this quadrant of supervision include cultural obligations and protocols, storytelling and yarning, connection with land, family, environment, cultural integrity, relationships, oneness, belonging, deep listening, values and well being. Other topics in supervision for this area may include team dynamics, professional relationships and how the supervisor encourages, appreciates and demonstrates the valuable role of the supervisee.

Educative/Professional Development

The E (Educative/Professional Development, bottom left) quadrant is all about the continual development of the supervisee in their professional role. Development and growth are a gradual process and the small circles in this quadrant provide the message that from smaller things larger things grow. The E (Educative/Professional Development) quadrant shows the smaller circles that progressively grow to become large circles depicting ongoing development of knowledge. The smaller circles are the seeds of knowledge, as we all continue to transfer our knowledge into practice. The use of the green tone signifies growth, awakening, enlightenment and insight. Learning and growing is passed on from generation to generation, and cultural knowledge is maintained and shared over time. The dots around the larger circles show the transfer of knowledge from the smaller circles, and how they are placed within the large circles to keep over time. Agenda topics that may be discussed in supervision include how knowledge is shared between the supervisor and supervisee and how they engage in the ongoing process of growth. Visual 10.8 overviews some of the agenda topics that may be discussed in each of the quadrants. As outlined in Chapter 4, the topics can be discussed

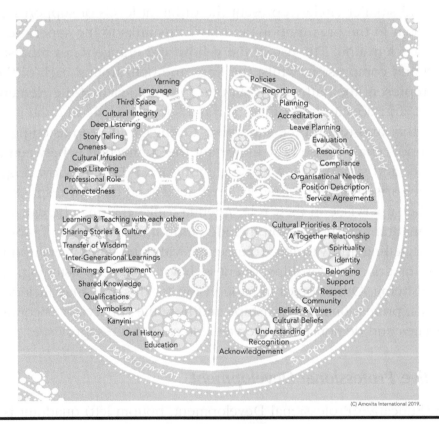

(C) Amovita International 2019.

Visual 10.8   CASE™ detailed Yarn Up Time model.

from any of the quadrants where the supervisee changes the focus of the discussion.

The lines around the outside of the CASE Yarn Up Time model show footprints and a dot painting that represent the journey that the supervisor and supervisee take together. Through the supervisor's skills and knowledge, they ensure the supervisee performs the role to the level required by the organisation, monitors their practice, feels supported to do their job well and engage in continual development (Harris & O'Donoghue, 2019; Harris, 2018).

Summary

This chapter has explored cultural supervision practice and the importance of having a cultural supervision model. When using a supervision model that considers the cultural background of the supervisee, the CASE Yarn Up Time model can be used to consider the needs of the supervisee. Reflect on the following questions about the cultural aspects of supervision.

What have been the key things you have gained from reading this chapter on cultural supervision?
What have been your reflections about this chapter?
List three things that you will take from this chapter to incorporate into your supervisory role.
What do you think will be useful to talk to your supervisee/s about regarding this chapter?
What steps are important to ensure supervision incorporates cultural?

Chapter 11

The Feedback Loop

Key focus for this chapter

- The importance of providing effective feedback
- The language of feedback
- Providing neurosocial feedback
- Using resource in the feedback process
- The process of feedback
- Open communication in feedback discussions
- The conversation framework

Introduction

Feedback is something that occurs in most conversations between two people. Knowing how to provide effective feedback takes skill. Understanding how to prime the other person's brain, how to be developmental even when the discussion may be difficult, knowing the right language to use, words or terms takes practice. Providing feedback is a professional activity and ethical responsibility that comes with being a supervisor and line manager. Feedback can be particularly difficult when someone is not performing well in their role, the supervisee is experiencing well-being issues, or when they are stressed, exhausted or burnt out. Having open conversations in these situations requires particular care and a clear framework.

Providing feedback and having open discussions in supervision are crucial for practice excellence, maintaining self-care and ensuring the supervisee meets organisational requirements in the role. Too often feedback is undertaken in a way that is not useful, does not consider appropriate language and does not follow a framework that is developmental. This chapter explores the importance of helpful feedback using a conversation framework. It provides a range of tools and resources that can be used in a way that the supervisee feels supported with clear outcomes. I am sure when you read this chapter you will remember the times where you have experienced feedback that was useful, and other times where the feedback was delivered in a way that made you feel terrible. As a supervisor, it is important when taking supervisees through the intake questions in supervision that there is a discussion about how the supervisee would like to receive feedback, how to have open conversations and how any performance or conduct issues follow a different process that sits outside of the supervision discussion. Initially, all feedback needs to be discussed from the *Support/ Person* (S) quadrant in any of the supervision models outlined in Chapter 4. When the supervisee needs to move into a performance process, a different discussion will take place.

When feedback is provided, it is to be undertaken using a clear framework and incorporate neurosocial principles, i.e., mindful of the use of language, understand the other person's beliefs and values around the issue, be developmental at all times and have clear outcomes where the supervisee has the opportunity to recorrect the situation so they see success.

Consider for a moment when you have provided feedback to your supervisees.

1. What framework or process do you use when providing feedback either as a line manager or professional supervisor? What approach do you use to ensure you seek a positive outcome?

_____

_____

_____

_____

_____

2. How do you like to receive feedback from your own line manager or supervisor?

_____

_____

_____

_____

_____

3. What do you see as the key principles of providing feedback?

_____

_____

_____

_____

_____

4. What do you believe are important skills to have as a supervisor in providing difficult feedback?

_____

_____

_____

_____

_____

The Feedback Loop

Engaging feedback in a looped process provides the supervisee with the opportunity to participate proactively and feel what they have to say is important and heard. In a communication loop, it is always a shared experience and the supervisor primes (prepares) the supervisee to reduce any threat response, i.e., the fight–flight–freeze mechanism. When feedback is provided without adequate priming, there is a high risk of the supervisee assuming what the feedback is about and will consider the feedback to be negative. As a threat response, the brain will dump cortisol and result in the supervisee not clearly hearing the feedback (Farmer, 2009; Harris, 2018).

The next feedback framework, The SPIRIT Feedback Framework includes six elements in the feedback process. The S (Be specific), P (Purposeful), I (Innovative), R (Relational), I (Intuitive) and T (Timed) framework assist supervisors to be focused in the feedback process. It also ensures that

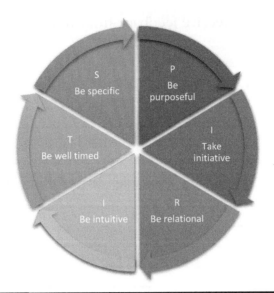

Visual 11.1   SPIRIT feedback framework.

the relevant areas are covered in the conversation, so the supervisee understands what is included in the process (Visual 11.1).

S: Be Specific

Our brains do not like surprises. They are designed to be well prepared for conversations, particularly when we are receiving feedback for different reasons. It is important to prepare the person for the conversation by letting them know what is to be discussed, how long the conversation will take and what the intended outcome is. Providing feedback in a loop assists both parties to contribute to the discussion and stops the risk of the discussion being one sided. Even in discussions about performance, it is important that the supervisee feels they are contributing to the discussion and feel heard. Feedback is harder to hear when it is too broad. When the discussion is specific, both parties stay on track and come back to key points if either party diverts from where the discussion needs to be. When multiple topics are needed in a feedback discussion, try to group them into themes and discuss the specifics of each of them. If there are too many topics in the agenda, it can overwhelm the supervisee and be counter-productive. Feedback topics can be explored from each of the PASE™ (Professional/Practice, Administrative/Line Management, Support/Person, Educative/Professional Development) supervision model quadrants as they relate to the relevant topic. For example, if feedback needs to be provided about policy it could be discussed from the *Administrative/Line Manager* (A) perspective. If feedback needs to be given in relation to practice, it could be discussed from the *Practice/Professional* (P) perspective.

P: Purposeful

Feedback needs to be purposeful at all times. Ensure that the necessary preparation has been done before the feedback is provided. Have a plan of what to say, how to say it and why you are saying those things. Providing positive feedback and acknowledgement is easy for the supervisee to hear, whilst the difficult conversations are hard to hear. Going off on a tangent is not helpful, unless it needs to be provided in another context to stay on track even if the other person takes the conversation in different directions. Purposeful feedback enables the supervisee to feel supported and can motivate change as required. When feedback is not purposeful, the supervisee's cognitive and decision-making biases can impact the thinking process and therefore influence how the supervisee understands the feedback. It is hard to receive feedback particularly when it is challenging, so making it meaningful and purposeful helps to work through the agenda.

I: Initiative

Be proactive in being able to explore the topic, not looking back too much but being future focused. When one or both people get stuck in any negative loop such as judgement or blame, this is an indication that they are coming to an adolescent or child space rather than from an adult mindset. If you notice the other person getting stuck, is unable to hear, becoming emotional or engaging in negative language – change tact, take a break or shift the conversation to a place where both people move forward. For example, if the conversation is challenging, language that may be helpful could be … 'this seems to be a difficult conversation where we are stuck at the moment, let's take a five-minute break and see if I can change my language or how the message is coming across' … or 'it seems we are both stuck in this point, what language would you use to move us forward'? Be kind, have empathy, engage in leadership skills around assessing what may be going on for the other person and use communication skills to shift the conversation if required.

R: Relational

Despite how positive or difficult the feedback is, it is the challenging conversations that are often not delivered very well. For this to be done well, supervisors need to have communication skills that include how to prime the other person for the conversation, how to reduce a threat response for the other person, understand how decision making and cognitive biases impact in the feedback process, the role of cortisol when the other person is under stress and understand how the brain engages its braking system through the use of language.

Despite the nature of the supervisor/supervisee relationship, any feedback needs to be provided through a positive exchange to maintain the professional relationship. This requires the supervisor to be highly skilled in the feedback process, know what words, terms and language to use that maximises opportunity for the professional relationship to remain intact. Where the supervisor has a dual role of line manager and professional supervisor, this can be difficult when providing feedback that is challenging to hear. Where the supervisor maintains the relational aspect of the discussion, specific language is used throughout, for example the supervisor might say … 'this conversation may be difficult due to …. However, as your line manager and supervisor, my focus in this discussion is to work through the issues together and find the right solution that will move things forward. I will use language that demonstrates support of you in this discussion and let's focus our discussion and language on how we will work through this together…'

I: Intuitive

Our enteric or gut brain is highly intuitive and can sense things before our conscious mind recognises the thinking process. When we connect to our intuition on a regular basis, it assists to support our decision making. Supervisors who are highly attuned to the use of self as a professional have a professional identity framework, hold values around integrity and trust as important in relationships and can read different contexts; they can tailor feedback and language that has a positive influence in the feedback process. Supervisors need to trust their own skills and abilities to provide feedback with language that ensures an effective outcome.

T: Timed Well

Our brain does not generally like surprises, particularly where feedback is challenging and there has been no prior discussion about the particular topic. Our brains are designed to be primed for conversations and know what is going to be clearly discussed either before the conversation begins or at the beginning of the discussion and then given time to prepare for it. It is important not to provide challenging feedback when the supervisee is already overwhelmed, is unwell or not in a space to hear what is going to be discussed. Where this is the case, the supervisor needs to explore the timing of the feedback or assist the supervisee to be in space to hear detail of the conversation.

Now that we have looked at the SPIRIT (Specific, Purposeful, Initiative, Relational, Intuitive, Timed) feedback framework consider your messaging and communication style. What messages do you want to impart and what might the other person pick up from you with the message you give. If you know this and some things about the other person, then even the most difficult conversations can have a positive outcome. As a supervisor we have discussed cognitive biases and therefore there will be times where you will not know how the other person is going to respond to feedback. This means it is important to prime the other person in almost all conversations you have. This will keep you conscious and remember what the best language and communication might be. Consider the following prompts in the feedback process:

■ What is the purpose of the feedback? Are you looking to receive feedback?
■ How might your feedback be perceived?

- How will you prepare the supervisee for the feedback?
- What do you need to say, want to say and how to say it?
- What do you know about the supervisee's self-perception, beliefs and values?
- What is the purpose of your message?
- When you provide the feedback, what do you think will be the response or reaction? This will assist you as the supervisor to consider what to follow up with.
- How will you check how the supervisee has received the message you have provided?
- Use your interpersonal skills – listen, mirror, reframe, paraphrase, use empathy, reality check, question, make statements, listen and then listen some more. If you are providing feedback and you have a situation where you are not wanting to enter into a conversation, then consider how you do this but at the same time, ensure the other person is okay in the process.
- What are you going to focus on in the conversation? (i.e., the supervisee's behaviour, feelings, emotions, content of what they are saying, conduct, etc.). When you are clear on this, it will make it easier to focus and tailor your message.

Here are some statements that can be useful to focus on the different areas.

Focus on feelings or emotions.

- 'Mel, as you know the other day, I sensed you were frustrated about … and your reaction indicated that…'
- 'I picked up from your reaction that you may not have been happy with my comments about that case … and let's see how we can discuss that and move to a positive outcome'.
- 'It was evident that you did not feel satisfied with the meeting outcomes last week, so if we have a conversation about that, we may be able to work through your comments successfully'.

Focus on content

- 'Mel you stated in the team meeting that you believed we were not dealing with … appropriately, and from the language you were using, let's have a conversation about the way you mentioned … and I may be able to assist you to consider different language if or when that occurs again'.

■ 'When you use those types of statements, is there a remote possibility some of the team could have mis-interpreted the intent of what you were saying? 'Let's unpack that and see how it could have been reframed so the other could have received your message better'.

Focus on conduct or behaviour

■ 'To support this conversation, I am keen to understand how your thinking or mindset was driving the behaviour/conduct the other day. From a support perspective, let's work through this together and see if we can find out what was happening to prevent the same thing from occurring again in the future'.

■ 'Mel, as your supervisor and line manager, you know that I enjoy having open and transparent discussions so we can work through anything that may be outside of how you are normally in your role. In relation to the behaviour/conduct that was evident in the meeting, I am keen to ask you some useful questions, that may help me better understand what was occurring. Let's keep this conversation open, transparent and within a support process...'

■ 'Mel, there have been some challenges lately in understanding what has been occurring for you given there have been concerns reported about conduct/behaviour that is outside of your position description. Together let's work through this and I will guide us in the conversation with questions that help us to change things moving forward'.

Question Types

The feedback process is hard enough without thinking of the right questions to include in the conversation. Asking the right questions makes all the difference in securing a particular outcome. We ask questions to lead the conversation, resolve things, take the person on a journey, to understand, to show we care and to get relevant outcomes. As a supervisor, it is important to be highly aware of the types of questions being asked in order to maximise the outcome you are looking for. Table 11.1 outlines example questions to guide you when you are looking for a particular question type.

Table 11.1   Question Types

Action questions	What do we need to take action about?
Appreciation questions	I would appreciate you telling me about…
Clarifying questions	Can you please clarify what happened when…
Closed questions	Did you attend the…
Curious questions	I am curious to know if … can you please…
Diagnostic questions	If you were to assess or diagnose what is going on, what would…
Evaluative questions	If you were to evaluate … what do you think is important?
Explanatory questions	If you were to explain, what do you think I need to know…
Extension questions	Take that further for me, what do you think about…
Factual questions	Can you tell me the facts in this…
Hypothetical questions	Hypothetically, what would you say about…
Leading questions	If you were to take that on board, how would that be?
Multiple choice questions	Do you think a) xxx, b) xxx or c) would work?
Observation questions	If I was observing you in your work, what would I…
Open questions	Can you tell me about…
Outcome questions	What outcome do you think…
Prediction questions	What is your prediction given that…
Probing questions	If I was to probe a little further, what was the purpose of…
Process questions	As you process what we have talked about, what would…
Priority questions	Of all the things that took place, what is a priority to tell me about?
Reality checking questions	One the one hand you indicated that … and on the other hand, you mentioned … which would be the better option?
Reflective questions	If we reflect on … what would suit you better?
Solution questions	What do you think is a solution to…
Summary questions	As we summarise what we have discussed, how does…
Supplementary questions	Further to my question, how does that…

Other useful statements and questions in the feedback process include

- What do you think occurred when...?
- If I was observing you ... what would I see?
- What would others see?
- What would others notice about...?
- What do you think we can do to resolve...?
- What outcome would you like to see?
- What options do you think we have available?
- What is the message in all of this?
- What else is important for me to know in this situation?
- Can you think about what could have been done differently?
- Upon reflection, what other decision could you have made?
- What needs to be different?
- What changes do you think need to be made?
- What was your reflective process?
- What was it about your approach that impacted on?
- What do you think you did really well in handling that?
- What could be different in the way we relate in the workplace/ supervision?
- What do you need to consider...?
- I have a duty of care to... how might I...?
- How are you going to change things in this situation?
- What do you think others are observing?
- Are you motivated to change...?
- What other things do you think we need to discuss?
- What I am looking for is...
- What are your expectations of?
- My responsibility is to... what would your advice be?
- How do you think others see you?
- How would you like them to see you?
- What do you think we could do first?
- What approach are you currently taking?
- How do you see that this approach may not be working?
- How can I support you better?
- What suggestions would you have for...?
- I am conscious that I am... I wanted to check with you if... How would you see that?

The Blocked Professional

There will be times when you are wanting to provide feedback and the supervisee will have barriers or blocks to be able to receive the feedback. They may not understand what you are saying, not understand the context in which you are saying things or have communication challenges such as misinterpreting what you are saying. If the person is feeling stressed or is burnt out, they may not hear what you are saying. When providing feedback, consider if there are any barriers or blockages that are present as that will change the way you provide feedback and change the language and wording used in the conversation. If the supervisee's brain is in a threat state, i.e., in flight, fight or freeze, it can also be hard for that person to hear particular things as well (Visual 11.2).

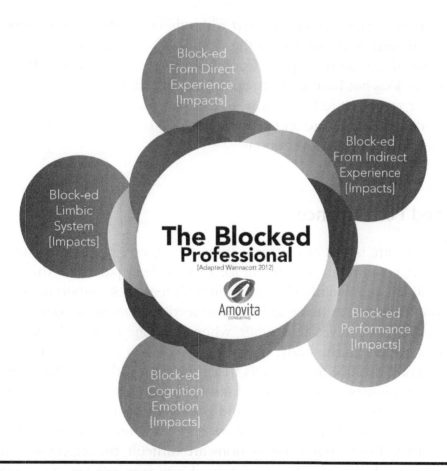

Visual 11.2   The blocked professional.

Blocked from Direct Experience

If the supervisee has had direct experiences that have been negative, i.e. trauma experiences in their life or in their work, this can impact how they receive information. The vicarious nature of complex work over time can result in the supervisee being blocked in receiving particular information particularly if they see what is going to be discussed impacts vicariously. If this occurs, it is important to consider what is said in the conversation and check in regularly to ensure the supervisee can hear and interpret what is being said or discussed.

Blocked from Indirect Experience

Equally, if the supervisee has worked with others who have experienced vicarious trauma or complexity in the workplace, this can impact other people and there can be impacts from those indirect experiences. If a supervisee does not have regular supervision in order to debrief and talk about their work in a reflective way, then other stories and the impact of their work can accumulate and cause blockages, i.e., the person may not understand aspects of conversations.

Blocked Performance

Where there are issues or concerns with the supervisee's performance in the role, it can often be difficult for them to hear particular things in conversations, particularly if there is difficult feedback. Supervisors need to be highly skilled at being able to give feedback where it could be perceived as a negative. Remember, when someone feels under threat, it increases cortisol in the body; therefore, the person is on high alert and may interpret positive messages as negative. Even if the supervisee has performance issues, it is crucial to know how to provide feedback that can be supportive, developmental and positive. Consider what words are unhelpful and what language can show care and consideration of the other person. Even when conversations are difficult, the supervisee needs to be respected and provided with natural justice principles of responding to any concerns.

Blocked Cognition/Emotion

If the supervisee has a barrier or blockage in their cognition or emotions, this can cause issues in the communication process. Blockages in cognition can be caused by stress, fatigue, exhaustion and burnout. It can also be caused by illness or if there are health or well-being issues. If the supervisee has negative self-perception (i.e., negative self-talk, beliefs or values), this can influence how they receive information and interpret the intent of the conversation. When a supervisee is also emotional or distressed, this can impact how they receive information and respond.

Blocked Limbic System

If the supervisee has a negative self-perception, is in fight, flight or freeze, the limbic system registers there is a threat and remains in an aroused state. If the threat is perceived as high, the supervisee may be hypervigilant and the ability to hear what the supervisor is saying is reduced. This significantly impacts the opportunity for the supervisee to reach a positive outcome and you must consider how to communicate to the supervisee in order to reduce the threat response and engage the brain's braking system. This can be achieved through the use of language that is supportive, acknowledges the supervisee and ensures the supervisee feels the supervisor is going to be with them in the conversation and work together to reach a positive outcome. Where feedback is negative or results in the supervisee being dismissed, it is important that the supervisor uses language to engage the supervisee in a way that despite the negative context of the conversation, the supervisee knows that there is still care in the delivery of the message (Farmer, 2009; Harris, 2018; Wonnacott, 2012).

In thinking about feedback, the key messages when providing feedback are as follows:

■ Be clear in the intent and purpose of the conversation. Do not play games with the supervisee – be genuine and authentic, even if the conversation is difficult. People like honesty even when tough feedback is given.
■ Be considerate; know your own communication style and that of the other person. It's important to consider what makes the other person

tick and go with that. Be positively assertive so that your message is received in the correct way and you are considerate in your approach.

■ Be aware of any negative self-talk, beliefs or values the supervisee may have, as this will give you ideas of what language to use.

■ Before the conversation know if the supervisee is fatigued, exhausted or burnout, this will dictate how you have the conversation.

■ Be approachable – open, warm, positive and caring.

■ Use your listening skills, clarifying skills, summarising skills throughout the feedback loop. Pick up on important things the supervisee says as this could assist you to reach a positive outcome.

■ Stay on point, do not stray off down any conversation pathways that will take you off track. Write things down if you need to cover them later in the conversation or at another time but stay focused.

■ Mirror the supervisee if appropriate, with body language or words if that assists to reach a positive outcome. If the person gets angry, stay calm, but consider what tone and pitch in your voice is important to keep the situation positive.

■ Set clear expectations for both parties.

■ Provide feedback often, just not when things are not going so well.

■ Practice and plan what you are going to say, things will then stay on track. You are not going to know at times how the other person is going to respond, so being prepared will assist in the process.

■ Think about how you are feeling in giving the feedback.

■ Check that your own energy is positive, and if you are not exhausted, this will impact the outcome.

■ Maintain the relationship post the feedback.

■ Be clear on the language and words you are going to use, positive and clear statements.

■ Be consistent in your message, no ambiguity.

■ Ask lots of questions – this will give you more information and show a pathway to resolve. Be curious in the conversation, this may assist the supervisee to open up.

■ If you need to engage in feedback that does not require a discussion or ask questions, be clear with the supervisee about why you are making statements, providing direction or a clear outcome without a response being required. This may take place where previous discussions have occurred, and you are delivering an outcome.

■ Be appreciative, considerate, and clear; validate the other person – you will never know what is going on for them.

Communication Skills

Just like having relevant questions, it is important to consider what communication skills are useful in the feedback process. The skills listed in Table 11.2 can assist you to reach a positive outcome.

Table 11.2   Communication Skills

Acknowledgement	Acknowledgement assists to reduce a threat response
Anchoring	Repeating messaging in different ways
Challenging	Questioning motivation, intent or purpose of something
Diversion	Moving the person away from what they are saying
Empathy	Showing consideration for the person through use of language to show understanding and respect
Humour	Smiling, making appropriate comments to keep connections
Inverting up and down	At the end of a sentence, the voice sounds up like a question, the voice sounds down sounding like a statement
Inviting engagement	Using language that encourages the person to engage
Listening	Being present without jumping into ask the next question or make statements
Mirroring	Consciously use particular skills and language similar to the person
Non-verbals	Engaging without talking, using body language to connect and show respect for the other person
Paraphrasing	Feeding back what the person is saying in a slightly different way
Priming	Preparing the person for the conversation or what is to be discussed
Reality testing	Showing the discrepancy in what the person is saying and what they would like the outcome to be
Reflecting	Feeding back what the person has said in a curious manner
Reinforcing	Feeding back what the person has said in a way to validate
Reported speech	Feeding back what the person has said, i.e., you mentioned that, then you went onto say that, you indicated that, etc.

(Continued)

Table 11.2 (*Continued*)   Communication Skills

Reframing	Feeding back what the person has said but in a different way that can open up the conversation or change the intent of the conversation
Round up summarising	Summarise in a way that rounds up what the person is saying, acknowledge or take the conversation in a different way
Silences	Use silence to demonstrate what is being said is being heard
Use of breath	Slow or increase breathing to mirror in the conversation
Validating	Acknowledge what the person is saying

The following checklist can assist when having conversations where any resistance appears in the conversation. Be patient and consider what skills and questions or language is important when resistance arises. Try to address it quickly and acknowledge the person to invite them to re-engage in the conversation.

1. Check yourself first – what triggers may be present for you? Do you need to change tact or your language?
2. Ensure you are coming to the conversation with positive energy, present and mindful.
3. What beliefs and values can you see that are impacting on the conversation?
4. Is there anything that is getting in the way of you connecting with the supervisee, anything bugging you?
5. What is your assessment of the situation?
6. Ensure you know the stages of change to assess if the person is pre-contemplative, contemplative or in a planning or action phase. This will tell you what language to use, your approach and how to reach a positive outcome.
7. What action needs to be taken if the person continues to be resistant or avoidant?
8. Assess where the resistance is coming from, i.e., fear, inability to engage in the conversation, communication issues, well-being issues, the supervisor's style, biases, self-perception, procrastination, negativity, game playing, etc. (Prochaske & Di Clemente, 1983).

Summary

This chapter has explored the importance of providing feedback and some of the barriers and challenges that can occur to ensure the process is positive. Consider the following questions to review what you have gained from this chapter.

What have been the key things you have gained from reading this chapter on the feedback loop?
What have been your reflections about this chapter regarding the importance of providing feedback and having key skills to do so?
List three things that you will take from this chapter to incorporate into your supervisory role.
What do you think will be useful to talk to your supervisee/s about regarding this chapter?
What steps are important for you to ensure feedback is done well as a supervisor?

Chapter 12

Supervision Experiences

Contributions about experiences of supervision

Elyse Leonard, Director Clinical Services and Programs, Amovita
International
Gerard Jeffries, Field Education Manager, University of Sunshine Coast
Jem Mills, Practice Excellence Manager, Social Futures

Elyse Leonard: Director, Clinical Services and Programs, Amovita International

My supervision journey began on my first social work placement at
university. I was considered lucky amongst my peers as I had a reliable
supervisor who met with me for formal supervision on a weekly basis.
However, it was not until my final university placement with Amovita that
I was able to fully comprehend the extent in which supervision influences
the positive development of an emerging professional in the sector.

Whilst on placement at Amovita, I was introduced to the PASE™
(Professional/Practice, Administrative/Line Management, Support/Person,
Educative/Professional Development) supervision model and was fortunate
to attend four by two days training on supervision which helped me to
implement the PASE supervision model; learn how to communicate what
I needed in supervision; understand how to engage in supervision so I
got the most from it and learned how to set a dynamic agenda. It quickly
became evident to me that supervision was more than just a conversation

or 'tick and flick' exercise. The whole framework in which the PASE model is founded allowed me to feel supported and valued as a student in the organisation, and the supervisor was able to support and guide me as I juggled the competing expectations of the agency, university and my workplace commitments.

Discussions in supervision proved to be some of the most memorable experiences on student placement, particularly from a developmental and reflective perspective. On placement, I was faced with an ethical dilemma in which the other student who was also on placement was not meeting the minimum expectations, and I found myself taking on additional responsibility and a higher workload. Bringing this scenario to supervision, I was able to debrief from an S perspective to better understand the impact of this on myself. Taking on a facilitative style, the supervisor worked with me to explore the self-talk, beliefs and values that were influencing my approach to working with the other student, and how this was contributing to the stressors I was experiencing.

After focusing in the S quadrant, the supervisor changed the focus of the conversation by asking me – 'From a P perspective, what elements of your professional excellence framework are important for you to consider when navigating this situation?' This was a 'lightbulb' moment for me, as it switched my mindset to think in a professional space. From a P perspective, I was able to reflect on the knowledge and skills I have as an emerging professional to problem solve a scenario like this and use my language framework to communicate effectively with my peer. Exploring my professional excellence and professional identity framework in supervision was critical in the transition phase of student to social work professional and allowed me the space to reflect on how my personal self-talk, beliefs and values were playing out with the other student. By switching how I was thinking about the situation from a personal viewpoint, I was then able to consider how to reframe my experience from a personal to a professional perspective.

Now, I am nearly a year into my professional career post-placement, I have found new value in supervision. I can genuinely say that I look forward to supervision and feel confident in leading the supervisory discussion, which is seamless when using the PASE model. It is also interesting to see the progress in the supervisory relationship – the more frequently we have supervision, the more I feel comfortable as a supervisee to explore particular elements of myself and my role at a deeper level. I attribute this to structured yet flexible supervision model and framework, as well as the high capability of my professional supervisor. I have also noticed myself using the PASE language on a daily basis, even when having discussions with my colleagues outside of supervision. My hope for all the sectors is that more emerging and experienced professionals have the same positive and developmental experience of supervision as I did and continue to have.

This supervision model and framework has followed and scaffolded me on the journey from student to social work professional. The PASE model and its associated tools and resources are an integral component of my professional excellence framework and is a practice that I will continue to utilise as I develop into a future supervisor and leader in the social work and human services sector.

Gerard Jeffries: Field Education Manager, University of the Sunshine Coast Queensland Australia

I have been a supervisor for approximately fifteen years, and like many supervisors early on in my career, I was asked to supervise junior staff because I was in a supervisory role. I can remember feeling a lack of confidence about taking on this role given as I was required to provide supervision due to my work experience, rather than knowing how to supervise. I can recall feeling totally out of my depth. I had not had any training or supervision myself, so it was a nerve-racking experience.

Since that time in different roles, I have provided line management and professional supervision to both staff and students in our social work program. One of the most memorable moments providing supervision was when I was working with a student who was highly engaged in supervision and had a keen interest in developing their own practice. Bringing things to supervision they were challenged by, they were actively engaged in the process and discussion. Because of the reflective process in supervision, I was able to support the student to grow and develop over time. The discussion allowed them to utilise strategies developed in supervision and take it back to consider how they would put these into their practice. This was incremental over time and the student benefited from what they were experiencing and learning from the discussions.

When I think about some of the challenges I have experienced, I consider my own supervision when I was in the role as a team leader. This was a very difficult situation as my own supervisor was not that experienced as a professional supervisor, and focused more on performance outcomes in my role, rather than providing supervision that was supportive and developmental. Agenda topics only ever focused on how I was performing in the role and over time – this approach did not feel that great.

My passion for supervision is the same as when I have been a supervisee. I enjoy developing new knowledge in supervision. I really like to support others in their journey to grow as well. I also believe that we learn something in every interaction we have with others. It is important to be aware of what we can learn in conversations and take into our roles. Supervision is fundamental to growing our skills and knowledge as professionals. When I think about how we evaluate supervision at the University, I think it could be a lot better. We only do a broad evaluation with the students we provide supervision to, and it is not that focused or useful. We do not gain valuable feedback that provides us with useful information about how to improve supervision.

We have used the PASE supervision model and it has changed the way we think about supervision. It has transformed the way we have our discussions with students and made our process better. We have started to think more proactively and professionally about supervision. The PASE supervision model really assists us to put all aspects of practice on the table and have more open and effective discussions. It is really useful for new supervisees that have not experienced supervision before, as it makes them feel more comfortable in the process and discussion. It ensures that supervision is transparent and the model really helps to set an agenda that is more meaningful. It also helps supervisees to discuss things that are important for them, rather than the experience I talked about before, where one of my supervisors talked more about performance than what was really important to me.

I would really like to see supervision become a mandatory part of social work practice and more broadly for supervisees across the human services sector. There are so many supervisees that do not have access to supervision or organisations that do not value it. If supervision was mandatory for social workers and not just encouraged, then it would not only provide development opportunities, but it would be better valued in the social work profession.

Jem Mills: Manager, Social Futures, New South Wales Australia

I first encountered the PASE supervision framework whilst working on a key project at Social Futures to embed our organisation-wide supervision policy.

Its unique quality as a fully integrated supervision model and system made PASE ideal for this type of project.

A large part of my fascination with the PASE model comes from the fact that it disrupts a central principle that has historically underpinned my supervision practice throughout my career. As a backdrop, my training and development as a mental health nurse, researcher and lecturer took place between the late 1980s and early 2000s in the United Kingdom (UK). During that period, supervision became a focus for government policy, professional training and research. One of my mentors and clinical supervisors was Alec Grant, whose 2001 PhD research 'Clinical Supervision Activity Among Mental Health Nurses' explored the resistance to the uptake of supervision and how that was of concern to the sector at the time. The training, evidence base and practice that I was exposed to revolved around a central theme that management and clinical practice supervision should always remain separate. Whilst the two activities share common aims, the dividing line is drawn in response to, what was taught to me as, two immutable facts. Clinical practice development requires a person to expose feelings of vulnerability in order to grapple with the personal and professional issues at play in their work. Line management involved monitoring and developing a person's professional performance that align to a certain set of expectations. Two quotes from research participants illustrate a common experience of supervision practice delivered by nursing management.

These responses highlight the need for supervisors utilising the PASE model, particularly in the context of line management to have the knowledge, skills and attributes required to build secure, trusting relationships. Some of the ways we support this at Social Futures are described in this overview.

It is becoming increasingly common to explore ways of bringing our authentic self into the work we do in the community and human services sector. Whether this happens in the context of specific lived experience roles or the intentional diversification of the workforce to include a broad array of experiences and qualifications. An increased focus on well-being and support can result in the work environment feeling like a safer place to be open about the personal thoughts and values that inform our work. The PASE supervision model provides an opportunity to address some of the common challenges that arise from trying to balance our professional and personal identities. How these show up in PASE conversations and ways in which the model has helped us to effectively address them are also explored below.

A Secure Base for PASE

A subtle but intended consequence of utilising the PASE supervision model within organisations is that it requires line managers to develop these and other professional leadership and coaching skills. Like any framework, with inadequate training and ongoing support, it can be misapplied. However, implemented properly, PASE has the capacity to surface and address professional development needs that will enable leaders to rise to the challenge of supporting our sector to face this volatile, uncertain, complex and ambiguous work with confidence and capability.

At Social Futures, we are constantly building and reviewing the structures and processes staff need to deliver evidence-based best practice, so that when it counts, the people accessing our services have the experience they need to find and maintain their journey towards their definition of a meaningful, connected life. We refer to this as our 'Practice Excellence Model', of which supervision is a critical part whether in the form of internal, external or group supervision as well as reflective practice groups. Each of these processes follows the PASE model, and when married with particular approaches from our practice framework, we have found the process to be highly effective.

Two theoretical approaches from our practice excellence framework have been particularly useful in informing our supervision practice alongside two structural tools.

These are

1. Attachment theory applied through the Secure Base Leadership approach;
2. Strength-based practice and coaching principles;
3. Streamlined organisational, service level and individual Practice Frameworks and
4. An accountability framework to support clear, kind feedback on performance at all levels of the organisation.

These four aspects of our practice excellence framework are outlined here with reference to how they are applied in practice. Attachment theory informs our efforts to build the foundations of the supervision relationship. Whilst there are clear differences between the supervision relationship and other caring relationships, both require a sense of security from which transformational learning can emerge. Secure base leadership principles suggest that supervision needs to be a secure place in which the supervisee can feel supported and valued. Supervision validates to the supervisee that their capability is developed and maintained through a sense of calm, predictability and responsiveness.

Four foundations of this approach for the supervisor are

1. Emotional Regulation
2. Attunement
3. Consistency of Responses
4. Routines and Rituals

Emotional Regulation

This involves the supervisor being self-engaged and attuned in awareness and know how to manage their own emotional reactions and to role model the activities and approaches to work required to nurture personal well-being from a mature perspective. We have found that providing specific reflective practice group sessions for supervisors has been helpful in this process as well as providing a forum from which common supervision issues can be discussed and development needs can be drawn. Essentially our view is that part of the supervisor's responsibility is to do what is necessary for them to be present and a calming influence in their interactions with supervisees. Self-regulation brings with it a way to communicate with influence when calm even when having difficult conversations.

Attunement

Being calm and present allows the supervisor to focus fully on the supervision process and to be open to and aware of subtle cues and shifts in the other person's presentation. Listening attentively to what is being said and also what is not being said reinforces the value of the opportunity to pause and reflect deeply on our work. This level of responsiveness gives the supervisee a sense that the supervisor and by extension the organisation values their contribution. The attunement process comes from the supervisor having the appropriate range of capabilities and competencies that come together in perfect symmetry whereby these align to ensure that supervision is an experience that the supervisee looks forward to and feels validated.

Consistency of Responses

Consistency is one key to providing a sense of predictability in supervision. Human beings need predictability and consistency so highly that we often prefer consistently difficult people over those whose presentations are less predictable. How many times have we heard the phrase 'at least you know where you stand' with reference to someone's consistently negative response? Building a consistent response requires the supervisor to be aware of all of the factors influencing their coaching approach. This requires knowledge of the supervisee's context, including position description, program guidelines, policy frameworks, legislation and being clear when more information or clarification is required before offering advice. This can be challenging in a fast pace changing environment like the community and human services sector, but signposting to the supervisee that all reasonable attempts are being made to provide calm, consistent support and development helps to establish the security needed to engage best practice and feel supported.

Routines and Rituals

Routine and ritual are another aspect of supervision that is most easily influenced by both parties and includes having a structure and clear practices in supervision sessions. Attachment theory informs our approach to scheduling a regular supervision pattern and to basing each meeting on a standard agenda format. In this way, a set of predictable routines and rituals can be established that contribute to providing the secure base mentioned above. Whilst the content of the supervision session may change from month to month, having the familiarity of a standard process and consistency in the relationship and style of the supervisor helps to contain and hold the space for the supervisee. This encourages both parties to embrace the opportunities for personal and professional development that effective supervision offers.

Strength-Based Principles Applied to Supervision and Coaching

1. Every individual, team and organisation has strengths, and the focus is on these strengths rather than deficits
2. The whole workforce is a rich source of resources
3. Development activities are based on individual self-determination
4. Collaboration is central with the supervisor–supervisee relationship as primary and essential

5. Supervision takes place in the supervisee's space
6. All people have the inherent capacity to learn, grow and change.

The Service Practice Framework

It is easier to consider individual development and support needs when we have a clear idea of the key skills and knowledge required to make our teams work effectively.

Monthly supervision sessions and Individual Development and Support Plans are informed and supported by a Service Practice Framework and for a successful team.

The Service Practice Framework helps connect individual roles to the wider program and organisational context including the Social Futures Practice Framework. It makes clear the various team and individual attributes required for success. It is co-created by the team over a period of time and reviewed periodically depending on the needs and development of the team. Although not written like this, the Service Practice Framework essentially enables teams to complete the blanks in the following paragraph:

For example:

'Our team exists to achieve [BLANK] which we do by systematically acting like [BLANK] and [BLANK]. We need to be skilled at [BLANK] and to understand [BLANK] & [BLANK] theories & evidence. This enables us to make the following service promise to our clients/agency partners. People will be able to see this in our practice because our actions are like [BLANK], & [BLANK]. When all of this is working and aligned we will recognize our team culture as [BLANK] & [BLANK]'.

The eight sections of the Service Practice Framework are defined as

Our Purpose	The reason our program or team function exists and the impact we are aiming to have.
Our Principles	The fundamental propositions that serve as the foundation for our systematic way of practicing and thinking about our work.
Our Skills	The skills we deem to be particularly crucial to doing our work effectively.
Our Knowledge	The theoretical and practical knowledge that we deem to underpin the skills we need.

Our Values	The principles or standards of behaviour that we judge to be important in our work, these may include but are not limited to the organization's values.
Our Commitment	The pledge we make to the people whom our work serves. The expectation we invite them to hold us accountable to.
Our Actions	The characteristics of our actions that exemplify our values, skills and purpose.
Our Culture	When our work is aligned to this Service Practice Framework, the culture of our team will be clear.

References

Abbey, D., Hunt, D., & Weiser, J. (1985). Variations on a theme by Kolb: A new perspective for understanding counselling and supervision. *The Counselling Psychologist. 13*(3). 477–501. DOI: 10.1177/0011000085133016.

Argyris, C. (1970). *Intervention Theory and Method.* Massey: Addison-Wesley.

Argyris, C. (2010). *Organisational Traps: Leadership, Culture, Organisational Design.* New York: Oxford University Press.

Bhabha, H. (1994). *The Location of Culture.* London: Routledge.

Bogo, M., & McKnight, K. (2005). Clinical supervision in social work: A review of the research literature. *The Clinical Supervisor. 24*(1-2). 49–67. DOI: 10.1300/J001v24n01_04.

Bunting, M. (2016). *The Mindful Leader. 7 Practices for Transforming Your Leadership, Your Organization and Your Life.* Australia: Wiley.

Carroll, M. (2007). One more time: What is supervision? *Psychotherapy in Australia. 13*(3). 34–40.

Carroll, M. (2010). Levels of reflection: On learning reflection. *Psychotherapy in Australia. 16*(2). 24–31.

Carroll, M., & Shaw, E. (2012). *Ethical Maturity in the Helping Professions: Making Difficult Life and Work Decisions.* London: Jessica Kingsley Publishers.

Chapman, A. (2005). David Kolb's learning styles model and experiential learning theory (ELT). Retrieved from www.businessballs.com/self-awareness/kolbs-learning-styles/.

Collins, J. (2001). *Good to Great.* New York: Harper Business.

Cousins, C. (2004). Becoming a social work supervisor: A significant role transition. *Australian Social Work. 57*(2). 175–185. DOI: 10.1111/j.1447-0748.2004.00130.x.

Davys, A., & Beddoe, L. (2010). *Best Practice in Professional Supervision: A Guide for the Helping Professions.* London: Jessica Kingsley Publishers.

Dimitriadis, N. (2016). *Neuroscience for Leaders: A Brain-Adaptive Leadership Approach.* London: Kogan Page.

Egan, R. (2012). Australian social work supervision practice in 2007. *Australian Social Work. 65*(2). 171–184. DOI: 10.1080/0312407X.2011.653575.

Egan, R., Maidment, J., & Connolly, M. (2016). Supporting quality supervision: Insights for organisational practice. *International Social Work. 61*(3). 353–367. DOI: 10.1177/0020872816637661.

Falender, C., & Shafranske, E. (2012). The importance of contemporary-based clinical supervision and training in the twenty-first century: Why bother? *Journal of Contemporary Psychotherapy. 42*(3). 129–137. DOI: 10.1007/s10879-011-9198-9.

Falender, C., & Shafranske, E. (2017). Competency based clinical supervision: Status, opportunities, tensions and the future. *Australian Psychologist. 52*(2). 86–93. DOI: 10.1111/ap.12265.

Farmer, D. (2009). *Neuroscience and Social Work: The Missing Link*. Thousand Oaks, CA: SAGE Publications.

Harris, T. (2017). Excellence in supervisory practice: Developing a supervisory capability framework for effective professional supervision in social work practice in Australia. *Unpublished PhD thesis*, Griffith University, Brisbane, Australia.

Harris, T. (2018). *Developing Leadership Excellence: A Practical Guide for the New Professional Supervisor*. New York: Routledge.

Harris, T., & O'Donoghue, K. (2020). Developing culturally responsive supervision through Yarn Up Time and the CASE supervision model. *Australian Social Work. 73*(1). 64–76. DOI: 10.1080/0312407X.2019.1658796.

Holloway, E. (1995). *Clinical Supervision: A Systems Approach*. Thousand Oaks, CA: SAGE Publications.

House of Commons. (2003). *The Victoria Climbie Inquiry Report*. Health Committee, House of Commons. pp. 1–33.

Knowles, M. (1990). *The Adult Learner: A Neglected Species*. Houston, TX: Gulf Publishing Company.

Kolb, D. A., & Fry, R. (1975). Toward an applied theory of experiential learning. In C. Cooper (Ed). *Theories of group process* (pp. 33–38). London: John Wiley.

Lencioni, P. (2012). *The Advantage: Why Organisational Health Trumps Everything Else in Business*. San Francisco, CA: Jossey-Bass.

McAuliffe, D., & Chenoweth, L. (2008). Leave no stone unturned: The inclusive model of ethical decision making. *Ethics and Social Welfare. 2*(1). 38–49. DOI: 10.1080/17496530801948739.

Milne, D. (2007). An empirical definition of clinical supervision. *British Journal of Clinical Psychology. 46*(4). 437–447. DOI: 10.1348/014466507X197415.

Milne, D. (2010). Can we enhance the training of clinical supervisors? A national pilot study of an evidence-based approach. *Clinical Psychology & Psychotherapy. 17*(4). 321–328. DOI:10.1002/cpp.657.

Mor Barak, M., Travis, D., Pyun, H., & Xie, B. (2009). The impact of supervision on worker outcomes: A meta-analysis. *Social Service Review. 83*(1): 3–32. DOI: 10.1086/599028.

Morrison, T., Wonnacott, J., & Frankel, J. (2009). *Guide to the Supervision of Workers during the Early Development Period*. Leeds: CWDC.

Mullarkey, K., Keasley, P., & Playle, F. (2001). Multiprofessional clinical supervision: Challenges for mental health nurses. *Journal of Psychiatric and Mental Health.* *8*(3). 205–211. DOI: 10.1046/j.1365-2850.2001.00376.x.

O'Donoghue, K., & Tsui, M. S. (2012). In search of an informed supervision practice: An exploratory study. *Practice: Social Work in Action.* *24*(1). 3–20. DOI: 10.1080/09503153.2011.632678.

Pillay, S. (2011). *Your Brain at Work: The Neuroscience of Great Leaders.* Upper Saddle River, NJ: Pearson Education.

Prochaska, J., & DiClemente, C. (1983). Stages of processes of self-change of smoking: Toward an integrative model of change. *Journal of Consulting and Clinical Psychology.* *51*(3). 390. DOI: 10.1037//0022-006X.51.3.390.

Ray, L. (2018). The ugly truth about leadership and engagement. (Blog Post). Retrieved from: www.neurocapability.com.au/category/leadership/.

Rock, D. (2009). *Your Brain at Work: Strategies for Overcoming Distraction, Regaining Focus and Working Smarter All Day Long.* New York: Harper Collins.

Schon, D. (1983). *The Reflective Practitioner: How Professionals Think in Action.* Aldershot: Ashgate Publishing.

Scott, K., Ingram, M., Vitanza, S., & Smith, N. (2000). Training in supervision: A survey of current practices. *The Counselling Psychologist.* *28*(3). 403–422. DOI: 10.1177/0011000000283007.

Shelley, S. (2003). *Clinical Supervision Framework.* London: The Society of Radiographers. pp. 1–10.

Stoltenberg, C. (1981). Approaching supervision from a developmental perspective: The counsellor complexity model. *Journal of Counselling Psychology.* *28*(1). 59–65. DOI: 10.1037/0022-0167.28.1.59.

Sweitzer, H., & King, M. (2004). *The Successful Internship: Transformation and Empowerment in Experiential Learning.* Belmont: Thomson Brooks/Cole.

Tversky, A., & Kahneman, D. (1974). Judgment under uncertainty: Heuristics and biases. *Science.* *185*(4157). 1124–1131. DOI: 10.1126/science.185.4157.1124.

Wonnacott, J. (2012). *Mastering Social Work Supervision.* London: Jessica Kingsley Publishers.

Wyles, P. (2007). When the bough breaks the cradle will fall. Child protection and supervision: Lessons from three recent reviews into the state of child protection in Australia. *Communities, Families and Children Australia.* *2*(1). 49–58.

Index

For Product Safety Concerns and Information please contact our EU
representative GPSR@taylorandfrancis.com Taylor & Francis Verlag GmbH,
Kaufingerstraße 24, 80331 München, Germany

Printed and bound by CPI Group (UK) Ltd, Croydon, CR0 4YY
01/05/2025
01858389-0010